# FLOOD HAZARDS MANAGEMENT: A COMMUNITY APPROACH

## Natural Hazards and Disaster Management

Dr. Kishor Dandapat

## Notion Press

Old No. 38, New No. 6
McNichols Road, Chetpet
Chennai - 600 031

First Published by Notion Press 2020
Copyright © Dr. Kishor Dandapat 2020
All Rights Reserved.

ISBN  978-1-64869-987-0

Dedicated to my parents who gave supreme
sacrifice for my education

# CONTENTS

# FOREWORD

I am glad that the book titled "Flood Hazards Management: A Community Approach" written by Dr. Kishor Dandapat, Lecturer in Geography, Seva Bharati Mahavidyalaya, Midnapore, West Bengal is being published by the international publishing House i.e. Notion Press, Chennai in 2020. This book is an outcome of an in-depth research study under taken by the author in the Post Graduate Dept. of Geography, Utkal University, Bhubaneswar under my guidance and supervision.

This book is first of its kind to provide some useful information to the people engaged in flood hazard studies and related disaster management with emphasis on community-based risk reduction strategies. This book deals with the problems of flood disaster management with a case study on the Kangsabati, Kaliaghai, Subarnarekha and Silabati river of Paschim Midnapore district of West Bengal. The book also illustrates the application of the tools of geospatial technology in vulnerability analysis and risk assessment of flood hazards at a regional scale. Management techniques of SWOT analysis is used for addressing the key issues of community level flood hazard management.

In India, Disaster Management Act of 2005 and Disaster Management Policy of 2009 had brought a paradigm shift in our disaster management activities focusing on community-based disaster preparedness and mitigation. The author has made all possible efforts to that the book has a contemporary relevance for its stake holders. I am sure the book will be a useful reference for academicians across diverse disciplines of science, engineering, humanities, management practitioners, Government and Civil Society Organizations working in the areas of flood hazard management.

**Dr. Gopal Krishna Panda**
Emeritus Professor of Geography
Dept. of Geography, Utkal University
Bhubaneswar, Odisha, India – 751004

# PREFACE

From the time immemorial, river plays a very significant role for the development of civilization. The ancient civilizations could not be built up without river as the basis and all the civilizations were riverine. Even now dams continue to act as bulwarks against dangerous flood of its destruction all over the world. Since early1940s river water utilization and river control structures have been forming the mainstay of planning policy in decolonized developing countries in their quest for self-reliance. Inspite of these huge benefits, river control has sometimes had serious social and environmental consequences. It is not surprising that the large-scale ecological damage and human suffering associated with river control.

I was born and brought up in the Ganga Valley of South Bengal. The River Ganga was a constant companion in my childhood. I decided to pursue an academic career focusing my interest on understanding the riverine regime and its paradoxes. As a graduate student of Geography, I had been privileged to visit and study the Ganga (Hooghly-Bhagirathi), Ajay, Subarnarekha, Kaliaghai, and Kangsabati Rivers.

With a keen interest I observed everywhere how indigenous technological innovations helped better water resource management and how flooding was accepted by the riparian communities as a positive factor. The disadvantage of floods in one season was converted into an advantage in another. Human impact on the riverine system and the socioeconomic environment has become a matter of great concern in the contemporary world. Geographers, ecologists, planners, engineers and scientists all over the world are paying close attention to the relationship between humans and the environment.

The book has been designed and its subject matters have been arranged in 6 divisions keeping the aforesaid facts into consideration wherein different aspects of flood hazard viz. community approach to flood and locational characteristics of flood, characteristics of flooding and flood prone areas, impacts of flood on people and economy, factors associated with flooding and flood intensifying condition, risk and vulnerability of flood and flood management process by community level.

**– Kishor Dandapat**

# ACKNOWLEDGEMENT

I gratefully acknowledge the sincere guidance and valuable instructions of Dr. Gopal Krishna Panda, Emeritus Professor, Post Graduate Department of Geography, Utkal University, Vani – Vihar, Bhubaneswar, Odisha for his constant guidance, valuable suggestions and deeply involvement the completion of this work in the present form would have not been possible. It is not only his guidance but also his zeal and interest as a geographer in this field has inspired me to work in this branch of Geography.

I am deeply indebted to my family members, specially my parents Mrs. Namita Dandapat and Mr. Saktipada Dandapat for their constant encouragement and uttermost patience.

The project has been benefitted from the efforts of numerous field assistants over the years. Among them I would like to mention Tapas, Chiranjeet, Samir, Prasanna, Puja, Riya, Aloka, Pritha, Uttam, Raju, Kalyan, Sital and Pijush without whose assistance my field survey could hardly be completed and also tabulation the data.

Finally, and most importantly, I wish to thank to Notion Press and entire publishing team, without whose patience, immense competence and support this book would not have come to the present form.

I would like to thank all these people for their generosity.

# ABBREVIATION

| | |
|---|---|
| ADRC | Asian Disaster Reduction Center |
| AHP | Analytical Hierarchy Process |
| CBFM | Community Based Flood Management |
| CCI | Composite Vulnerability Index |
| CDF | Composite Flood Distribution |
| CGWB | Centre Ground Water Board |
| CI | Consistency Index |
| CR | Consistency Ratio |
| DDMA | District Disaster Management Authority |
| DDMO | District Disaster Management Officer |
| DDMP | District Disaster Management Plan |
| DFFD | Derived Flood Frequency Distribution |
| DRR | Disaster Risk Reduction |
| DL | Danger Level |
| EDL | Extreme Danger Level |
| FMCS | Community Level Flood Management Committee |
| GMP | Ghatal Master Plan |
| HRVC | Hazard, Risk, Vulnerability and Capacity |
| ILGUS | Institute of Local Govt And Urban Studies |
| IMD | Indian Meteorological Department |
| IPCC | Intergovernmental Panel on Climate Change |
| LISS | Linear Imaging Self-Scanning Sensor |
| MBGIS | Model Builder Geographical Information System |
| NIDM | National Institute of Disaster Management |
| NRSC | National Remote Sensing Centre |
| PHED | Public Health Engineering Department |
| PVI | Physical Vulnerability Index |

RI            Random Index
RS & GIS      Remote Sensing and Geographical Information System
SDRF          State Disaster Response Force
SIPRD         State Institute of Panchayat and Rural Development
SRTM          Shuttle Radar Topography Mission
SVI           Social Vulnerability Index
UNDP          United Nations Development Programme
WLC           Weighted Linear Combination
WAPCOS        Water and Power Consultancy Services

# FLOOD HAZARDS AND ITS MANAGEMENT

Nomenclature of Flood; Types of Flood; Problems of flood hazard; Flood hazards in Indian situation; Literature Review; Flood hazards assessment

## 1.1 Nomenclature of Flood

The word "Flood" comes from the old English 'flod', a word common to Germanic language. Flood is a state of high-water level along a river or on coast that leads to inundation of land which is normally submerged for several days in continuation. Generally, floods are considered to be associated with rivers and people conceive floods as the outcome of accumulation of huge volume of water coming out of the rivers through overtopping of river banks during peak discharge period. In Webster's New International Dictionary, flood is defined as a "great flow of water.... especially a body of water, rising, swelling and overflowing land not usually covered; a deluge, a freshet, an inundation". Any high stream flow which overtops natural or artificial bank of a stream is called flood (Rostvedt, 1968). Floods, relatively high flow of water which overtakes the natural channel provided for run-off (Chow, V.T. 1956). Normally the level at which the river overflows its banks and inundates the adjoining area is called the flood stage (Subramanya, K. 1994). Rather than, floods have different meaning in different disciplines. The hydrologist looks upon floods in terms of precipitation in excess of drainage capacity. To engineers, floods indicate uncontrolled run-off. For agriculturalist floods signify water in excess of crop requirements and submersion. For dwellers in towns and villages, floods indicate interference with communication, damage to dwellings and interruption in normal activities of man. But for a geographer, floods are comprehensive phenomena covering all aspects indicated above.

## 1.2 Type of Floods

A flood can be defined as relatively high-water levels caused by excessive rainfall, storm surge, dam break or tsunami that overtop the natural or artificial banks in any part of a stream, river, estuary, lake or dam; and/or local overland flooding before surface runoff enters a watercourse; and/or inundation resulting from super-elevated sea levels and/or waves overtopping the coastline or the banks of an estuary. The India is exposed to eight different types of floods, as shown in Table 1.3, each with its own characteristic behaviour and degree of hazard.

### 1.2.1 Rainfall Floods

#### *1.2.1.1 Mainstream Floods*

Mainstream floods occur when excessive rainfall causes the River to overflow its banks. Typically, the mainstream flood season is from June to November, with flood levels peaking in August-September. In the Middle and Lower River Reaches of Lao PDR and Thailand, mainstream floods inundate the relatively narrow Mekong floodplains for 1-2 weeks or thereabouts and cause backwater flooding along the Lower Reaches of tributaries. In Cambodia and Viet Nam, mainstream floods inundate vast areas of the Cambodian Lowlands and the Cuu Long Delta to depths of 3 m and more for periods of 2-4 months or longer. In 1998, when the mainstream flows and flood levels were amongst the lowest recorded in recent times (see Figure 3.3), some 26,000 km2 of Cambodia and Viet Nam were flooded; in 2000, when flooding across the Cambodian Floodplain and Cuu Long Delta was the most severe in the last 20-50 years (see Figure 3.3), some 45,000 km2 were inundated (MRC, 2005a).

Mainstream floods passing through Cambodia and into Viet Nam are moderated by 'the Great Lake' of Cambodia, which reduces downstream flood levels and extends the duration of the flood season by storing an average of 30 km3 of water on the rising limb of the mainstream flood wave and returning this water, plus local wet season inflows, on the recession limb of the flood. During this process, the surface area of the Great Lake swells from a dry season average of 2,500 km2 to a wet season average of 15,000 km2 (MRC, 2005a).

**■ Table 1.1: Floods of the Lower Mekong Basin**

| Flood category | Name | Cause | Characteristics |
|---|---|---|---|
| Rainfall | Mainstream | Excessive RF over Mekong Basin catchment. | Generally slow onset and slow moving. Average annual flood volume flowing into South China Sea is 460 km3. Duration can last for 2-4 months. |
| | Tributary | Excessive RF over Tributary catchments. | Rapid onset and fast moving because of small, steep catchments. Duration typically several days to one-week. |
| | Local | Excessive RF over Local Catchments. | Rapid onset. More of a nuisance and less hazardous than Mainstream and Tributary floods. Duration typically hours to one-day. |
| Dam-Related | Dam release | Excessive Release of Water from Dams. | Onset can be rapid and unexpected, especially for emergency releases. Hazard levels can be high. |
| | Dam break | Structural Failure of Dams. | Immediate onset and rapid increase in water levels. Destructive velocities and extreme hazard. |
| | Dike breach | Structural Failure of Dikes. | Similar to a Dam break flood, but water levels and hazard tempered somewhat by generally low height of dikes. |
| Maritime | Storm surge | Tropical Cyclones, Depressions & Storms. | Slow onset. High water levels and flood, wind and saltwater damage can occur. Can be very hazardous. |
| | tsunami | Undersea Earthquakes. | Immediate onset. Extreme and immediate increase in water levels. Very destructive and extremely hazardous. |

## 1.2.1.2 Tributary Floods

Tributary floods occur when excessive rainfall causes Mekong tributaries to overflow their banks. Three types of tributary floods can be distinguished: 'flash floods', 'combined floods' and 'landslips'. A flash flood can be defined as "Sudden and unexpected flooding caused by local heavy rainfall or rainfall in another area of the catchment often defined as flooding that occurs within six hours of the onset of the flood-generating rainfalls". (DIPNR, 2005)

In the LMB, all floods in steeper Upper and Middle Reaches of tributaries can be considered to be 'flash floods'10. Significant floodplains have developed around the confluence of the Mekong and its tributaries. These areas are subject to combined flooding from both mainstream and tributary floods and to backwater flooding from mainstream floods. 'Landslips' are rainfallinduced landslides or mudslides that occur in the relatively steep upland areas of the LMB and often accompany tributary floods. Landslips occur because of slope instability and happen abruptly and with little warning. Although not floods per se, they are treated as 'floods' because they generally occur in concert with tributary floods. Landslips are frequently more hazardous and destructive than any accompanying tributary flood. In 2001, landslips in Phetchabun province of Thailand, which is adjacent to the Western edge of the Khorat Plateau, caused about 100 deaths.

### 1.2.1.3 Local Floods

Local floods occur when runoff from heavy rainfalls overwhelms the local (typically urban) drainage system. Local floods are generally of a 'nuisance' nature: they affect relatively small areas and are generally characterised by shallow flood depths, low flood velocities and low hazard.

### 1.2.2 Dam-Related Floods

Dam Release Floods Dam release floods occur when released water from a dam overtops the banks of the receiving stream. Day to day dam releases, for hydroelectricity generation and other purposes generally do not constitute a 'flood'. However, to cater for an incoming flood in an emergency situation, it can be necessary to release high discharges, which can flood downstream communities and imperil lives. In recent years there have been several instances of serious dam release flooding in the LMB; lives have been lost, as have riverside gardens and possessions. Dam release floods are largely controllable; their frequency, size and impact should be assessed during the investigation phase of a new dam. Appropriate inflow forecasting and dam operations minimize the need for emergency releases. If necessary, warning systems can be installed to alert downstream communities of unexpected releases.

Dam break Floods Dam break floods occur when a dam wall breaches because of overtopping, structural failure or the undermining of its foundations. Because of its high water velocities and a rapid and extreme rises in water levels, a dam break flood wave can cause catastrophic damage and extreme flood risk as it races downstream. To date, no dam failures have occurred in the LMB, but proposed dam building programs in China, Lao PDR, Cambodia and Viet Nam will increase the number of dams. The risk of dam failure can be controlled (i.e. reduced to an acceptably small level) by ensuring that dams are built to strict design, construction and maintenance standards and areappropriately monitored during their life. Spillway capacities should be regularly checked and enlarged if found wanting. These days, it is usual to undertake a 'dam break analysis' of both new and existing dams to assess the hazard of the resulting flood wave to downstream communities should the dam fail, and to put in place emergency management measures if necessary.

Dike Breach Floods Dike breach floods occur when flood protection dikes fail or breach in a similar way as described for dams. The dikes that protect flood-prone areas of the LMB are typically 2-5 m high, and whilst much lower than dams, dike breach floods can impose significant risks to people and assets within 'protected' areas. The likelihood of dike breach floods can be minimized by appropriate design, construction, maintenance, and monitoring.


## 1.2.3 Maritime Floods

Storm Surge Floods Storm surge floods occur when storm-induced increases in coastal water levels inundate coastal and estuarine areas. Such storms include the tropical weather systems (TWSs) described in Section 3.2b. Coastal water levels are raised by the effects of reduced atmospheric pressure of the storm and by the action of onshore winds and storm-driven waves pushing water against the coast (see MRC, 2007b). In the LMB, only the coastal waters of the Cuu Long Delta and the Lower Reaches of its waterways are exposed to storm surge flooding. The northern and central coastal regions of Viet Nam are considerably more prone to storm surge effects of TWSs than the Cuu Long Delta. Over the 49-year period, 1945-98, the coastal provinces of the Delta were affected by TWSs on only 5 occasions, predominately in October and November (DMU, 2005). Notwithstanding their rarity, even a modest storm surge will increase flood levels in the delta reaches of the Mekong and Bassac rivers, perhaps substantially if it coincides with mainstream flooding.

Tsunami Floods Tsunami floods are caused when the ocean floor is thrust up or down by an undersea earthquake, the greater the movement of the ocean floor, the higher the resultant tsunami waves. In the LMB, Tsunami Flooding is limited to the coastline of the Cuu Long Delta and the Lower Reaches of the Mekong and Bassac Rivers. The risk of significant tsunami flooding around the coast of the delta is small to very small: locally generated tsunamis would be less than 0.5 m high; substantial tsunamis generated around the Philippines would be moderated by the favourable orientation (approximately East-west) of the coastline of the delta (MRC, 2007b).

## 1.3 Problems of flood hazards

Since the beginning of civilization man has suffered from the effects of natural hazards. These create chaos in society, for they disrupt the order and routine of civilized life. Among these disasters we find floods, which have been more frequent and devastating as time has passed. It is because of this that their study is necessary.

Flood is defined as extremely high flows or levels of rivers, lakes, ponds, reservoirs and many other water bodies whereby inundates outside of the water bodies area. Flooding also occurs when the sea level raises extremely or above coastal lands due to tidal sea and sea surges. Flood is a natural phenomenon is response to heavy rainfall but it becomes a hazard when it inflicts loss to the lives and properties of the people.

In recent years there has been a significant increase in floods around the world, both in developed and developing countries. Not only the frequency, but the severity of floods has increased to such an extent, especially in developing countries, that 100 years floods are becoming annual occurrences (Alho et al. 2008; ISDR 2004; Klijin 2009; Shamaoma, Kerle & Alkema 2006; Wisner et al. 2004).

To date, floods are the most frequently occurring natural disaster with the greatest loss of life. Fatality during a flood hazard event is largely due to drowning and severe injury. The long-term secondary effect is, however, more rigorous where affected communities are hampered by impacts such as disease and starvation (Pilon 2004; Watts 2007; Wisner et al. 2004). Economic losses due to floods are higher than for any other hazard (Pilon 2004; Wisner et al. 2004). Poor communities are more at risk due to the vulnerability of their livelihoods. Especially in rural areas where access to services and infrastructure is limited (Garawta & Bollin 2002; Pilon 2004; Wisner et al. 2004.)

Flood is the most expensive and devastating natural hazard (Wilby and Keenan 2012; Sanyal and Lu 2004), and it continues to be a concern in many parts of the world (Jha et al. 2012; Kundzewich et al. 2010; Chang and Franczyk 2008). For instance, the Intergovernmental Panel on Climate Change Assessment Report 4 (IPCC AR4) indicated that fl o od is likely to be a major cause of regional concern under warmer climates (Solomon et al. 2007). Floods accounted for 40% of the total number of natural disasters that occurred between 1985 and 2009, and they resulted in massive destruction in terms of economic loss and persons affected (Ferreira et al. 2011) (see Table 1.1). During the last decade of the twentieth century, floods killed 100,000 people and affected 1.4 billion people (Jonkman 2005). On average, floods affected 99 million people every year from 2000 to 2008 (Johnson 2010). Floods are currently one of the greatest threats to social security and sustainable development, and it is estimated that floods affect around 20–300 million people every year (Hirabayashi and Kanae 2009).

■ **Table 1.2:  Number of reported disasters and humans affected, 1985–2009**

| Disaster Type | Numbers of Events (%) | People killed (%) | People Affected in Million (%) |
|---|---|---|---|
| Floods | 2893 (40) | 175453 (13) | 2677 (53) |
| Storms | 2251 (31) | 414425 (31) | 722 (14) |
| Extreme Temperature | 339 (5) | 101638 (8) | 92 (2) |
| Earthquake | 656 (9) | 601302 (45) | 136 (3) |
| Drought | 352 (5) | 7512 (1) | 1425 (8) |
| others | 829 (11) | 47825 (4) | 16 (0) |

*Source: Ferreira et al. (2011).*

**Fig. 1.1:** Number of reported flood events between 1950 and 2011 (Source: EM-DAT/CRED, v. 12.07)

Figure 1.1 shows the trend of flood events around the world since 1950. Data from EM-DAT/CRED (v. 12.07) showed that 3,954 flood events (out of 7,849 hydrometeorological events) occurred between 1950 and 2011, of which 52.2% occurred during 2000–2011. In addition, the data showed that only 2% occurred during 1950–1959, 3.9% during 1960–1969, 6.6% during 1970–1979, 13.2% during 1980–1989, and 21.9% during 1990–1999. Although fatalities from floods have declined considerably around the world, economic losses have become more pronounced, causing enormous monetary losses (see Fig. 1.2). Floods that occurred during 2000–2011 resulted in an estimated loss of more than US $285 billion. Likewise, the economic damage was more than $211 billion during 1990–1999. In contrast, fl o od-related losses were $1.8 billion during 1950–1959, $4.9 billion during 1960–1969, $8.8 billion during 1970–1979, and $43 billion during 1980–1989. However, the economic losses are disproportionate among continents. For example, Asia experienced the highest economic losses from 1950 to 2011, amounting to more than 60% of the global damage. This was followed by Europe (19%), the Americas (16.8%), Oceania (2.5%), and Africa (1.2%).

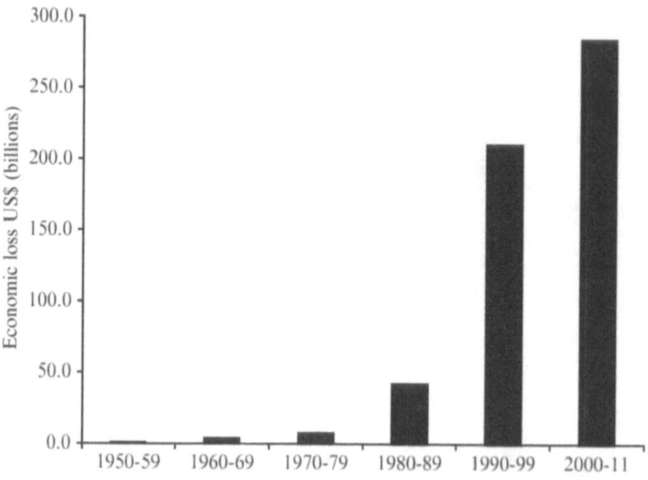


**Fig 1.2:** Economic losses from floods, 1950–2011 (Source: EM-DAT/CRED, v. 12.07)

The most irreversible effect of fl o od is the loss of human lives, which is significantly higher in developing countries. Between 1950 and 2011, floods killed 2.3 million people and affected 3.5 billion people around the world, including more than two million during the 1950s and 68,361 during 2000–2011. Estimates show that over 95% deaths attributed to large floods occurred in developing countries, despite fewer large flood events (Ferreira et al. 2011). Of the deaths attributed to floods between 1950 and 2011, 96% occurred in Asia, 2.6% in the Americas, 0.9% in Africa, 0.4% in Europe, and 0.02% in Oceania (see Table 1.2). During 2000–2011, 68.8% of flood related deaths occurred in Asia, followed by the Americas (15.7%).

Studies demonstrated that floods are expected to bring significant levels of misery in the coming years as a result of global climatic change (Whit field 2012; Mirza 2011; Bouwer 2011; Pall et al. 2011; Hirabayashi et al. 2008; IPCC 2007a; van Aalast 2006; Kundzewich et al. 2010, 2005; Milly et al. 2002; Wetherald and Manabe 2002). A recent modelling study on climate change and fl o od probabilities suggested that up to 20% of the world's population is at risk of increased flooding due to climate warming (Kleinen and Petschel-Held 2007). This number is expected to increase with a further rise in global temperatures (Hirabayashi and Kanae 2009).

■ Table 1.3 Deaths from floods, by continent, 1950–2011

| Continent | Persons killed | Percent |
| --- | --- | --- |
| Asia | 2268968 | 96.13 |
| Europe | 7846 | 0.33 |
| Americas | 61857 | 2.62 |
| Africa | 21134 | 0.90 |
| Oceania | 463 | 0.02 |
| Total | 2360268 | 100 |

Source: EM-DAT/CRED, v. 12.07

However, a general consensus is that poor countries will be disproportionately affected by water-related disasters that are driven by climate change because of their high rates of population and poverty and their poor adaptive capacity (Tol 2008; Adger 2006; Senga 2004). South Asia, one of the most impoverished regions in the world, is at a high risk of fl o oding for many reasons (Kale 2003, 2012; Mirza 2011; Varis et al. 2011; Osti et al. 2011; Kumar et al. 2010; Gupta and Chakrapani 2007; Chowdhury and Ward 2007; Ferdous and Hossain 2005; Ahmad and Ahmad 2003; Chowdhury 2003a; Mirza 2003; Mirza et al. 2003; Anon 1993). With South Asia's extreme population density and rampant poverty, the problem of flooding is likely to exacerbate with climate warming, as intense precipitation is projected to swell (Solomon et al. 2007; Cruz et al. 2007; Milly et al. 2002; Palmer and Rälsänen 2002).

Overall, the number of fl o od events in the region is increasing, with an average occurrence of nine per year, but, the peak discharges of major rivers have not been changed noticeably (Mirza 2003). The spatial distribution of floods in the region during 1950–2011 shows that India has the highest incidence of floods, followed by Bangladesh (see Fig. 1.3). Between 1950 and 2011, 0.14 million deaths were attributed to floods, while 1.2 billion people were affected in South Asia (see Table 1.3). Losses from floods in the region totalled $65.3 billion between 1950 and 2011, of which India had the highest economic damage (54.9%), followed by Pakistan (22.9%) and Bangladesh (18.5%).

## 1.4 Flood hazards in Indian situation

India is one of the most flood prone countries in the world. The principal cause for flood in this country, namely, the monsoon, the highly silted river systems, the steep and highly erodible mountains, particularly those of the Himalayan ranges. The average rainfall in India is 1150 mm with significant differentiate across the country. The annual rainfall along the western coast and Western Ghats, Khasi hills and over most of the Brahmaputra valley amounts to more than 2500 mm. Most of the floods occur during the monsoon period and are usually associated with tropical storms or depressions, active monsoon conditions and break monsoon situations.

Twenty-three of the 36 states and union territories in the country are subject to floods and 40 million hectares of land, roughly one-eighth of the country's geographical area, is prone to floods. The National Flood Control Program was launched in the country in 1954. Since then sizeable progress has been made in the flood protection measures. By 1976, nearly one third of the flood prone area had been afforded reasonable protection; considerable experience has been gained in planning, implementation and performance of flood warning, protection and control measures (CWC, 2007). Table 1.8 presents the flood affected area and damages for the period 1953 to 2004 in India as per Water Data Complete Book 2005 and Central Water Commission, 2007).

NIDM mentioned in its document that in Bihar 100% and in U.P. 82% flood is caused due to land depression and well-marked low pressure. In W. Bengal main reason for flood is cyclonic circulation. Whereas in Punjab, Gujarat, Rajasthan & Jammu & Kashmir the main reason of frequent flooding is low pressure areas. Flood in Orissa and Andhra Pradesh is due to monsoon depression. Now days metropolitan cities are facing repeating episodes of the flood. This flood is caused by mismanaged drainage and sewer system which get chocked due to careless dumping of the wastes in the drains and poor maintenance by the responsible agencies. The coastal flood is mainly because of the cyclones and tsunami. Rashtriya Barh Aayog (1980), mentioned that India's 12% land comes under the flooded areas which were comprised nearly 40 million hectares of land. This has exceeded upto 49.815 mha as per the database maintained by CWC based on the flood damage data reported by States for the period from 1953-2010 (Report of Working Group on Flood Management and Region Specific Issues for XII Plan (2011).Annual average area and population affected due to flood: 7.2 M ha and 3.19 million respectively.

India has faced 649 disasters from 1915 to 2015. Out of these 649 events 302 disaster were caused by flood with on an average of 3 flood per year. This accounted approximately 47% of total disasters took place in India in the last 100 years. These floods can be further divided into Riverine Flood, Flash flood, coastal flood and other type of flood. The summary of the affected people, death and economic damage to the India is given in the following table.

■ **Table 1.4 Flood and related damage in India during 1915-2015**

| Flood disaster type | Event count | Total deaths | Total affected | Total damage ('000' US $) |
|---|---|---|---|---|
| 1. Riverine Flood | 143 | 29810 | 333442962 | 41404929 |
| 2. Flash Flood | 23 | 7,436 | 23443526 | 416200 |
| 3. Coastal Flood | 4 | 569 | 11500000 | 275000 |
| 4. Others | 132 | 33,611 | 462703212 | 11898059 |
| | 302 | 71426 | 831089700 | 53994188 |

Decadal change of flood in India distinguishes an alarming picture. If we look at the flood trend based on CRED data we find that in the last five decades India has witness continuous rise in flood disasters. The occurrence of flood disasters reached approximately 100 in the last decade. (It should be noted that the number mentioned here is talked about those incidences which turns as disaster as per the CRED conditions). The lives claimed by these floods have gone from an average of 1000 per year in the 1965-75 decade to 1700 per year in 2005-15 decade. The cumulative economic loss in the last decade i.e. 2005-2015 was nearly 2% of current GDP of India. Compare to previous decadal loss last decade shows a steep rise on economic burden caused by flood. The decadal economic burden burgeoned from USD 11.6 billion in 1995-2005 to USD 34.5 billion in 2005-2015. This because the most affected five floods took place in last five years only. Uttarakhand flood (2013), Leh-Laddakh flood (2010), Assam flood (2012), Jammu Kashmere flood (2014) and recently Manipur Flood (2015) are some example of the biggest floods in India.

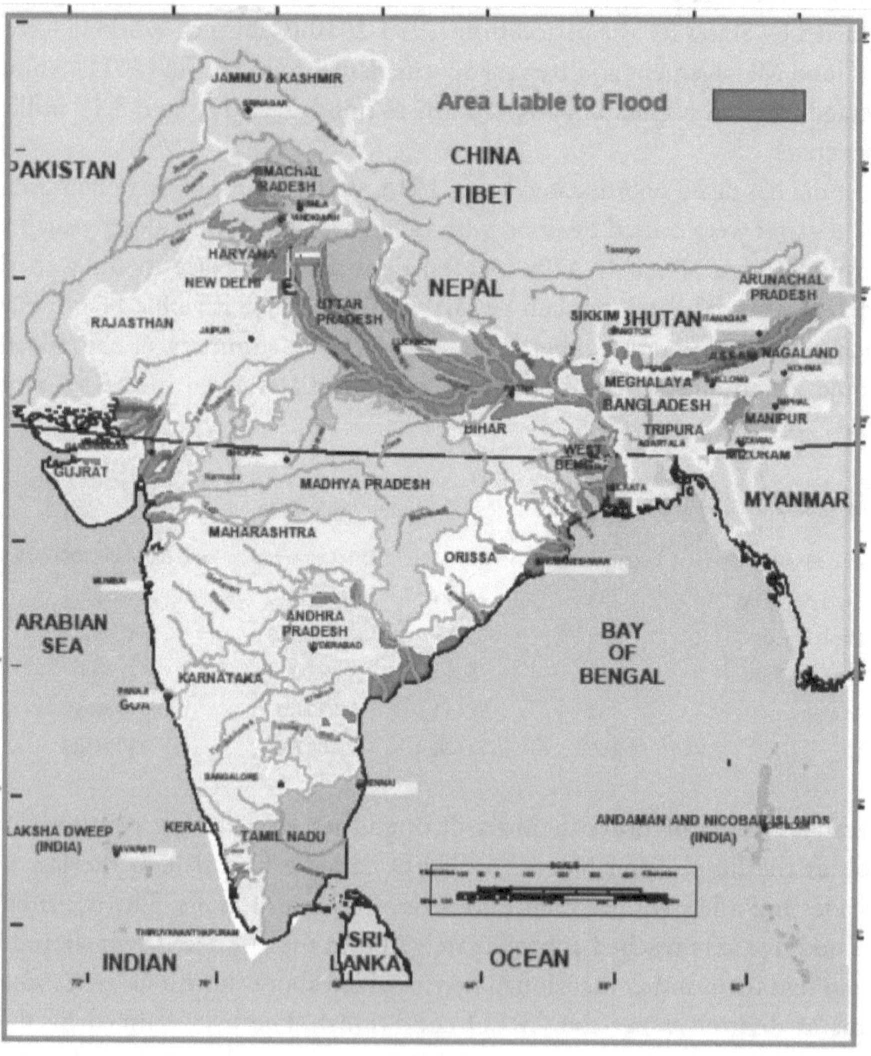


**Fig. 1.3:** Normal Flood Map in India (source: NIDM)

## 1.5 Literature Review

Our very own survival on earth essentially depends on two basic resources – soil and water, nature's two valuable gifts to mankind. Water means life. This veracity from long past has enacted the hallmark of reality as how numerous civilizations flourished with its assurances. Even until this day, inspite of great advancement of modern science and technology for mankind, nothing but the water bodies specially the river signifies the unique bond, which exists between man and nature. Throughout the history it is seen that people are attracted to lands adjacent to rivers. The reason behind it could be easily perceived. This is due to the deposits of alluvium forming fertile soils in the river basins, which help in rising of different crops. Probably this was the prime factor for the down of Mesopotamian civilization in the bank of the rivers Tigris and Euphrates. Availability of level lands for easy means of transport and communication and human occupation through settlements etc. have also attracted people. The rivers while embracing the heartlands of civilizations, nature numerous stories. There are numerous descriptions of these aspects scattered in the pages of journals, books, monographs etc. Floods are repeatedly in the headlines of local, national and international media. Most of the stories concerned with comparatively minor events of floods, which cause little damage, are soon forgotten. But those, which are most directly effective, are always mentioned or remembered.

Floods events as well as their studies and management practices attracted people since the dawn of human civilization. The history of many countries like Egypt, china, Turkey etc. reveals the fact. However, modern studies on the line based on observed data are very recent. In country like U.S.A, such a study had begun only in 1928 with the adoption of proposal by congress to expand the food control measures of the river Mississippi. In U.K, modern study on floods was started in 1933 after the formulation of a proposal for the study of reservoir practices by the Institute of Civil Engineers. However, in the present-day context, plenty of works have been done both in theoretical as well as in applied aspects relating to flood hazard. The important areas of study in this line are characteristics of floods, flood control and management; flood damage assessment and its impact on human society; environmental aspects of flood control measures etc. The study of watershed and flood plain management, impact of floods on human occupancies and response to floods etc. are also important aspects associated with flood hazard. Studies on impact of floods on the areas of human occupancy have now become a field of attraction, because such evaluation may help the sustainability of life in the society.

**N.K. Goel, R.S. Kurothe et al., (1999),** Studied on 'Flood Frequency Distribution for Correlated Rainfall Intensity and Duration'. In this paper, authors analyze a derived flood frequency distribution (DFFD) combines a stochastic rainfall model with a deterministic rainfall – runoff model to obtain a physically based probability distribution of flood discharges. Previous DFFD studies have either assumed that rainfall intensity and duration are independent or negatively correlated. This study is more general than previous studies because it accommodates both positive and negative correlations between rainfall intensity and duration. Rainfall – runoff processes are modelled using a $\phi$-index infiltration model and a geomorphoclimatic instantaneous unit hydrograph. Application to four Indian watersheds and one US watershed demonstrates that (1) the correlation of rainfall intensity and duration has an important impact on the DFFD and (2) the DFFD provides a potentially useful alternative for estimating flood flow quantiles at ungaged sites. The DFFD model for the four Indian watersheds the CDF of flood discharge is illustrated 95% confidence intervals assuming a lognormal distribution of flood discharge. The confidence intervals were constructed by fitting a lognormal distribution to the flood discharge observation at each site and estimating 95% confidence limits about the true distribution. The confidence intervals reflect our uncertainty regarding the underlying CDF of flood discharges at each site, and hence provide a useful and informative basis for evaluating the results of the DFFD models.

**According to Chambers (2000),** Vulnerability is difficult to cope with the community experiences as it is exposure to contingencies and stress. So, the vulnerability has two sides i.e. (a) External Side: is related to the shock and stresses exposure to the individual or households. (b) Internal Side: is related to the defencelessness which means the incapability to cope without damaging losses. Losses makes physically weaker, economically poor, psychologically harmed, social dependent.

**Bohle, (2001),** Expended the concept of vulnerability of Chambers. As seen in Chambers, (2000) the vulnerability is having the two sided: External and Internal sides. Figure 1.1 shows that the external side is related to the exposure and shocks and is influenced by the political economic approaches, human ecology perspectives and the entitlement theory. While the internal side is the theory is related to the coping and is influenced by crisis and conflict theory, action theory approaches and models of access to assets.

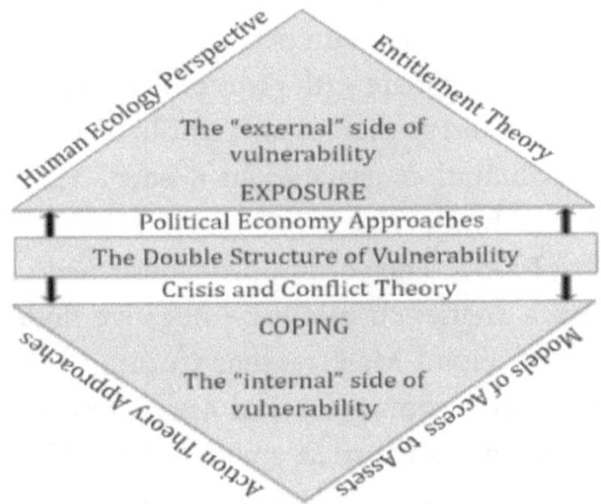



**Fig. 1.4:** Bhole'sconcept about vulnerability.

**Annual Report Brahmaputra Board, Government of India (2002),** The community-facilitated coping measure generally requires planning, participatory operationalization, monitoring, and continuous evaluation of overall implementation of various related activities. To run a smoothly functional 'temporary flood shelter' (here after called flood shelter), formation of a community-based Flood Management Committee is essential. People expressed in one PRA that the Union Disaster Management Committee, as mandated by the Ministry of Home Affairs, must be activated in order to facilitate CBFM activities at the block levels, operationalize "Community-Level Flood Management Committee". Develop a participatory management code for undertaking day-to-day activities of the proposed flood shelter. Clearly marks escape routes, preferably showing signs along the escape routes. Assess the overall requirement of space within the flood shelter and if needed, increase capacity elsewhere and or within the premises. Clean up the premises; provide room for the privacy of the females. Check where to place cooking utensils and stoves. Create sufficient number of sanitary latrines, based on capacity assessment. Make cleaning up schedules for the latrines. Keep frequent contacts with the Thana Health Officer and arrangements for health check-ups at regular intervals. Create separate spaces for storage of

(a) medicine, (b) food items, (c) register books/logbooks, (d) money, (e) dry fuel etc. Provide rooms for treating patients, privacy of lactating mothers and adolescent girls and overall administration of the activities. Liaise with Local Government Institutions and NGOs for various supplies (food items, drinking water, fuel, medicine etc.). Based on capacity assessment, assess weekly demand for various supplies. Maintain charts and logbooks on utilization and supply of such material. Negotiate with government authority to help create a community-based trust fund so that it may be utilized for carrying out various preparedness and rehabilitation activities, as needed. Maintain ledgers while spending from the trust fund.

**UNDP Report (2003),** The community concerned generally take note of the following few activities to minimize negative flood impacts activate the 'Community-Level Flood Management Committee's (FMCs). If there is none, they form such a committee and assign responsibilities/duties to the members, individually and or in small groups. Quickly assess needs of the poor, females and the disadvantaged in the community. Prepare plans based on needs assessment for relocation, preparedness and relevant action. Identify safest means and road-plans for relocation/evacuation in those designated flood shelters. Prepare the designated flood shelter(s) in terms of (a) cleaning up the premises, (b) preparing large-size cooking stoves, (c) sinking afresh or elevating the existing tube well above flood danger level, (d) making smaller rooms available for health care check-ups, lactating mothers and children, chambers for privacy of adolescent girls, storage of medicine and food items, and for storage of fuel wood/biomass and or kerosene, and arrange lanterns for lighting. Identify alternative shelters and expand capacity of shelters to prepare for the worst. Ensure that a few boats, maintained in working condition, are at the disposal of the VDMC (Village Disaster Management Committees) to facilitate relocation of the elderly, the children and ailing/pregnant women. Make a few cages, using low-cost material, collect fish fingerlings and begin 'cage fish culture'. Nilotica and Pungash varieties of fish grow very well under confinement of the cage, especially when adequate feed is supplied to the growing fish. Growing fish fingerlings in confinement, during the course of the entire flood season, would enhance income by the end of the flood season – which in turn would enhance greater financial opportunity for carrying out post-flood rehabilitation.

**ADPC Report, (2004),** There is a general perception among people living in flood vulnerable areas about flood events which are generally damaging. According to people's perception, annually occurring low-level flood events are most usual and they do not worry about such flooding. People call it 'barsha' and often find it useful for replenishment of top soils. On the other hand, there are events, which disrupt life, to some extent cause extent cause damage to agriculture and to a lesser extent to the infrastructure. These moderate events are called 'bonna' in local terms. People also can identify unusual flood events, which they call 'plabon' or 'moha-plabon'. These are, according to local perception, most damaging- causing damages to crops and cropping potential during 'kharif' season; completely disrupting life and economic activities; lasting for a long period, often weeks together; wreaking havoc on the physical infrastructure etc. People find 'flood preparedness' as the most viable tool for them to manage floods, as reported during the PRA/FGD. The community must be part of flood risk identification, prioritization, plan formulation, implementation, monitoring, and evaluation. People are involved in all aspects of the flood risk management process, beginning with assessment. Community-based risk assessment allows all community members to participate, and to identify the flood hazard they face and understand it. The assessment provides them with the information they need to enable them to participate in decision making. Risk mapping can be a community project that encourages participation and awareness. It as an exercise that not only produces a risk map that is understood by the participants, but also informs them of potential hazards, vulnerability of risk elements, and potential exposure.

**According to Dwyer, (2004),** The vulnerability cannot be determined by one factor but the combination of various factors which influence people prone to more vulnerable due to the certain hazards. Also they justified their saying by one example " the elderly people has high vulnerability not because of their age but also the accompanying condition if he or she lives alone, being disabled and also low income, but if they live with another persons may has some health insurance, has some savings etc then it decrease their vulnerability". Some of the factors that are considered in vulnerability quantification are water depth, flow velocity, flow duration, wave height, time of onset etc. The vulnerability is also influenced by social, economic and political factors. So to get the better understanding of vulnerability it is necessary to identify the social, economic and political dimensions of risk assessment that contributes to vulnerability.

**Delica-Wilson, (2005),** Expressed that it highlighted the role of NGO and community based coping strategies. It is found that many of the NGO activities face the problem of sustainability over a longer period of time, especially once the NGO withdrew from the field of flood management. Many of the NGO programs are poorly designed and so they are unable to either attract continuing support or transfer project ownership to communities. Continuation of community activities over a longer period of time at local level, as well as local institutions can continue the CBFM activities. Thus, even though the initiatives are started with the NGO interventions, it is important to link them to the local community activities, and incorporate them into Flood Preparedness plan (FPP) to ensure its sustainability and replication of innovative efforts to other parts of flood prone areas. Thus, the major challenges of the Community Based Disaster Management (CBDM) are: 1) sustainability of the efforts in the community level, and 2) incorporation of the CBDM issues in the planning level. To be effective and to create sustainable impact, the application of the CBDM must go beyond the initiative of communities, NGOs and a handful of local governments. As part of an advocacy for more responsive and effective governance, national and state level governments should look at integrating CDBM in their policy and implementing procedures.

**According to IPCC, (2007),** Flood vulnerability is the degree to which the system is and unable to cope with adverse effects of climate change, including climate variability and extremes it is the function of the character, magnitude and rate of climate change and variation to which a system is exposed, its sensitivity and its adaptive capacity.

**The 5th International Conference on Flood Management Report (ICFM5, 2008),** It marks the continued advancement of flood management practices and policies around the world. The name change from "Defence" as used in the previous four events to "Management" is reflective of the more integrative approaches to flood management that nations are increasingly employing. The ICFM5 theme is 'Floods: From Risk to Opportunity", reflective of the continued trend towards a broader understanding of how we collectively make use of the opportunities provided by floods and flooding, cope with risks posed by them and plan for and respond to flood events. It provides a unique opportunity for these various specialists to come together to exchange ideas and experiences. Societies continue to occupy floodplains and delta areas that are highly susceptible to the incidence of severe flooding. At the same time, the threat from climate change continues as witnessed by the changes in frequency and severity of inland floods and coastal storms. International and regional cooperation and collaboration is critical to the success of the overall flood damage reduction process.

**Samanta. S (2008),** Study on Land-Use Land-Cover Mapping and Issues of Floods and Its Management- A Case Study on Tapasia Mouza In the Kaliaghai River Basin, Paschim Medinipur district using Remote Sensing and GIS Techniques. In this study carried out to prepare a land-use/land-cover map of the Kaliaghai river basin by using satellite imagery through digital image processing and to prepare a land-use/land-cover map and flood map of Tapasia Mouza using cadastral map through GIS methodology. In this study find some result like- flood is the major problems of this village in the monsoon period. About 60% of total geographical areas of the village inundated frequently in the time of flood occur. Channel depth decreases every year due to excessive sedimentation. So, the channel can't contain and pass out excess water and spill during the rainy season. Peak discharge, textural conditions of alluvial, heavy rainfall in short time, heavy rainfall on the upper catchments area are responsible for flash flood.

**According to Van Westen, et al., (2009),** The elements at risk mapping can be carried at in various scale levels and also depend upon the requirements of the study. The scale levels range from small scale to the detailed scale. Table 1.1 shows the elements at risk mapping versus the scale, adopted from (Van Westen, et al., 2009).

**P.Guhathakurta, O.P Sreejith & P.A Menon, (2011),** Studied on 'Impact of climate change on extreme rainfall events and flood risk in India' analyze some of the extreme rainfall indices using reliable, consistent and sufficient amount of rain gauge station data and to study the changes in the frequency of rainy days, rainy days as well as heavy rainfall days. For this study the data was collected from Indian Meteorological Department (IMD) Pune. Mann-Kendall (MK) trend test of non-parametric and 'Least square linear fit' method use. The outcome of the study rainy days and heavy rainfall days can be seen over most parts of central, north and eastern parts of the country using both MK and t test. Wet days have increased in peninsular India particularly over Karnataka, Andhrapradesh and parts of

■ **Table 1.5:** Elements at risk mapping in different scale

| Elements at Risk | Scale Analysis | | | |
|---|---|---|---|---|
| | Small (<1:100000) | Medium (25-50000) | Large (10,000) | Detailed (>1:10000) |
| Buildings | By municipality -Number of Buildings | Mapping Units -predominant Types e.g Residential, Commercial, Industrial. -Number of Buildings | Building Foot Print -Generalized Use -Height -Building Types | Building Foot Prints -Detailed Use -Buildings Types -Construction Types -Quality/Age -Foundation |
| Transportation Networks | General location of transportation networks | Roads and Railway network with general traffic density formation | All transportation networks with detailed classification including viaducts and traffic dates etc. | All transportation networks with detailed engineering works and detailed dynamic traffic data. |
| Population Data | By municipality -Population Density -Gender -Age | By Ward -Population Density -Gender -Age | By mapping Units -Population Density -Daytime/night time -Gender -Age | Population per Buildings -Day time/night time -Gender -Age -Education |
| Agricultural Data | By municipality -crops type -yield information | By homogeneous -crops types -yield information | By cadastral Parcel -crop types -crop rotation -yield Information -agricultural buildings | By cadastral Parcel, for a Given period of the year -crop types -crop rotation and time -yield information |
| Ecological Data | Natural protected area with international approval | Natural protected area with national relevance | General flora and fauna data per scale cadastral parcel | Detailed flora and fauna data per cadastral parcel |

Rajasthan and some parts of eastern India while most parts of central and northern India showed a decreasing trend in frequency of rainy days. Significant increasing trends also are clearly noticed in the frequency of rainy days over Rajasthan, parts of Gangetic West Bengal and adjoining parts of Jharkhand. This indicates that the great desert areas of India are becoming wet.

**According to S. Chaudhury, (2012)** the development of human civilization has always been very closely related to water availability and river valleys. On the contrary, flood hazard is one of the natural hazards better understood by riverain populations and the presence of the river is a permanent reminder of the dangerous situation that may occur. In Silabati river basin especially it lower reaches large number of people (approximately 100000) and their livelihoods are affected by flooding which covering larger part of Ghatal and Daspur of Paschim Medinipur district, West Bengal.

**L. Mandal & D.K Khan (2012),** Studied on 'Flood risk reduction in lower Damodar basin, West Bengal' analyzed the risk reduction from flood by examining the factors influencing local communities to adopt both structural and non-structural flood mitigation strategies in lower Damodar basin in Eastern India. The hydro-meteorological condition of the study area is dominated by monsoon confined to four months in a year. The intense rainfall during monsoon and discharge from upland reservoir leads to severe flooding in various parts of the area in varying magnitude almost in every year. The river Damodar, known as 'sorrow of Bengal' due to its flood ravages in entire Damodar valley caused much unhappiness and distress in lower Damodar region. In this study, the annual peak flow is taken to determine the flood frequency analysis. The damage due to flood in terms of economic loss and the probability of flood occurrences are used for assessing flood risk and magnitude of vulnerability in the study area. This paper briefly describes the flood problems of lower Damodar basin, the magnitude of flood damages and outlines of important flood management practices. As a severe flood prone zone, lower Damodar basin requires mitigation of the diverse impacts of flooding by local decision makers. The adopted structural measures in this area have not yielded sufficient results to mitigate the chronic flood problems. Therefore, some non-structural measures are taken into consideration like flood forecasting, alternative cropping arrangements and capacity building through self-help group. Particular attention is paid to the role of organizational capacity to address floods in addition to various geophysical and socio-economic characteristics.

**Rudra. K (2012),** Opined that continuing colonial legacy in management of rivers of West Bengal. The drainage system of West Bengal has changed appreciably during known historical periods. Many rivers have been disappeared and many have gone dry. The changing courses of rivers have drawn attention of the Geographers, Historians and many concerned academicians. It is also an interest of common people. But our understanding about his life support system is incomplete. The British took over the control of Bengal in the mid 18[th]centaury when Britain itself was in the thrones of the industrial revolution. The road-rail and urban-industrial model of development was implanted into an inappropriate geographical setting leading many environmental changes. Since the roads and railways intercepted the drainage there was expansion of floodable area, outbreak of malaria and decline food production. The urban sector externalized their cost of living on to rural poor since early 19th century; the engineering intervention into the fluvial regime of Bengal delta was started with the construction of embankment to achieve a freedom from flood. It was denied that flood was not exclusively the evil but had many beneficial roles.

The British Raj ended in 1947 but the river management continued to be guided by the colonial legacy and reductionist engineering logic. A concentration on purely traditional hydrological engineering solutions to augment lean season flows and to combat flood and erosion, continue to imperial the ecological security and delicate hydrological balance of the densely populated Gangetic Delta.

The vast and intricate mesh of tributaries and distributaries in its lower deltaic region are characterized by some unique hydrological and morphological features which give rise to certain ecological processes typical in the region. The region has been experiencing difficulties adjusting to the combination of accelerated process of natural and anthropogenic change owing to which certain human ecological and social problems has changed. The second phase of engineering investigation was the construction of massive dam across the rivers with the multipurpose objectives of irrigation, power generation and flood control. The Damodar valley corporation generates mostly thermal power. The Farakka Barrage was constructed to resuscitate the navigation channel leading to Kolkata port. But the induced water from the barrage failed to flush the navigation channel and vessels found it difficult to approach to port. On the country, increasing bank failure and expanding flood control upstream of the barrage have posed a formidable challenge to the government.

**Mandal. M (2012),** Studied on People's Perception on Flood Management at Daspur-I Block, Paschim Medinipur district in West Bengal, revealed a number of important facts about the interaction between people and floods.

Focus group discussions and in-depth interviews were the most effective data collection tools because they focused on psycho-social factors and drew out in-depth responses from respondents about what they think and how they feel. Local resources available for flood risk reduction should be more utilized with less reliance on external aid to ensure sustainability. The use of existing administrative authorities and community primary health workers should be entrusted to promote food security, water, and sanitation and health services. Additional training and incentives could extend their services concerning flood control and proper understanding of early warning system. Community links with government agencies and NGOs should be strengthened in order to ensure community of efforts at flood risk reduction. Flood risk management needs to be considered within development strategies and planning at all levels.

**Md.A.Asad, S.Kar et al, (2013),** Studied on 'Flood Frequency Modeling Using Gumbel's And Powell's Method for Dudhkumar River'. This paper aims at estimating return period associated with flood peaks of varying magnitudes from recorded floods using statistical methods. Gumbel Distribution, Powell Distribution and for the Goodness of Fit Chi-square test are used. Flood Frequency Analysis (FFA) has been done for Dudhkumar River for 14 years discharge data. The results tell that, Gumble and Powell distribution clearly describes the flood magnitude while a Chi-square test derives no significance differences (p=1) between the predicted and observed floods. Probability distribution function also fit with the flood data. Due to goodness of fit and probable fitted value of the flood, the distribution should be used in calculating design flood magnitude. Hence the distribution models can be used to predict the occurrence of flood event for Dudhkumar River.

**K. Mujiburrehman (2013),** Studied on "Frequency Analysis of Flood Flow at Gurudeshwar Station in Narmada River, Gujrat, India". This paper studied on maximum monthly flood data in Narmada River at Garudeshwar station using widely used frequency distributions for periods from 1949 to 1979. The Normal, Lognormal, Log Pearson Type III and Gumble Extreme Value Type I are proposed and tested together with their single distributions to identify the optimal model for maximum monthly flood analysis. The selected model will be determined based on the minimum error produced by some criteria of Goodness of Fit (GOF) tests. The results indicated that Normal distribution is better than the other distributions in modelling maximum monthly flood magnitude at Garudeshwar station in Narmada

River. However, the flood data should be further analyzed and corrected for missing data, historical data and zero flood values. The study should be further extended to account for outliers involved in the data. Based on this study the Normal distribution curve has been found as most suitable distribution for analysis of maximum monthly flood data of Narmada River at Garudeshwar station. This study can be further extended for preparation of flood inundation map for various return periods. The study can be also applied in flood forecasting management.

**V.Kamal, S.Mukherjee, P.Sing et al, (2016),** Studied on "Flood Frequency Analysis of Ganga River at Haridwar and Garhmukteshwar". This study is in a part of the upper Indo-Ganga plains subzone. Statistical distributions applied on the discharge data at two stations found that for Haridwar lognormal and for Garhmukteshwar Gumble EV1 is applicable. The importance of this study lies in its ability to predict the discharge for a return period after a suitable distribution is found for an area. The study has shown that the recent technique of GEV distribution that uses L-Moments does not fits well with the discharge data of Ganga in Haridwar for long term data but Log normal (3P) fits and prove more reliable for flood frequency analysis. Goodness of fit tests validated that Gumble EV1 distribution stand high in ranking for short term data of Garhmukteshwar at 145 km downstream. The comparison of result if we have more historical data, with values neither overshooting nor undershooting.

## 1.6  Flood hazards assessment

The primary objectives of the study are to explore some of the basic characteristics, causes and controlling variables and consequence of the floods in Paschim Medinipur district as well as low lying areas of the river basins. It has been stated that the floods are due to surface run-off and therefore all the factors that affect surface run-off also affect flood flows. These factors can broadly be grouped into three categories i.e. one of them determines the intensity of storms and rainfall that are likely to visit the drainage basin. The other one is the physical characteristics of the basin which affect and determine the disposal of the rainfall. The last one is the geological, geomorphological, and hydrological and other environmental conditions of the lower reaches of the rivers accompanied with that of the tides. The flood problem is very much complicated because in the upper reaches, the problem takes the shape of river spill and bank erosion and lower part of the river basin is inundated.

Thus, the objectives of the study are not to confined the investigations within the limits of geographical interest rather than understanding a wide range of environmental variables responsible for floods with the aim of successful prediction and effective environmental management. Thus, the study aims at understanding the wide range of environmental parameters from geomorphology, hydrology, climatology which are responsible for floods with a sense of their application in environmental management. Thus, the objectives may be summarized as follows-

(1) Understanding and analysis of causes of flooding and other associated flood intensifying condition. An investigation into the causes and controlling variables of the floods as manifested in-a) The physical characteristics of the drainage basin i.e. drainage area, shape, stream length, drainage density and nature of the drainage channels') Geomorphological and hydrological setting of the flooded area i.e. the nature of the drainage channels, their meandering, channel slope, ground water condition, tidal bores and storm surges. c) Type of precipitation; duration of rainfall and intensity and its distribution over the basin and direction of storm movement. d) An examination of the effect of the detention reservoirs on the upstream of the rivers on flood control and flood routing and an estimation of the flood devastations. (2) Characteristics of flooding with respect to magnitude, frequency and periodicity of floods. (3) To determine the flood prone areas with respect to flood of different magnitude. (4) Impact of floods on people and economy. (5) Flood hazard management practices. (6) Impact of flood prevention measure on flood control.

"Identification and marking of flood lines in high flood-prone rivers will help to reduce the effects of flood hazard in adjoining villages or settlement". In order to fulfil the aforesaid objectives, some hypothesis have also been formulated as outlined below-

(1) The peculiar location of the study region, it is a region of rolling topography of Chhotonagpur plateau and its marginal end tough the Bay of Bengal. All the river of this region is charged with the rainfall in the total catchment area of Chhotonagpur plateau and rainfall within the respective basin area and to create recurrent floods and associated problems. (2) There prevails a serious hazard in the district due to recurrent floods. (3) Floods of different magnitudes, marked by specific return periods, create hazard conditions of different intensity and devastation.

(4) The middle and the lower plains of the district are subject to severe flood during monsoon and hazard prevails in these parts of the district. (5) Floods have significant impact on the serious-economic and cultural life of the people of the district. (6) The existing flood mitigation and management practices.

The study is based on both primary and secondary data. Primary data are collected through direct field survey and observations, whereas secondary data are collected from various Govt., private, public and semi-public institutions in the form of documents, literatures, charts, maps and diagrams. Most of hydrological data have been collected from the Department of Irrigation and Waterways of the Govt. of West Bengal. The climatic data also collected from the district level Irrigation and Waterways Department and IMD. The data pertaining to flood damage and flood devastations have been collected from the Revenue Department records Govt. of West Bengal. The demarcation of the flood prone areas has been done by the author basing the flood mappings carried out by the Irrigation and Waterways Department, Govt. of West Bengal and community response on flood hazard. The preliminary base maps have been drawn basing on the toposheets of different scales on the Survey of India and maps of the National Atlas Organization. Extensive field work has been carried out by the author along with the supervisor in the study region for observing the existing drainage channels and their distributaries; the condition of the dying channels and river mouths. The field work has been very much useful in field checking of the different features observed in the topographic maps and satellite imageries.

The data collected from the primary and secondary sources have been computed and tabulated and analysed with various quantitative techniques. Its results have been presented in a number of cartographic representations such as maps and graphs. The cartographic and quantitative methods have also been used for the analysis of the stream gauging records and flood stages and their magnitude and frequency. Characteristics of the floods have been shown through flood hydrographs. In the time-series analysis of the flood stage and damage, the fluctuations and long-term trends of the data has been studied through the "Moving Average". The magnitude and frequency and the probability of peak flood discharge has been studied with the "Gumbel's law of extreme value Distribution" adopted from the Ven-Te Chow's Hand-Book of Applied Hydrology (Chow, 1964).

**■ Table 1.6: Coordination Schema and Study Design**

| Objectives | Variables | | Method | Expected Findings |
|---|---|---|---|---|
| | Major | Minor | | |
| 1. Characteristics of Flooding | Socio- economic | a) Population b) Houses c) Area d) Human life e) Infrastructure f) Crop | Descriptive statistics and trend analysis | Frequency and Magnitude of Floods. Probability of Floods. |
| 2. Understanding and Analysis of Causes of Flooding and Flood Intensifying Condition | Basin characteristics | a) Drainage size b) Drainage shape c) Drainage area d) slope | Morphometric analysis, Association analysis, Trend analysis | Major factors which are associated with flooding and also responsible for flooding. |
| | Climatological characteristics | a) Type of precipitation b) Intensity of rainfall c) Duration of rainfall | | |
| 3. Zoning of flood prone areas | Frequency, Depth | a) Population b) Housing Units | GIS based approach | Flood Prone areas. |
| 4. Vulnerability Analysis and Risk Assessment | Physical | a) Elevation b) Land use c) Distance to active channel d) Geology | Analytical Hierarchy Process (AHP). | Physical and Social Vulnerability Mapping. Determine the vulnerability of Physical and Social variables. Flood Risk Mapping. Estimated the risk population and risk of housing units. |
| | Social | a) Demographic b) Socio-economic c) Infrastructure and lifelines | | |
| 5. Management Practices | Physical | a) Watershed management b) Flood plain zoning | Content analysis | Way of flood hazard management. |
| | Social | a) Afforestation b) Flood insurance c) Crop management | | |

From the point of latest advances or development in the field as an interdisciplinary subject, this will help in understanding the primary causes and finding out some effective means of controlling the floods in the lower reaches of the river basin. It is not only a severe environmental problem but has posed a challenge to the people. So, an understanding of the characteristics and controlling variables of the flood is necessary not only for academic interest but also for the people to get rid of the flood hazards. The available studies show a great deficiency of knowledge about the immerging dimensions of hydrology of floods in India and more specifically very little is known about the following question like-

a.    What are the primary causes of flood?

b.    What is the probable frequency of occurrence of floods?

c.  To what extent the flood detention reservoirs have been effective in controlling the floods?

Knowledge of the above aspects is not only essential towards understanding the nature of the floods but also it has practical implication in planning for flood control and resource management. The study is significant in so far it will through some light on some of the above aspects which will be of both practical and academic value.

## 1.7 Scope and Limitation of the work

Field survey has been done in more flood prone areas, which is the largest obstacle in marking continuous flood line. There are no alternative points to consider as flood marks in the villages. Therefore, the discussion with the local people is taken into consideration. Socio-economic damages or changes are measured by the collection of secondary data and in order to categorize other losses, for which the data through questioner is calculated, is given but that is also not in terms of numbers. Other things like loss of cattle could not be taken in to consideration because there is no such record in Government offices.

Some time immemorial floods have been responsible for loss of crops and valuable property and untold human misery in the India. An area of more than 40 million hectors in India has been known as flood prone. India, which is traverse by a large number of river systems, experiences seasonal floods. It has been the experience that floods arise almost every year in one part or the other of the country. The rivers of Paschim Medinipur are prone to frequent floods during the south-west monsoon season, particularly in the month of July, August and September. There is every option that this figure may increase due to population growth and developmental works taken up in the flood plains. The largest challenge for flood study is the underlying capacities of the state and district authorities as well as the lack of resources to undertake implementation of priority activities. In most cases, local resources and capacities are often overlooked, thus relying too much upon external assistance. For a successful flood study preparedness planning, it is imperative to learn from the experiences and best practices for greater collaboration and information sharing to enhance the synergy and to extend the resource base for more effective implementation of flood preparedness programs. It is also important to launch and add flood prone zone planning within the overall developmental plan for securing resources for better implementation.

# FLOOD HAZARDS AN INDIAN EXPERIENCE



Flood hazards of West Bengal and Paschim Medinipur District; Geographical Background of the study area: Paschim Medinipur; Geographical Location-Climate-Physiography-Geology-Geomorphology-Hydro-Geology-Soil Characteristics-Drainage Density-Ground water condition and water table-Land use/Land cover Characteristics-Active river channels-History of floods-Vulnerable population/Settlements.

## 2.1 Flood hazards of West Bengal and Paschim Medinipur District

### 2.1.1 Flood characteristics of West Bengal

The flood, water related disaster in the state of West Bengal has been an annual feature. Some parts of the state are victims of onslaughts of flood each year resulting severe loss to standing crops, cattles and human properties. The state has all possible facets of flood, drainage, bank erosion, cyclonic storms ravages and associated problems. It has been noticed that the furies due to flood have increased during the last two decades. A severe inundation took place twice in the fifties i.e.1956, 1959; once in the sixties namely 1968; twice in the seventies i.e. 1971, 1978; thrice in the eighties namely 1984,1986,1987; five times in the first decades of twenty first centaury i.e. 2000,2002,2005,2007,2008 and 2011,2012,2013. Flood and allied problems thus being on the rise, due to stress is to be meted out to both structural and non-structural measure for proper management of flood. 37660 Sq. Km. areas are flood prone out of the total geographical area of the state is about 88752 Sq.Km.

Due to its physical and geographical position, the state apart from the diverse characteristics likes physical, topographical and climatological variation as well. The average rainfall of the state is 1750 mm of which more than 75% occurs during the monsoon period while the hilly region at the foot hills receives the heaviest rainfall ranging from 2500 mm to 5000 mm and the southern districts in the plains receive average of 1125 mm to 1875 mm. Many factors such as intensity and duration of rainfall, sedimentation in river bed, natural and manmade obstruction etc. play a significant role in the occurrence of flood.

## 2.1.2 Flood characteristics of Northern Districts of West Bengal

The northern parts of the state receive high rainfall with the highest of 3600 mm in Cooch Behar district of the Torsa basin areas. In Cooch Behar and Jalpaiguri districts, the rivers originating from the Himalayas has a steep bed slope till they reach the foothill areas, Terai Plain. With the local rainfall of the districts is added the high volume of monsoon flow from upper basins of the Himalayan range. The heavy rainfall in the hills is carried quickly to the foothills with very high velocity. The excessive volume of water cannot be contained in the shallow confines of the riverbanks in the Terai region, this gives rise to flood situation. The flood in plains stays comparatively for longer duration and can be even longer if the Bramhaputra, with whom all rivers of North have their outfall, is in spate. The flood situation in Uttar and Dakshin Dinajpur districts is mainly depend on the rainfall at Bangladesh region. In Malda district, flood occurs due to high discharge carried by the Mahananda and the Ganga. If the upper Mahananda basin receive heavy rainfall then Malda district situated at the lower valley is sure to be flooded.

## 2.1.3 Flood characteristics of Southern Districts of West Bengal

The southern states of West Bengal receive 1250 to 1350 mm average annual rainfall. The major river of South Bengal Ajoy, Damodar, Bhagirathi, Rupnarayan, Kangsabati, Kaliaghai, Silabati and Subarnarekha. In the Jharkhand plateau and other adjoining basin area's high rainfall generates very high volume of overland flow. The nature of terrain, physical character and high rainfall together create the flood situation in this region and another one factor is, the situation becomes very serious when the tidal influence clogs the outfall at the Hoogly.

## 2.1.4 Flood characteristics of Paschim Medinipur Districts of West Bengal

A large proportion of Paschim Medinipur district in the state of West Bengal is also susceptible to flooding. The area of the district is 9295.28 Sq. Km while

1952 Sq. Km is flood prone. The district has four main river catchments i.e. Kangsabati, Kaliaghai and Silabati catchment are more vulnerability of flood than Subarnarekha. Kangsabati, Silabati, Subarnarekha River originated from Chhotonagpur plateau and rainfall within the West Bengal's respective basin area. On the other hand, Kalaighai River originates in said district and it's also very much flood prone in rainy season. Those are the rivers commanding huge catchment areas in and outside the district or state, brought enormous volume of water during the rainy season. Their nature of discharge varies from over 35 to 200000 cubic feet per second. In the monsoon period most of these rivers exceed their normal channel capacity attaining the flood stage and frequently overflows their banks causing great havoc to the life and property of the people. The flood occurring in great magnitude and with undesirable frequency has left their indelible marks over this region since its history and their ravages tell a grim and sorrowful tale of the suffering of the people. And also, reservoirs, the heavy rainfall in Chhotonagpur plateau result in large inflow into the reservoirs of Chandil, Galudi, Durgapur and heavy rain in Bankura and adjacent district result in large inflow into the reservoir of Kangsabati etc. causes the necessary release of large volume of water from reservoirs. The heavy discharge within a short span of time with onrush of water through the rivers causes inundation and water logging in vast areas and also river bank collapse is the great havoc to the life and property of the people in low land region.

## 2.2 Geographical Background of the study area: Paschim Medinipur

### 2.2.1 Geographical location of the Study Area

Paschim Medinipur district, located in the Southern part of West Bengal, has been curved from the erstwhile Medinipur District, the then largest district of India, and came into existence in the present from 1st January 2002. It is situated between 22°57′10″ North and 21°36′35″ North latitude and 88°12′40″ East and 86°35′55″ East longitude. Paschim Medinipur is bounded by Bankura district from the northern side and Purba Medinipur District from the South-eastern side. The Southern boundary of the district is merged with Balasore and Mayurbhanj district of Orissa and western boundary is merged with Singbhum district of Jharkhand. Geographical area of the district is 9295.28 sq. km. The district is further divided into 4 sub-divisions, 29 blocks and 8 Municipalities.

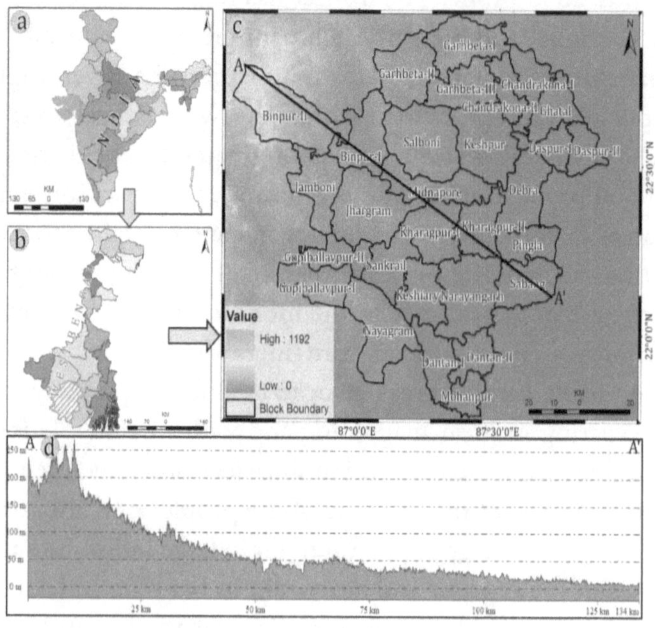



**Fig. 2.1:** Location of the study area: (a) The Indian state of West Bengal, (b) Paschim Medinipur district located in southern part of West Bengal &(c) Elevation variation and block boundary of Paschim Medinipur district & (d) Elevational cross-section of A-A'.

■ **Table: 2.1 Administrative set up of the Districts**

| Sub-Divisions | C.D.Blocks |
| --- | --- |
| Jhargram Sub-Division | Jhargram |
| | Binpur-I |
| | Binpur-II |
| | Jamboni |
| | Nayagram |
| | Sankrail |
| | Gopiballavpur-I |
| | Gopiballavpur-II |
| MedinipurSadar Sub-Division | Ssalboni |
| | Keshpur |
| | Garbeta-I |
| | Garbeta-II |
| | Garbeta-III |
| | Midnapore |

| Sub-Divisions | C.D.Blocks |
|---|---|
| Kharagpur Sub-Division | Debra |
|  | Pingla |
|  | Keshiary |
|  | Datan-I |
|  | Datan-II |
|  | Narayangarh |
|  | Mohanpur |
|  | Sabang |
|  | Kharagpur-I |
|  | Kharagpur-II |
| Ghatal Sub-Division | Chandrakona-I |
|  | Chandrakona-II |
|  | Ghatal |
|  | Daspur-I |
|  | Daspur-II |

## 2.2.2 Climate

The climate is characterized by hot summer, cold winter, abundant rainfall and humidity. The area is experienced by a great variation in climatic characteristics. The climate is very much tropical and exercising monsoonal characteristics with variations in micro-regions. The climate of the western part of the area is being characterized by arid climate having a vicious dry heat in summer, a short winter season and moderately rainfall. The climate of Eastern and Southern part is different in nature, characterized by hot and humid climatic condition. The seasons are however well marked for the entire area.

➢ Summer Season (March to May)
➢ South West Monsoon (June to September)
➢ Post-Monsoon Season (October to November)
➢ Winter Season (December to February)

Rainfall fluctuates widely over years and concentrates over a few months of a year under monsoon. The annual rainfall of the district varies from 1400 mm to 1500 mm while the annual temperature ranges from $9^0c$ to $43^0c$.

**Rainfall:** In the cold weather months of November and December only 12-25mmrainfall falls monthly, such rain as there is being due to the northward movement of cyclonic storms from the south of the Bay of Bengal. From about the end of December, when the northerly trade winds have become established, cold season storms are caused by shallow depression, which originates in the north-west of the Bay and move eastward. During their passage they cause general cloudy weather and light rainfall. At the end of January or the beginning of February a local breeze commence. The rainfall in March and April at an average 25-75 mm. Most of the rainfall occur (75%) in five months i.e. May to September in the district during the monsoon periods. According to state Agro Meteorological Department of West Bengal, averages of monthly rainfall data for PaschimMedinipur district has been calculated over the period of 1991-2014 (see Table 2.2 & Fig. 2.2).

**Temperature:** Western part of the district, where the surface soil is composed of red laterite and the hot westerly winds from central India penetrate of times, exceptionally high day temperatures are a feature of the hot weather months. Table 2.3 shows the monthly maximum and minimum mean air temperature of the district.

■ **Table 2.2:** Average monthly rainfall from 1991-2014 (Station:Medinipur)

| Months | J | F | M | A | M | J | J | A | S | O | N | D |
|---|---|---|---|---|---|---|---|---|---|---|---|---|
| Rainfall (mm) | 19.1 | 26.8 | 31.8 | 52.4 | 140.5 | 257.3 | 336.1 | 317.7 | 288.6 | 119.6 | 35.1 | 5.5 |

*Source: West Bengal District management Authority.*

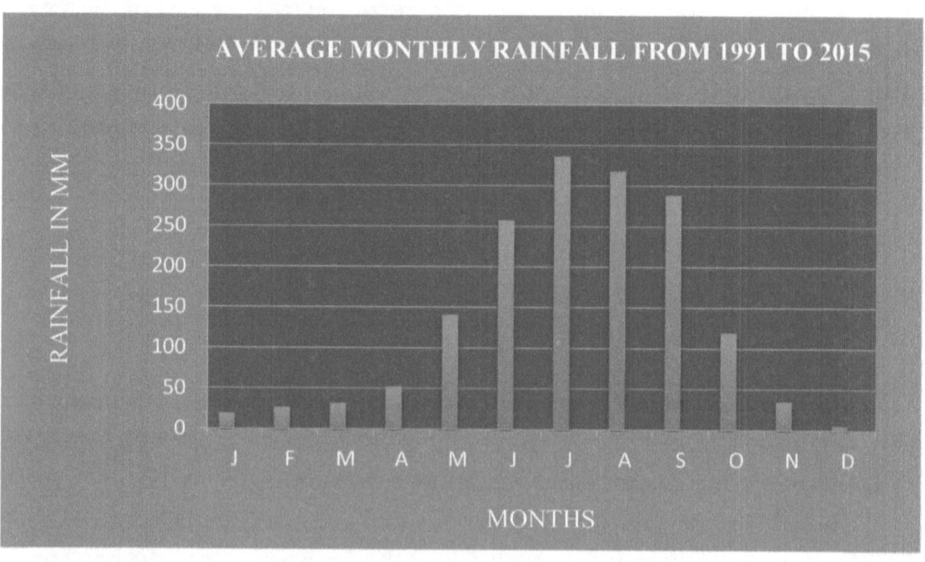


**Fig. 2.2:** Average monthly rainfall from 1991-2015.

■ **Table 2.3:** Mean Air Temperature (Station:Medinipur)

| Months | J | F | M | A | M | J | J | A | S | O | N | D |
|---|---|---|---|---|---|---|---|---|---|---|---|---|
| Maximum (⁰c) | 30 | 34.1 | 39.4 | 41.8 | 41.9 | 39.9 | 35.7 | 34.4 | 34.7 | 34.2 | 32.0 | 29.1 |
| Minimum (⁰c) | 9.4 | 12.1 | 16.3 | 19.8 | 21.0 | 22.7 | 23.3 | 23.6 | 22.9 | 19.4 | 14.3 | 10.6 |

*Source: IMD, Pune.*

**Winds:** From about the middle of March a strong breeze begins to blow from the south and continues through the hot weather. From the beginning of June these local sea breezes are replaced by the steadier sea winds of the South West monsoon, which blows till the month of October. This is followed by a short calm lasting till about the middle of November and broken only by cyclones, occasionally accompanied by storm-waves, which are never so severe oars disastrous as during this period. The north wind then sets in and lasts generally till about the end of February (see Table 2.4 & Fig. 2.3, 2.4).

■ **Table 2.4:** Monthly mean wind directions at 8 A.M and monthly average wind velocity km/ph

| Months | J | F | M | A | M | J | J | A | S | O | N | D |
|---|---|---|---|---|---|---|---|---|---|---|---|---|
| Mean wind direction of 8 A.M. (Degree) | N 3 W | N 6 W | S 16 W | S 4 E | S 8 E | S 16 W | S 8 W | S 33 E | S 43 E | S 3 E | N 2 W | N 9 W |
| Average wind velocity (km/ph.) | 2.1 | 2.7 | 3.4 | 4.6 | 5.2 | 4.2 | 3.2 | 3.2 | 2.7 | 1.9 | 2.1 | 1.9 |

*Source: Alipore Meteorological office.*

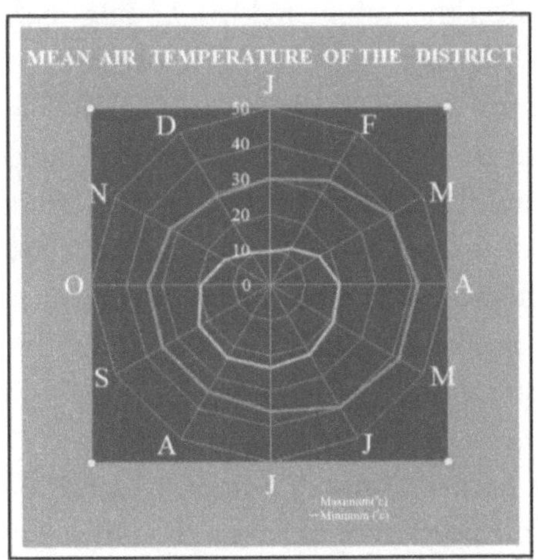


**Fig. 2.3:** Mean air temperature of the district.

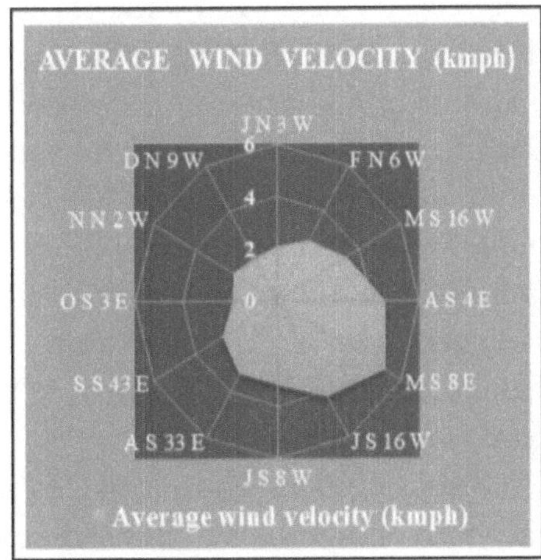


**Fig. 2.4:** Average wind velocity of the district (km/ph.).

### 2.2.3 Physiography

On the basic of the characteristics of the districts, the entire Paschim Medinipur district has broadly been divided into two natural divisions – the western upland including undulating lateritic Rarh Plain and the south eastern Gangetic alluvial plain. Physiographically, the region has been sub-divided into three macro-regions (see Fig. 2.5) and three micro-regions. The macro regions are:

a.   The Western Upland
b.   The Rarh and
c.   The Plain.

The micro-regions lie within these macro-regions are:

a.   Upland of PaschimMedinipur
b.   Shilai Plain and
c.   Lower Cossye Plain.

**Upland of Paschim Medinipur:** Paschim Medinipur is a neighbouring area of Bihar and Odisha. This very upland is of 2029 sq. km. and the lands look wavy in this area. Some small ranges and depression are found here. It is a part of chhotonagpur plateau which is formed with laterite. In the extreme north some hills can be seen which 82 mtr are. to 423 mtr. height. The land is sloping from north-west to south-east. In its hilly surface some rivers and streams course with their move. Among them, some rivers meet the flow of Cossye in the north and some of them meet the Subarnarekha. Among them the major one is Dulung, which is on the right side of the Subarnarekha. The Subarnarekha may be called the controlling river this upland region. The Subarnarekha comes from Jharkhand and entered into Gopiballavpur-I block of this district and then flows like a natural border of West Bengal and Orissa in the Western part of Datan-I Block. Soil surface of this Western region is dry, non-fertile and unsuitable for habitation and cultivation. In lower hilly areas bush and dwarf Sal trees are found. Block like Binpur-II, Sankrail, Jamboni, Gopiballavpur-I & II, Dantan –I, Western part of Jhargram are totally or partly included in this region.

**Plain of Shilai:** This plane-land is a part of Bankura border, which is on the north of this district. This is the middle portion of Shilai on the north and Cossye on the south. This is a portion of eastern Chhotonagpur plateau and of 2528.6 Sq.Km. Shilai is the main river of this area. Shilai River comes from

Purulia and enters into Garbeta-II Block. Due to regular alluvial deposition, the river bed gradually grows and in rainy season it causes floods in Daspur-I and Ghatal block. In Geographical aspect it is known as a depression area.

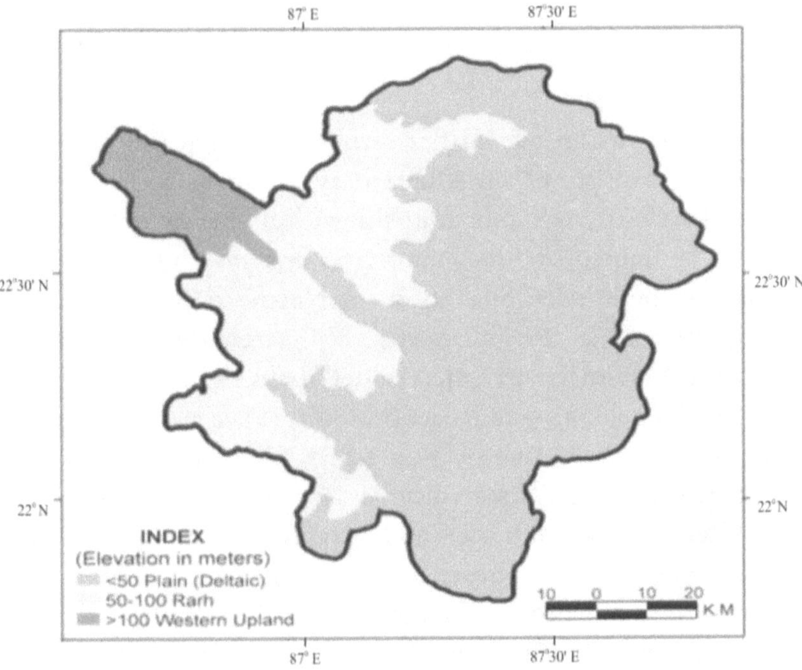


**Fig 2.5:** Physiography of PaschimMedinipur.

Alluvial and brown soil is found in southern side of this plane area. The upland of northern region is covered with bush and dwarf Sal trees. In this geographical area, Garbeta-I and Garbeta-II blocks, some portion of Binpur-I Block, Chandrakona-I and II Blocks, Ghatal and some portion of Daspur-I Block are included.

**Lower Cossye Plain:** This region can be marked in the both side of the Cossye River or its stream. Some portions have been formed with the eastern part of the Rupnarayan, which is a natural marking of Medinipur (undivided) district. The features of a delta plane are keenly found in the eastern part of the Rupnarayan and adjacent areas of Hooghly banks. Ebb and flow are very active in this region. It is a long and depressed area. This triangular depressed region is formed with delta plane of Cossye and Shilai. Due to gradual alluvial deposition, navigabitity of this river is totally lost. A huge depression is formed in the west and North West area on the Cossye and Keleghai confluence and causes flood situation. Places like Binpur, Jhargram, Salboni, Medinipur, Kharagpur, Keshpur, Ghatal, Daspur, Panskura, Mayna, Debra, Bhagwanpur, Pingla, Nandigram, Tamluk, Sutahata, Durgachak, and Haldia are included in this plane.

## 2.2.4 Geology

The district exhibits an overall flat terrain excepting the north western portion which consists of Pre-Quaternary group of rocks with cuestas and hogbacks along with monadnocks within the valley fill segments. The district is drained by four major river systems, Subarnarekha in the West, Kasai in the middle, Silabati in the Northeast and Kalaighai in the southeast. The area is covered mostly by Quaternary sediments, except in the North western parts, where older rocks are exposed. The older rocks of the area belonging to Palaeoproterozoic age are represented by (i) Singbhum Group Consisting of mica schist, phyletic, garnet – staurolite schist and quartzite (ii) Dalma volcanics, Consisting of Carbon phyletic, Volcanics, Pyroclastics, epidiorites and hornblende schist and (iii) Younger intrusives belonging to Mesoproterozoic age, consisting of Kuilapal granite and quartz –tourmaline rocks. Cainozoic lateritic in the area are observed at many places, representing a hard crust at the top, followed by a layer of nodular lateritic mass that grades down through a lithomarge (saprolite zone) to an unconsolidated parent material. There are numerous exposures of laterite in the area giving rise to bi-or-tri profile sequence indicating "in situ" nature. The Bhairab Banki formation constitutes clay, grit and at places conglomerate having a very low dip, except in the north-western part of the area. This formation has been assigned a Mio- Pliocene age due to the presence of leaf impression of dicotyledonous angiosperms on the rocks of this formation. The oldest Quaternary deposits exposed in the area comprise Lalgarh formation of early Pleistocene age consisting of fragments of quartz, phyllite, granite, pebbles and gravels occasionally lateritised. The Quaternary sediments in the area are mostly of fluviatile origin and have been deposited by Subarnarekha, Kasai, lower part of Silabati and Kaliaghai River. The Sijua formation constitutes the sediments of older alluvium, comprising hard clay and silt, impregnated with caliche concretions. The present-day flood plain deposits are composed of sand

and silts of different layers and it is mostly found in the lower reach of the rivers (see Table 2.5 & Fig. 2.6).

■ **Table 2.5:** Geological Stratigraphy in Paschim Medinipur District and their present area covered

| Lithostratigraphy | Area in Sq. Km. | Geological Unit | Age |
|---|---|---|---|
| Carbon Phyllite (Dcp) | 0.33 | DalmaVolcanics | Palaeoproterozoic |
| Epidiorite/Hornblende Schist (De) | 0.09 | | |
| Quartzite (Dq) | 0.01 | | |
| Garnet-Staurolite Schist with Kyanite (Sgs) | 0.06 | Singbhum Group | |
| Mica Schist (Sm) | 1.79 | | |
| Phyllite (Sp) | 2.11 | | |
| Quartzite (Sq) | 0.01 | | |
| Tourmaline-Quartz Rock (Yt) | 0.33 | Younger Intrusive | Mesoproterozoic |
| Kuilapal Granite (Yk) | 0.01 | | |
| Clay, Grit and Conglomerate (Mb) | 0.29 | Bhairab Banki Formation | Miocene to Pliocene |
| Gravels with different size (Tg) | 1.34 | Tertiary Gravel Bed | Cainozoic |
| Laterite with occasional ring like growth of Silica (L) | 0.02 | Laterite | |
| Fragments of Quartz, Phyllite, Granite Pebbles and Gravels occasionally lateritised ($Q_1$) | 38.85 | Lalgarh Formation | Pleistocene |
| Greenish Grey Clay, impregnated with Caliche Nodules ($Q_{1-2}$) | 36.17 | Sijua Formation | Upper Pleistocene to Lower Holocene |
| Sand with Silts, Clays associated with Fe-nodules ($Q_2$a) | 15.68 | Panskura Formation | Holocene |
| Sands, Silts and Clays deposited in different flood regimes, no oxidation effect ($Q_2$hb) | 0.56 | Basudevpur Formation | |
| Sands and Silts in alternate layers ($Q_2$pf) | 0.74 | Present day Flood Plain Deposits | |
| River | 1.62 | Flood Plain Deposits | |

*Source: Geology map of Medinipur, Kolkata, GSI.*

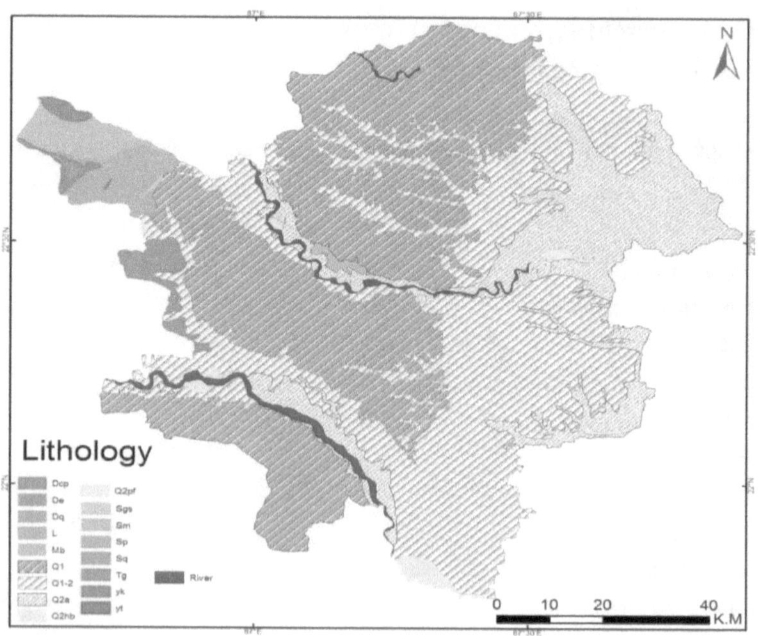


**Fig. 2.6:** Geological characteristics of the Paschim Medinipur based on Geology map of Medinipur.

## 2.2.5 Geomorphology

Geomorphologically the district is classified into seven units such as (i) Ridges/ Hills with intervening broad undulation plains which is found extreme west in the district, (ii) Planation surfaces in the east of hills with intervening broad undulating plains, (iii) Upland plains which is spread out maximum area with Binpur –I, Jhargram and northern Part of Gopiballavpur I and II block, (iv) Deeply weathered plains found at the some parts of GarbetaI and II blocks and also some parts of Jhargram and Gopiballavpur I blocks. (v) Badland topography is found in Binpur- I, Keshpur, Salboni, Garbeta II, Garbeta III and Medinipur Blocks, (vi) Younger deltaic plains also found in the lower reach of Silabati river basin, which are fall into Ghatal Blocks. During Creteous time, Ghatal area was under the influence of restricted lagoon environment, which was replaced by open marine shelf environment during the Paleocene and Eocene (Raman et al., 1986) (vii) Present day flood plains area found along the Kangsabati, Silabati, Subarnarekha and Kalaighai Command area and Para deltaic fan surfaces found both side of present day flood plains area (see Table 2.6 & Fig. 2.7).

**■ Table 2.6:** Geomorphologic characteristics in Paschim Medinipur District and their present area covered

| Geomorphologic Units | Area in Sq.Km | Percent area covered (%) |
|---|---|---|
| Valley Fill Deposits (VFD) | 991.56 | 10.91 |
| Flood Plain Deposits (FPD) | 2886.48 | 31.77 |
| Deep Buried Pediments (DBP) | 2009.47 | 22.12 |
| Deep to Moderate Buried Pediment with Lateritic Capping (DMBPLC) | 1913.87 | 21.06 |
| Moderately Buried Pediment with Lateritic Capping (MBPLC) | 834.83 | 9.18 |
| Pediment (Ped) | 95.53 | 1.04 |
| Denudational Terraces and Rocky Outcrop (DTRO) | 349.72 | 3.84 |

*Source: Geomorphological map of India, GSI.*

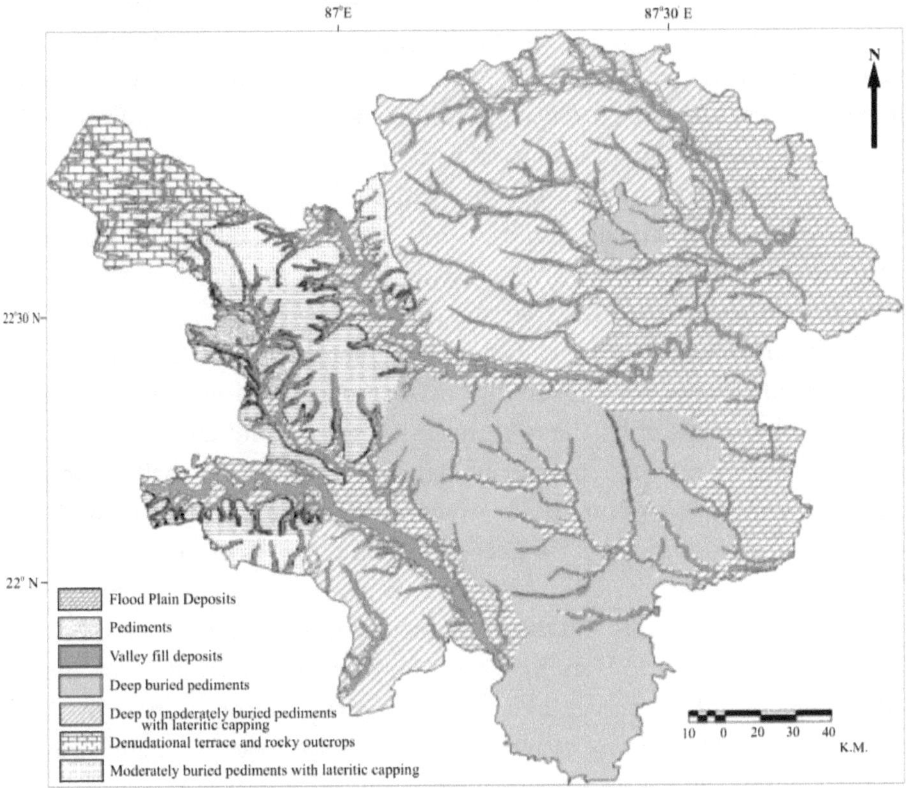


**Fig. 2.7:** Geomorphological characteristics of Paschim Medinipur based on morphological map of West Bengal (Source: Samanta, 2012).

## 2.2.6 Hydro Geology

The hydrogeological condition of the district can be divided into two broad divisions as (i) Fissured/Fractured formation (ii) Porous formation (see Table 2.7 & Fig. 2.8).

Hydrogeological condition of Fissured/Fractured Formation: Hard crystalline rocks occur around Binpur – II in the extreme north western part of the district. Where ground water occurs under water table condition in weathered residuum of the hard rocks and the interconnected fracture, fissures, joints etc. The thickness of the weathered zone varying from a very thin veneer to as much as 15 – 20 m. depth to water level in the zone of weathered and fractured rocks, vary from 2m.bgl to 13m.bgl during pre-monsoon period. Ground water in this unit forms limited ground water development scope and is mainly tapped by dug wells, dug cum bore wells and bore wells. However, the deeper fractures are also potential for ground water development and are mainly developed by bore well. Ground water exploration carried by CGWB in this unit reveals that existence of fractures within depth of 85m. bgl with the yield of the well ranges from 5 to 7 m. bgl.

Hydrological condition of porous formation: The porous formations are very extensive both laterally and vertically and can be sub divided into two categories a) Older alluvium and upper tertiary's in the platform area and b) Recent alluvium plains in the eastern part of the district.

a) Older Alluvium and Upper Tertiary in the platform Region: The upland region in the north western, northern and south western part of the district is characterized by the occurrence of laterite and lateritic soils at the top underlain by a thick sequence of clay, silt, sand. In the shallow phreatic aquifers ground water occurs under water table condition in this upland tract whose pre-monsoon depth of water level ranges from 4 m. bgl to 10 m. bgl during pre-monsoon period. The deeper aquifers occur under confined to semi-confined conditions and the piezometric surface in pre-monsoon period ranges from 5 m. bgl to 9 m. bgl. Auto flowing tube wells in Narayangarh, Lalgarh, Salboni, Jhargram and Garbeta areas are quite common.

b) Alluvial plains in the eastern part: The block areas of Ghatal, Daspur, Keshpur, Debra, Pingla, Sabong are mainly covered by recent alluvial deposits. Very significant and promising water bearing formations occur in Daspur – Debra. Block within the depth range of 130 – 164 m. Ground water here both in water table and confined conditions.

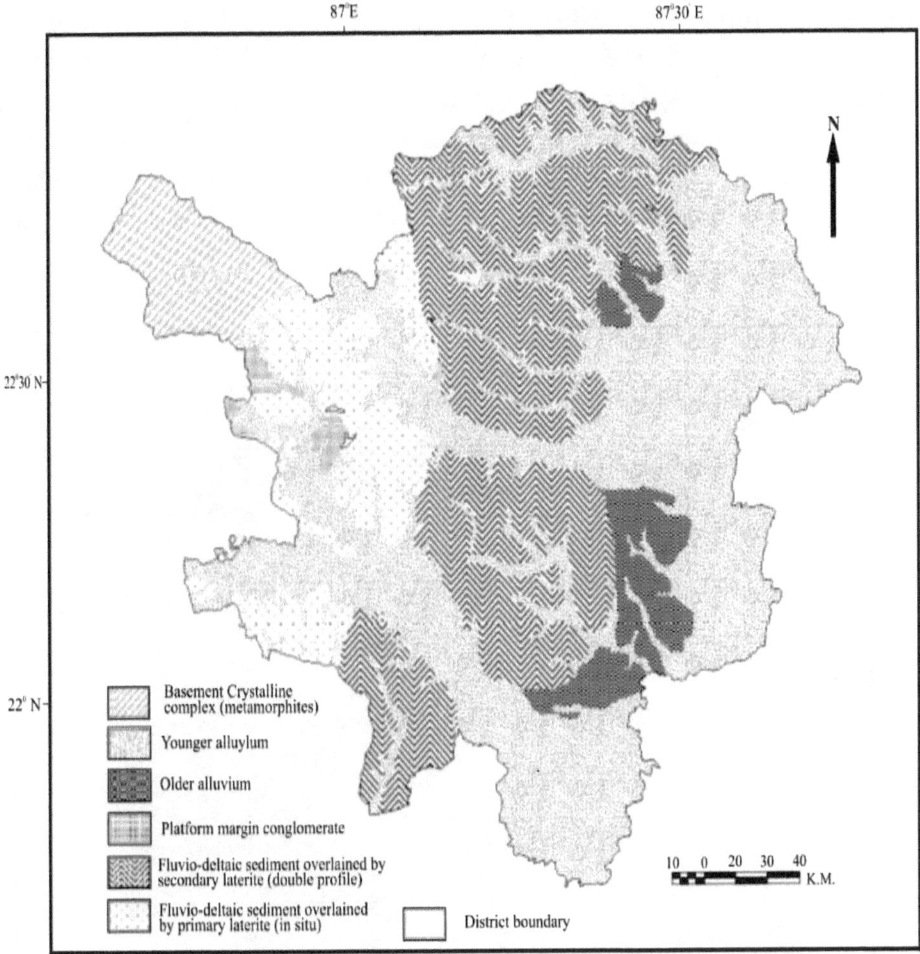



**Fig. 2.8:** Hydro – geological characteristics of the Paschim Medinipur based on geological map of West Bengal (Source: Samanta, 2012).

## 2.2.7 Soil characteristics

The soil characteristics of a region is determined by the relief, vegetation, the parent rock material, the nature and characteristics of the erosional activity in the region and the various soil forming processes. Soil type in the district are mainly consist of younger alluvial, group of entisols; older alluvial, red sandy, red gravel group of Alfisols and Lateritic, group of Ultisols. Red gravel is mostly found in the extreme north-western part of the district. Red sandy also found Binpur –II and Gopiballavpur –I block. Middle portion of the district are covered by the laterite soils. Older alluvial Soils mostly found in the side of river bank. Eastern margin of the district including Chandrakona -I, Daspur -I, Daspur-II, Debra, pingla, sabang and Narayangarh covered by the younger alluvial soils. In an extensive way the soil type of Paschim Medinipur district can be divided into sixteen categories (see Table.2.8 and Fig.2.9).

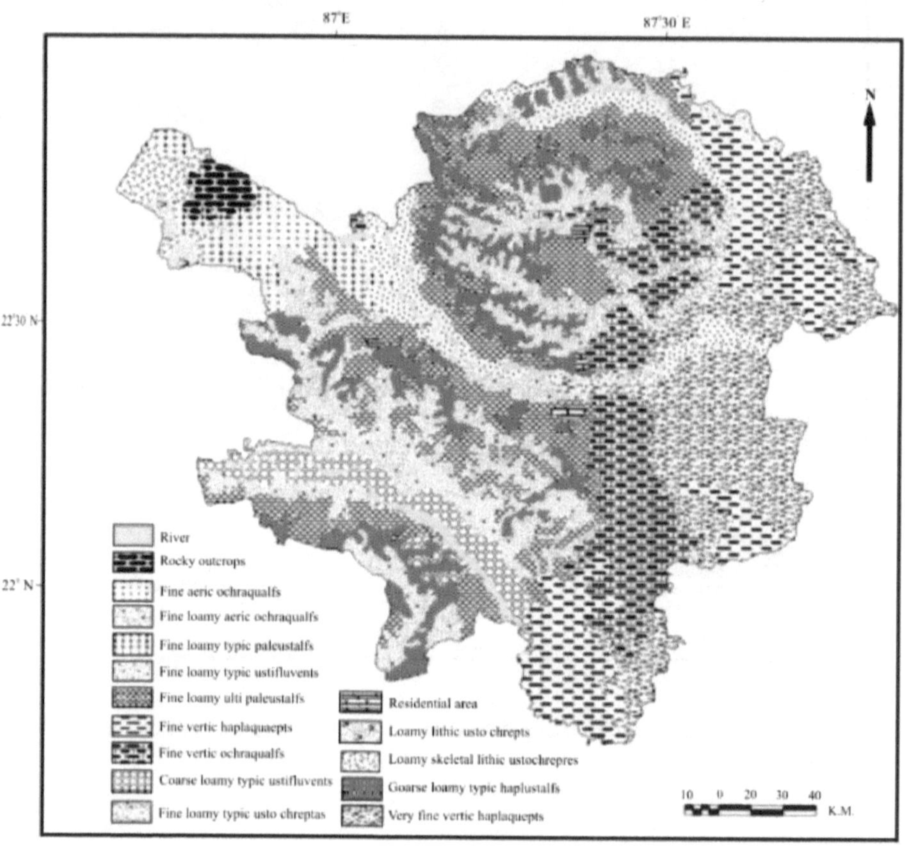


**Fig. 2.9:** Spatial distribution of Soil characteristics of Paschim Medinipur based on Soil map of West Bengal (Source: Samanta, 2012).

## 2.2.8 Drainage Density

Drainage density is one of the important parameters to understand the flood potential of a watershed. The drainage number (frequency) can express the drainage density property and it has the strong relationship with water recharge and discharge. Drainage network has been extracted from topographical maps (1:50000). The drainage of the study area mainly controlled by the Kangsabati and Silabati river and they are intersected by numerous Khals.

Different drainage pattern such as – dendritic, sub-dendritic and radial are predominantly seen in the study area. Very high drainage density is found in the western and northern part, whereas moderate to low drainage density is found in the southern and eastern part. Generally, lower drainage density area has been affected by long term flood situation (see Fig. 2.10).

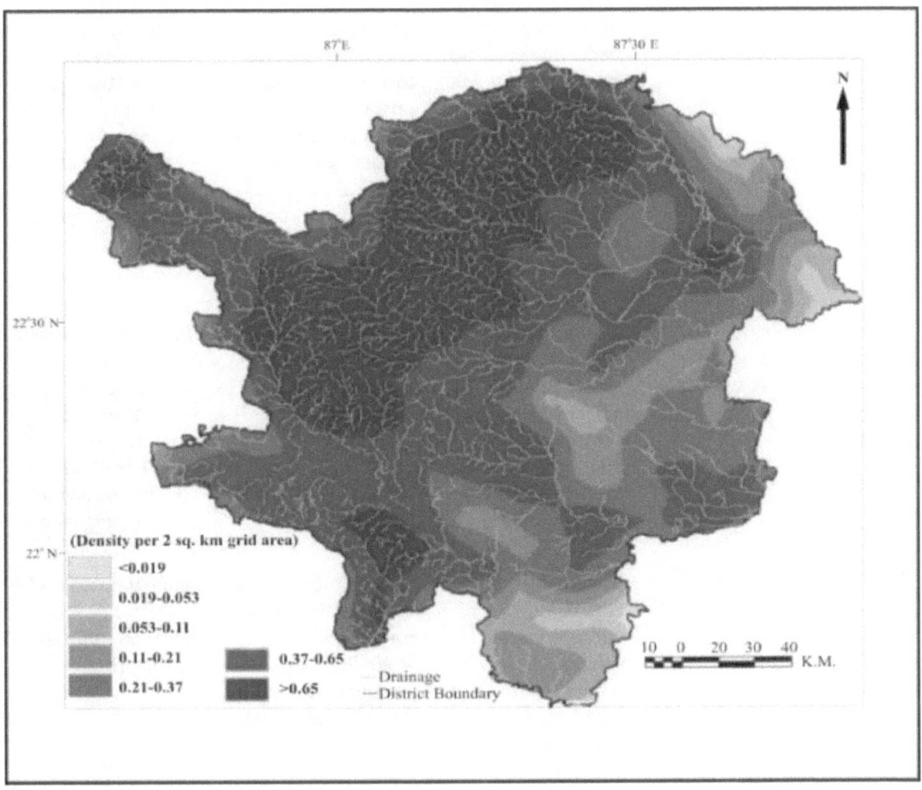


**Fig. 2.10:** Drainage density per Sq.Km grid area of Paschim Medinipur based on satellite imageries and topographical map (Source: Samanta, 2012).

■ **Table 2.7: Hydro geological characteristics in Paschim Medinipur District**

| Hydro-geologic units | Aquifer age | General Lithology | Aquifer deposition in mbgl | Aquifer character |
|---|---|---|---|---|
| Younger alluvium (YA) | Recent to late Pleistocene | Finer to medium sand with vertical and lateral facies change to sandy clay or clay. Prismatic sand bodies consisted mainly of moderately to well sort rounded to well round quartz with significant flaky minerals. | From top surface to a depth of 48.80 m bgl. In general subsurface deposition is between 5 – 36 m bgl. i.e. thickness variable from 30 -35 m. | Cumulative thickness of granular zones forming aquifers 10 – 20 m. ground water occurs with phreatic water surface and under semi confined condition. |
| Older alluvium (OA) | Late Pleistocene | Sand, medium to coarse with brownish tint, poorly sorted but texturally matured with ferruginous modules and kankarsghuttings (Calcareous concretional aggregates) are present. | Granular zones encountered down to a depth of 400 m. phreatic aquifer is underlained by semi unconfined aquifer below 25 from G.L. | Summer ground water level varies from 1 – 18 m bgl. Post monsoon water levels vary from 1 – 7 m bgl. Seasonal water level fluction has a wide range of 6 – 18m. |
| Fluviodeltaic sediment overlained by secondary laterite (FDSO$_{dp}$) | Middle to early Pleistocene | Laterite: hard crust 1.5 – 16 m thick molted clay 03 – 7 m thick lithomarge. Mio-pliocene sedimentaries: sand-silt-shale alternation. | Disposition of water bearing prospective aquifers are within 250 m. bgl. | The depth of phreatic acquifer varies from 12 – 30 m. bgl. Summer and post monsoon water level varies from 2-21 and 1.5-9 m. bgl. Range of G.W.L. fluctuation 6-19 m. |
| Fluviodeltaic sediment overlained by primary laterite (FDSO$_{pl}$) | Pliocene | Lateritic hard crust; highly porous in places with honeycomb weathering structures underlained by lithomergic clay. Mio-pliocene sedimentaries with indication of more oxidation and presence of ferruginous clay. | Lateritic profile: 0 – 25 m. bgl. With spring zones in places. Multiple aquifers are found down to a depth of 165 m. bgl. | Summer water level 6 – 21 m. bgl. Post monsoon water level 1.5 – 9 m. bgl. |

| Hydro-geologic units | Aquifer age | General Lithology | Aquifer deposition in mbgl | Aquifer character |
|---|---|---|---|---|
| Platform margin con-glomerates (PMC) | Early Miocene | Pebbles, cobbles and boulders in coarse sand matrix. Significant constituent lateritic gravel, cobbles and gneissic rocks. | Down to a depth of 30 m. bgl. | Hill slope discharge zone with springs and auto flows along Dulung river. |
| Basement crystalline complex (BCC) | Pre-Cambrian | Ortho and paragneissic complex, schists, metabasics, epidiorites, phyllites, pegmatites, granites with colluvial material. | Fracture conduits extend down to a depth of 150 m. maximum from G.L. Regolith thickness 5 -20 m. from G.L. | Unconfined anisotrphic, summer G.W.L. 2 -11 m bgl. Post monsoon G.W.L. 0.5 – 5 m. bgl. |

*Source: Hydro-geological map of India, GSI.*

■ **Table 2.8:  Soil characteristics in Paschim Medinipur District and their present area covered**

| Soil Type | Area in Sq.Km | Percent area covered (%) |
|---|---|---|
| Coarse loamy typichaplustalfs (CLTH) | 1008.53 | 11.11 |
| Fine loamy ultipaleustalfs (FLUP) | 1506.94 | 16.59 |
| Fine loamy aericochraqualfs (FLAO) | 1513.46 | 16.67 |
| Fine vertichaplaquaepts (FVH) | 940.03 | 10.35 |
| Fine loamy typicustifluvents (FLTUSTI) | 469.03 | 5.16 |
| River | 1521.52 | 16.75 |
| Fine loamy typicpaleustalfs (FLTP) | 226.71 | 2.50 |
| Loamy skeletal lithic ustochreprs (LSLU) | 126.27 | 1.39 |
| Very fine vertichaplaquepts (VFVH) | 123.93 | 1.36 |
| Rocky outcrops (RO) | 90.27 | 0.99 |
| Fine verticochraqualfs (FVO) | 878.77 | 9.68 |
| Loamy lithic ustochrepts (LLU) | 51.13 | 0.56 |
| Fine aericochraqualfs (FAO) | 122.86 | 1.35 |
| Fine loamy typicustochreptas (FLTUSTO) | 173.05 | 1.91 |
| Residential area | 35.44 | 0.39 |
| Coarse loamy typicustifluvents (CLTU) | 293.15 | 3.23 |

*Source: Soil map of West Bengal.*

## 2.2.9 Ground Water Condition and Water Table

The soil and sub-soil conditions of an area determine the nature and characteristics of seepage contributing to the ground-water conditions and depth of the water table. Normally a high-water table during the heavy rain and flood stage of the rivers create adverse conditions of water logging and drainage congestion. Ground water flow direction is from North-West to South- East. The flow gradient is very steep in the north western part, 1:10 which it is more or less flat in the south eastern part, 1:2000 and in the central part around Medinipur town it is 1:3000.

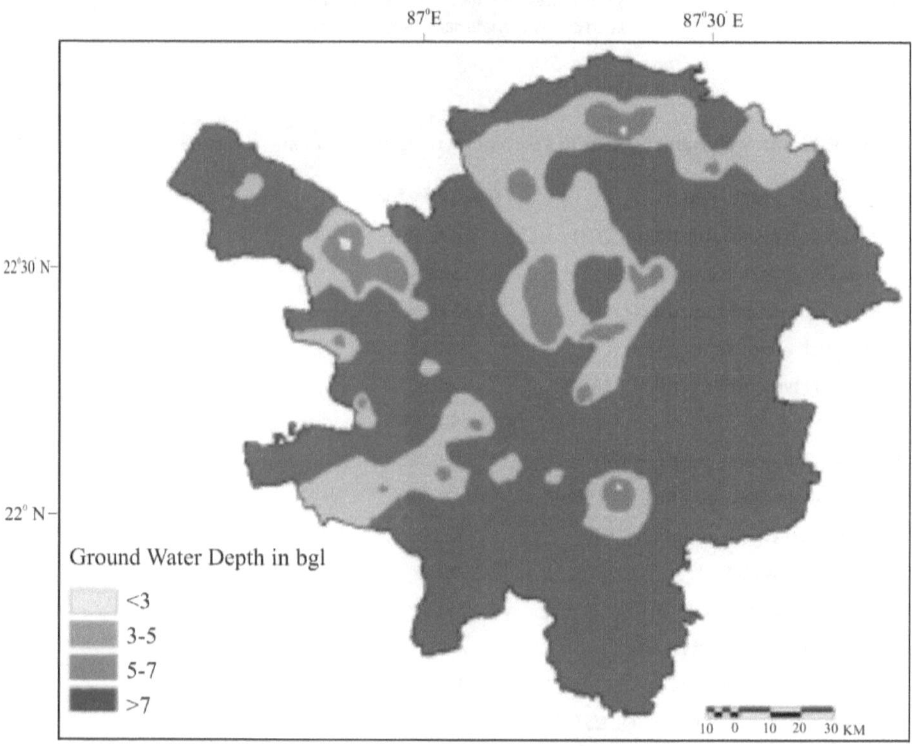


**Fig. 2.11:** Ground Water level of Monsoon Season of Paschim Medinipur District.

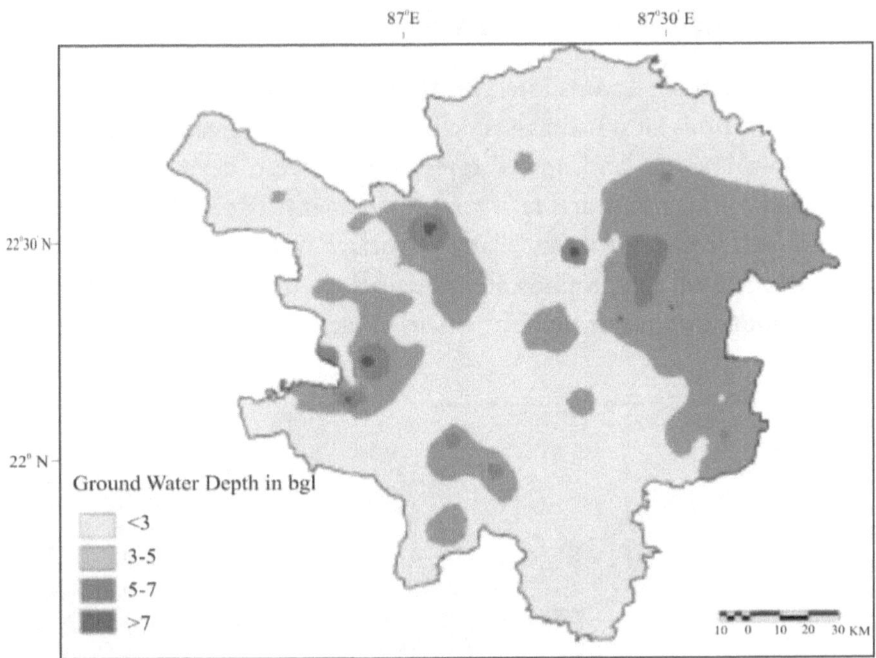


**Fig. 2.12:** Ground Water level of Post Monsoon Season of Paschim Medinipur District.

■ **Table: 2.9** Well frequencies for different ranges of depth to water level

| District | Year | No.of wells analysed | Depth to water level (mbgl) | | No./percentage of wells showing depth to water table (mbgl) in the range of | | | | | | | | | |
|---|---|---|---|---|---|---|---|---|---|---|---|---|---|---|
| | | | Min | Max | 0-2 | % | 2-5 | % | 5-10 | % | 10-20 | % | 20-40 | % |
| Paschim Medinipur | April 2014 | 69 | 1.3 | 21.5 | 2 | 2.9 | 11 | 15.9 | 26 | 37.7 | 29 | 42 | 1 | 1.4 |
| | August 2014 | 69 | 0.32 | 16.41 | 22 | 31.9 | 19 | 27.5 | 18 | 26.1 | 10 | 14.5 | 0 | 0 |

*Source: Central Ground Water Board.*

■ **Table 2.10:** Categorisation of change in water level (10 yrs mean from August 2004 to August 2014)

| District | No. of wells | Range of fluctuation (m) | | | | No. of wells/percentage showing fluctuation | | | | | | | | | | | | Total no. of wells | |
|---|---|---|---|---|---|---|---|---|---|---|---|---|---|---|---|---|---|---|---|
| | | Rise | | Fall | | Rise | | | | | | Fall | | | | | | | |
| | | Min | Mix | Min | Mix | 0-2 | % | 2-4 | % | >4 | % | 0-2 | % | 2-4 | % | >4 | % | Rise | Fall |
| Paschim Medini-pur | 31 | .08 | 3.15 | .02 | 11.7 | 12 | 38.7 | 2 | 6.5 | 0 | 0 | 7 | 22.6 | 6 | 19.4 | 4 | 12.9 | 14 | 17 |

*Source: Central Ground Water Board.*

## 2.2.10 Land Use/Land Cover Characteristics

Land-use pattern of the area interpret through remote sensing data (Land sat 5 TM) and various land use classes delineated includes river, sand, dry fallow, moist fallow, lateritic land, mixed forest, dense forest, degraded forest, open forest, crop land, agricultural fallow and settlement (Fig.2.13). Different uses of terrain surfaces result a miscellany of surface water recharge processes. In view of flood condition groundwater potentiality and river/surface water body are much more important than the others criteria.

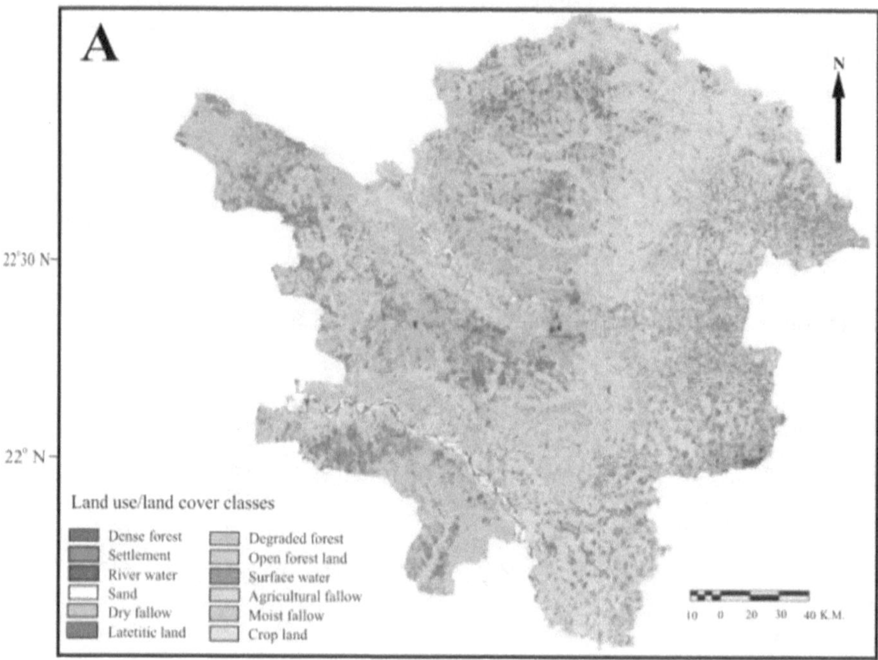

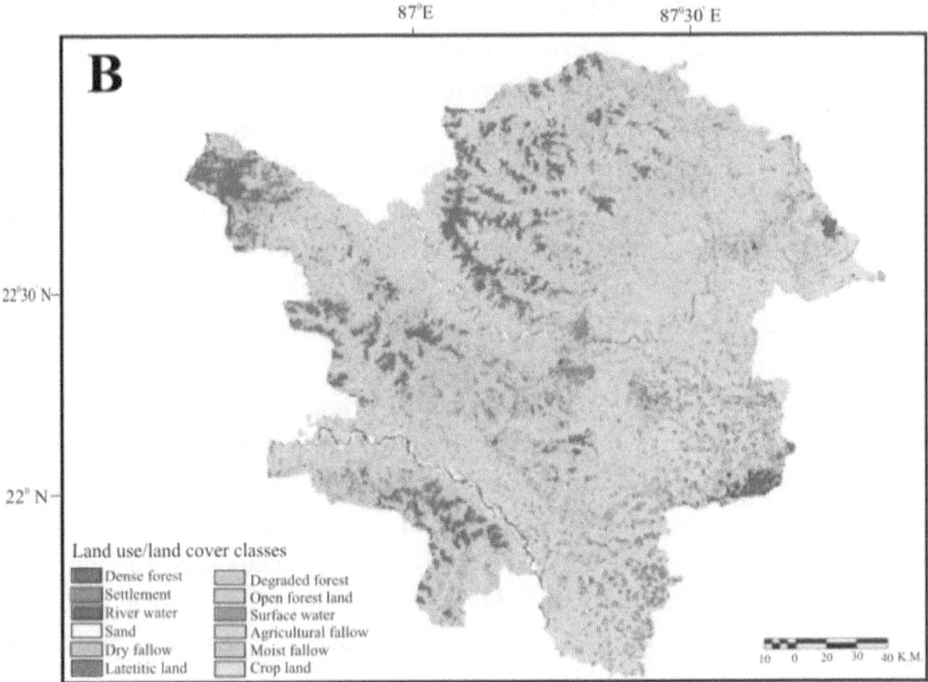


**Fig. 2.13:** Land use/Land cover characteristics in Monsoon season (A) and Post Monsoon season (B) of Paschim Medinipur district based on Landsat 5 (TM) Imageries (Source: Samanta, 2012).

## 2.2.11 Active River Channels

The river system of Paschim Medinipur district consists of the Kangsabati, Kaliaghai, Silabati and Subarnarekha.

**Kangsabati System:** The River Kangsabati originates from Jabarband at an elevation of 641 metres in the hills of Chhotonagpur range, about 48 Km. north-east of Purulia town. The principle tributary of the Haldi is the Kasai which enters the district in the north-east from Bankura. It follows an exceedingly tortuous course, running first south and south-west and then eastwards pass the town of Medinipur, which is situated on its north bank. The river up to Midnapore anicut at Mohanpur is known as kangsabati after which further down up to Kapastikri it is known as Cossye. At Kapastikri, the river bifurcates into two branches known as old Cossye and the New Cossye. The new Cossye passes through Panskura and after flowing for a length of 65 km. it meets river Kaliaghai forming Haldi. After old Cossyeflows for about 15 km below the bifurcating points, a branch known as Kanki Khal takes off. The

Kanki Khal meets Silabati River. The oldCossye after flowing for another 10 km. bifurcates into the Palaspai Khal and the Durbachati River. The Palaspai Khal precedes an easterly for 16 km before joining the Rupnarayan River near Gopigunj, while the Durbachati flows for about 25 km before joining the Rupnarayan near Sribora out falling of the river Hooghly. The Kangsabati in its upper reach has received some important tributaries of these the Kumari coming from Chhotonagpur hill range has joined the river on left bank near Ambikanagar of Bankura District. The Bhairab Banki and Tarapheni are two other rivers to meet the Kangsabati at two different locations on its right bank at its upper reach before reaching Jhargram town.

**Kaliaghai System:** The River Kaliaghai originates from Dudhkundi in P.S. Jhargram in the district of Paschim Medinipur. The general height of the area, from where the rivers start its journey is about 78 metres. During its course of Journey from the high land in the Western Part towards east, it meets with numbers of tributaries namely Deuli, Kapaleswari, Kalimondap, Ganpath, Chandia on its left and Baghai on its right. River Kapaleswari, one of its main tributaries meets Kaliaghai at Langalkata, P.S. Sabong and further down the river meets new Cossye at Dhewbhanga. After the confluence point, the river is named as Haldi and finally outfalls into river Hooghly. Kaliaghai is the second tributary of the Haldi.

**Silabati System:** The principle tributary of the Rupnarayan in the Silai or Silabati. This river originates from Chhotonagpur plateau of Jharkhand. It flows east for some distance then turns south west to form the border of Bankura and enters the study area on the north near Garbeta town in Medinipur Sadar Sub-division, then turns to the south-east and south through Ghatal Sub-division. Near Narajole the river takes a turn to northeast forming a loop. Combined flow of the Kubai, the Tamal, and the Sundar from West joins the river. It is also joined by the Parang. The Kanki River an off shoot of the old Cossye also joins it. The outfall of the Silabati to the Rupnarayan at near Bander.

**Subarnarekha System:** The River Subarnarekha originating from Chhotonagpur plateau near Ranchi, Jharkhand at an elevation of 610 metres flows through the district of Ranchi and Singhbum in Jharkhand, Paschim Medinipur district in West Bengal and Balasore in Orissa. The river finally falls into the Bay of Bengal. The main tributaries are kanchi and Karkai above chandil in Jharkhand, Kharkai in Orissa and Dulung in West Bengal. The only tributary of the river, Dulung in the district of Paschim Medinipur join the

River Subarnarekha above 2 km above Rohini. South of Datan at Sonakonia it enters the Balasore District.

## 2.2.12 History of Flood

Though flood is almost an annual feature in the District of Paschim Medinipur and it occurs fairly in a large area affecting a good number of villages, not much is known about the floods that took place in the district before the advent of the British. Some areas of the district like-Jhargram Sub Division and Garbeta areas under Medinipur Sadar Sub Division suffer from flood like situation due to rush of down flow of water due to heavy downpour and discharge of water from the dams. In eastern margins of the district Debra, Pingla, Sabang, Keshiary under Kharagpur sub-division; Ghatal, Daspur-I, Daspur-II, Chandrakona-I and Chandrakona-II under Ghatal sub-division etc. blocks in the basin as wells catchment areas of different rivers are affected by severe flood due to overflow of riverside embankments. The blocks are very much vulnerable to flood and water logging problems. Most of the rivers have been silted and have lost water holding and carrying capacity and it cause flood in the catchment areas. Cyclonic storm also pays visit to this district and causes immense damage to property and suffering to people. However, some flood events were recorded in the history of undivided Midnapore. In 1823, there was a devastating flood in Midnapore which destroyed crops and caused something like famine. In1831 to 1834 AD a recurring flood occurred in Midnapore district. Again in 1839 to 1840 AD a devastating flood occurred in Midnapore. In 1907 flood in Ghatal and Kharagpur sub-division appeared, this flood attempt to blow away train at Narayangarh station to kill Andrew Frazer. Midnapore Sadar sub-division faced devastating floods in 1914 AD. In 1919AD a devastating flood occurred in Ghatal and Midnapore Sadar sub-division. The then Bengal Governor Lord Ronald Shaw visits flood affected areas. In 1959 AD a devastating flood appeared in Daspur-I and Daspur-II block. The then prime minister Jawaharlal Nehruvisits flood affected areas. Leaving the disasters occurred in remote past in Paschim Medinipur district, if we recall some of those of recent years the intense flood during 2007caused large scale devastation and damage of dwelling houses, standing crops and publicutilities. The death toll reached to 97. Situation becomes so alarming that the Army and I.A.F personnel had to be deployed for rescue of the marooned people and relief operation. Midnapore (W.B), Oct 2 (PTI) around

50,000 people were affected in the floods in West Bengal's West Midnapore district, a top district official said 2nd oct.2007. District magistrate S.N.Nigam told a press conference here that around 50,000 people were affected and some 8000 mud houses were damaged in the flood in which crop worth around Rs. 200 crores were also destroyed. The worst affected in the flood was the Monoharpur I & II Grampanchayat under Ghatal Sub-Division, he said. The District administration had opened 105 relief camps in the district in which 21000 people had shelter, the DM said. Chief Minister Buddhadev Bhattacharyee would visit the flood affected west Midnapore district 3[rd]oct. 2007.

### 2.2.13 Vulnerable population/Settlement

Total population of the district 59,43,300according to 2011 census, within these 3032630 males and 2910670 female population. Rural and urban population one of the districts 5228308 and 714992.Percentage of rural population to the total population 87.97 and district mostly covered by the rural population. Total vulnerable population of the district by the flood 2265122. More than 20 blocks, 111 GP are affected by the flood hazards. The most vulnerable block is Sabong where 270018 persons having of risk during flood season and most vulnerable GP is jalibanda at Debra Block in Kharagpur Sub Division.

# CHARACTERISTICS OF FLOODING AND FLOOD PRONE AREAS AND ITS IMPACT



Characteristics of Flood: General Flow Characteristics – Nature of Peak Flood. Zoning of Flood Prone Areas: Flood Frequency – Flood Water Depth – Flood Hazard Map Impacts of flood on people and economy.

## 3.1 Characteristics of Flooding

Floods are both physical and socio-economic phenomena which are exhibited through a wide range of measurable characteristics (Panda, 1979). They are the seasonality of occurrence, the frequency of flooding, the flood magnitude, the area of inundation, the duration of inundation and overall, the depth of flood water. But, however, many of these characteristics can be described with the flood frequency curve and the flood hydrograph (Cook and Doornkamp, 1974). Undoubtedly the oldest and still probably the most common index of flood magnitude in the water depth or flood stage, read from the gauge posts located on the river banks from where flood heights may be measured directly (Panda, 1979). It has an immediate relevance if flood stage or danger levels are likely to be crossed. This index is very popular in India. But, later discharge volumes are computed by the Flood Control and Irrigation Departments. In study area only one river i.e. Kangsabati have a discharge station which is computed by the Irrigation and Waterways Department, West Medinipur Division.

Seasonality is one of the important measurable characteristics of flooding. Although theoretically floods may occur at any time, they tend to occur more frequently in certain seasons and months of the year than in others. Besides, flood frequency is a statistical measure of the probable occurrence of flood of a given magnitude. High floods occur relatively infrequently with large return periods or recurrence intervals of perhaps several years. But low floods occur very frequently and therefore, have a very small return period or recurrence interval. This statistical likelihood of a given flood occurrence of a given magnitude provides important evidences for the people concerned to the problem of floods. The average flood plain occupants warned of an incipient flood event will be more concerned with the time left to evacuate to safer places. The average time gap between the maximum rainfall in the catchment areas and the resulting peak stream flow at the gauging station is referred to as the "time lag" or "basin lag" which indicates the time from the centroid of a heavy rainfall to the centroid of runoff or peak discharge. The study of these characteristics also not only provide an insight for a better understanding of the occurrence of the natural phenomena but also provides the basis and signifies the relevance for the determination of the magnitude of the floods that may be expressed to occur on any stream with a given average frequency.

In this chapter, the nature and characteristics of the floods have been studied for four major rivers of the rolling topography of Chhottonagpur plateau and plain of PaschimMedinipur i.e. the Kangsabati, the Silabati, the Kaliaghai and the Subarnarekha.

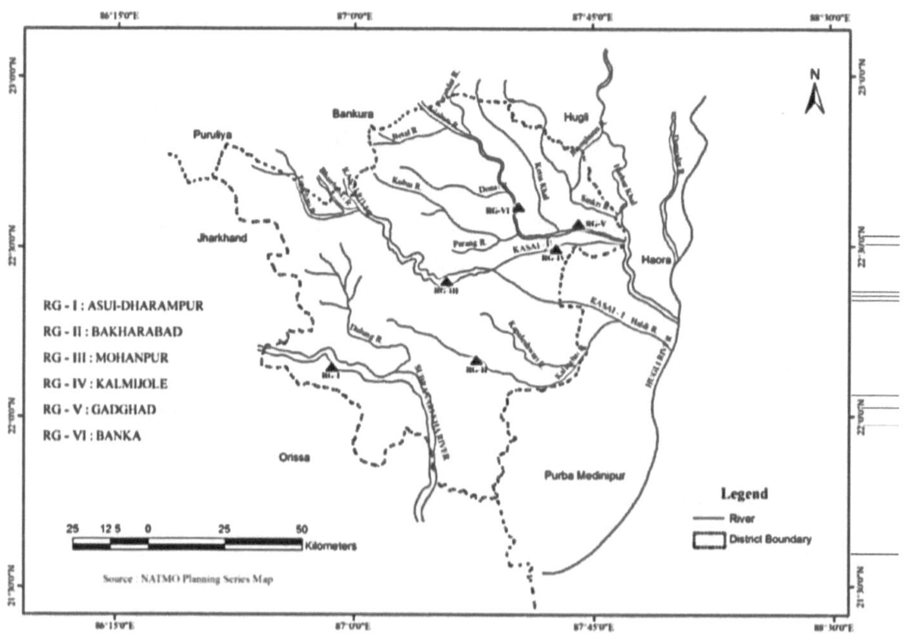


**Fig. 3.1:** Location map of River Gauge in Paschim Medinipur District.

### 3.1.1 General Flow Characteristics

Due to availability of only few discharge data of the River Kangsabati, the analysis of discharge hydrograph is found from July to October months appeared flood months of the study area and one day maximum peak discharge is found in the year of 1950 (See Fig.3.2). It has been observed from lower reach of the River gauge, that if above 1500 Cumec water discharge from Mohanpur station than all gauge station has been crossed the danger level in lower reach and high magnitude flood occurred in lower portion of the Kangsabati River basin. The available data set of a Flood Year (1978) and a Non-Flood Year (1998) when fitted with a hydrograph Flood Year shows very high peak of discharge level in respect to the Non- Flood Year (See Fig. 3.3). It has also been observed that, when amount of flood water discharge increased then height of water level also increased in a same way (See Fig. 3.4). It has been revealed that, in respect of available gauge height and flood water discharge data set, if above 65000 Cusec flood water discharge in Jamsole station than Asui-Dharampur gauge crossed the danger level and lower portion of Subarnarekha basin has been flooded automatically.

From the analysis of annual peak flood heights of the River Silabati and Kaliaghai it has also been revealed that, if River gauge of upper portion crossed the danger level than lower portion of the River basin has flooded automatically. In case of Silabati River if Banka gauge station has been crossed the danger level then lower portion of the River basin flooded and in case of Kaliaghai River if Bakhrabad gauge station has crossed the danger level then also been lower portion of the Kaliaghai River basin flooded. The annual fluctuation of one day peak flood stage of the major rivers has been studied at their heads. 2 year and 5 year moving averages has been computed to investigate into the prevalence of any short term and long-term trends and nature of fluctuations in the peak flood stage. From each river two-gauge stations are taken to showing the fluctuation of annual peak flood heights and for each two 2 year and 5 year moving average has been computed.

PATTERN OF ONE DAY MAXIMUM FLOOD WATER DISCHARGE
( At Mohanpur Gauge on Kangsabati River)
Discharge in Cumec
9000
8000
7000
6000
5000
4000
3000
2000
1000
0
Discharge In Cumec
12.08.50
28.07.52
22.08.54
27.09.56
16.09.58
30.08.60
04.10.62
25.08.64
01.07.66
04.08.68
11.09.70
13.09.72
16.08.74
13.08.76
02.10.78
28.08.80
15.08.82
11.08.84
27.09.86
18.09.88
04.08.90
29.09.92
22.07.94
08.08.96
22.1'0.98
24.09.2000
12.09.02
21.08.04
24.09.06
18.06.08
21.09.10
16.08.12
10.08.14
Years With Date

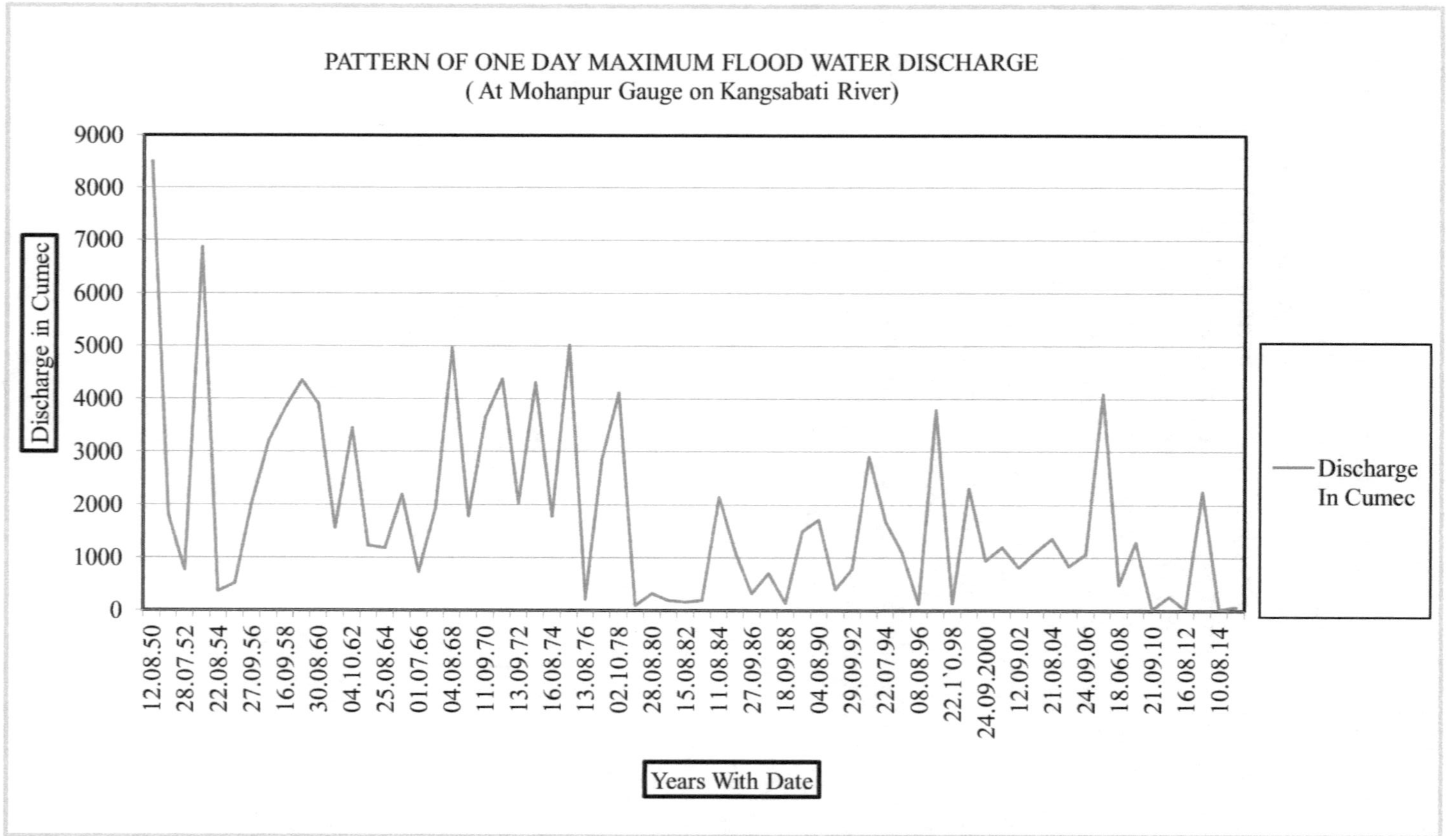

**Fig. 3.2**

PATTERN OF FLOOD WATER DISCHARGE IN A NON - FLOOD AND FLOOD YEAR
(At Mohanpur Gauge On Kangsabati River)
Discharge in Cumec
1200000
1000000
800000
600000
400000
200000
0
1978
1998
January
February
March
April
May
June
July
August
September
October
November
December
Months

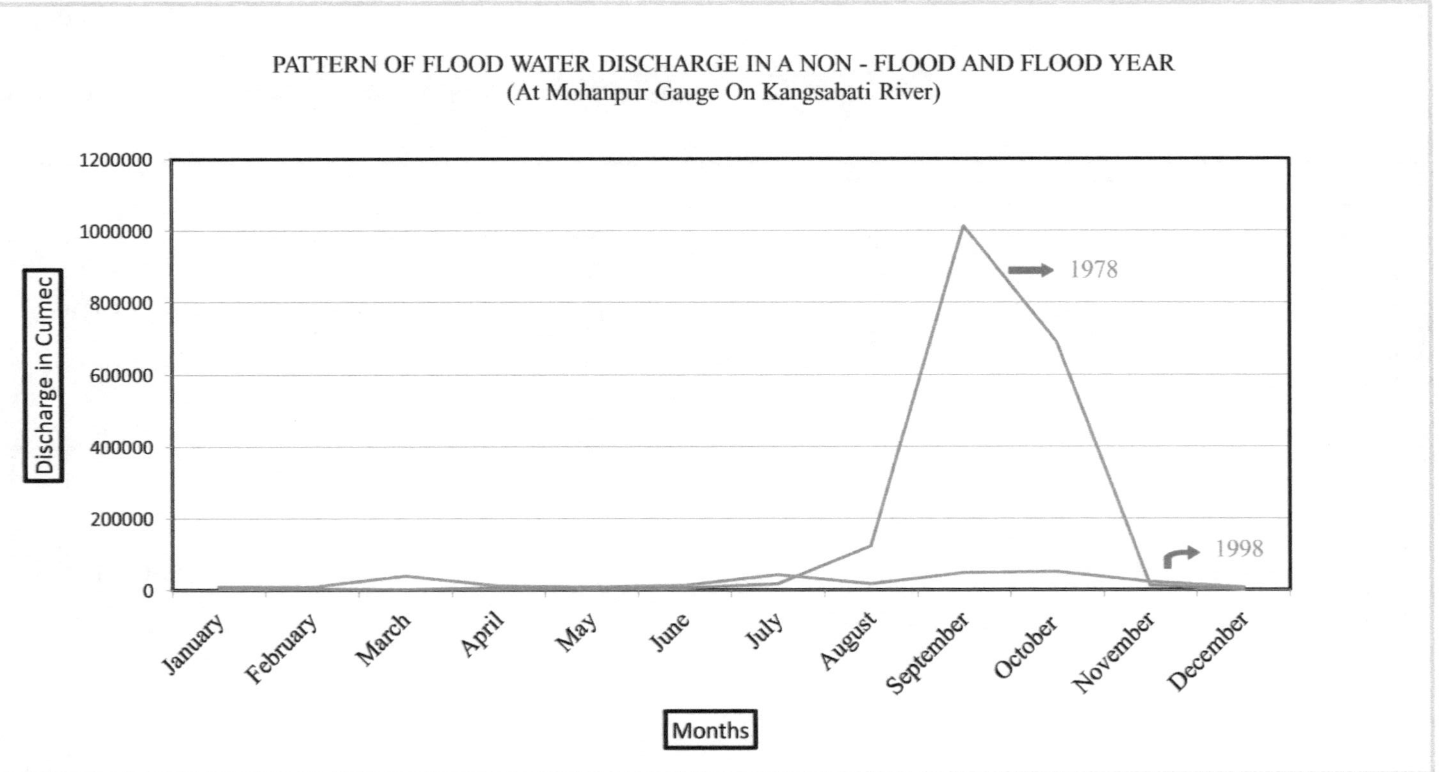

**Fig. 3.3**

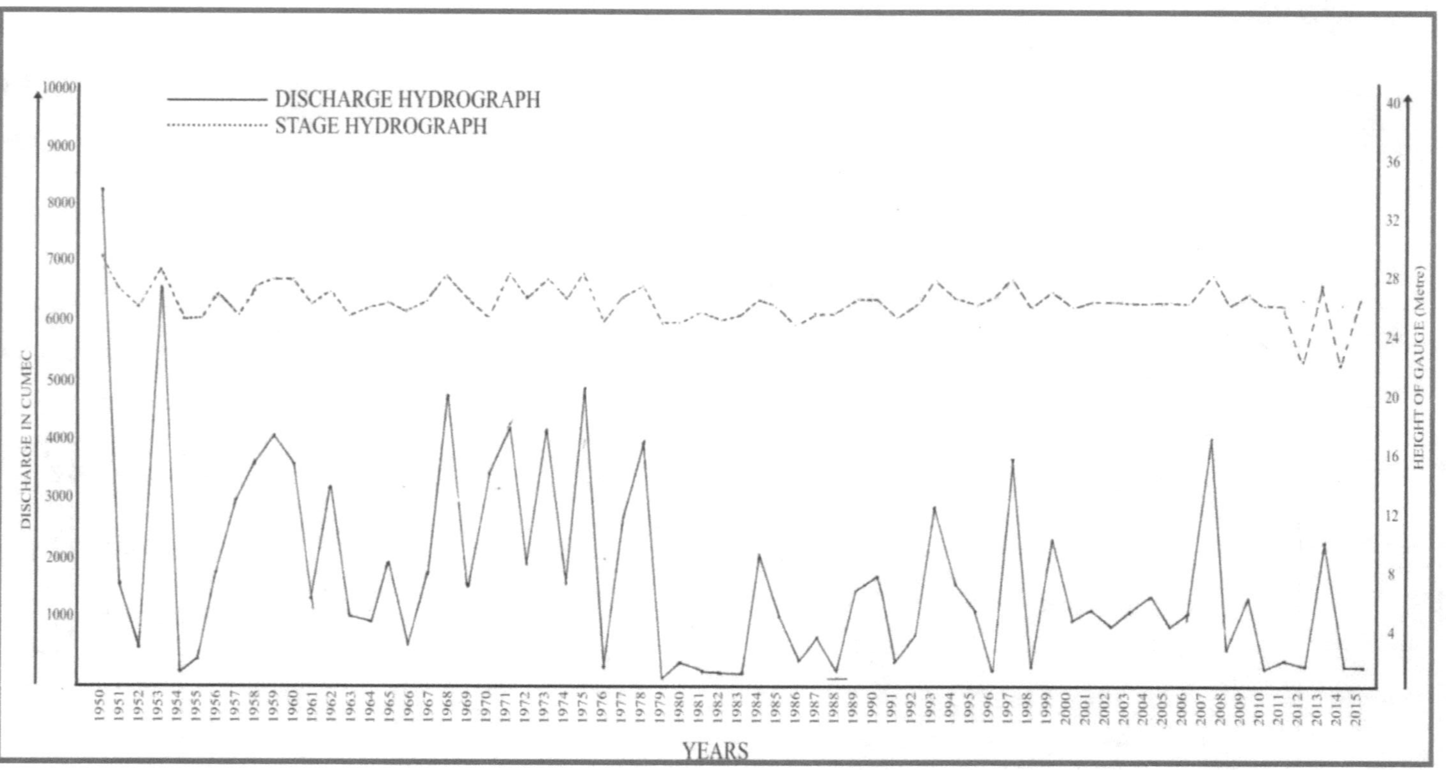


**Fig. 3.4:** Water Discharge and Stage Hydrograph on Kangsabati River at Mohanpur

PATTERN OF ONE DAY MAXIMUM FLOOD WATER DISCHARGE
(At Jamsola Gauge On Subarnarekha River)
Flood Discharge in Cfs
90000
80000
70000
60000
50000
40000
30000
20000
10000
0
1988
1989
1990
1991
1992
1993
1994
1995
1996
1997
1998
1999
2000
2001
2002
2003
2004
2005
2006
2007
2008
2009
2010
2011
2012
2013
2014
Years
Flood Discharge (cfs)

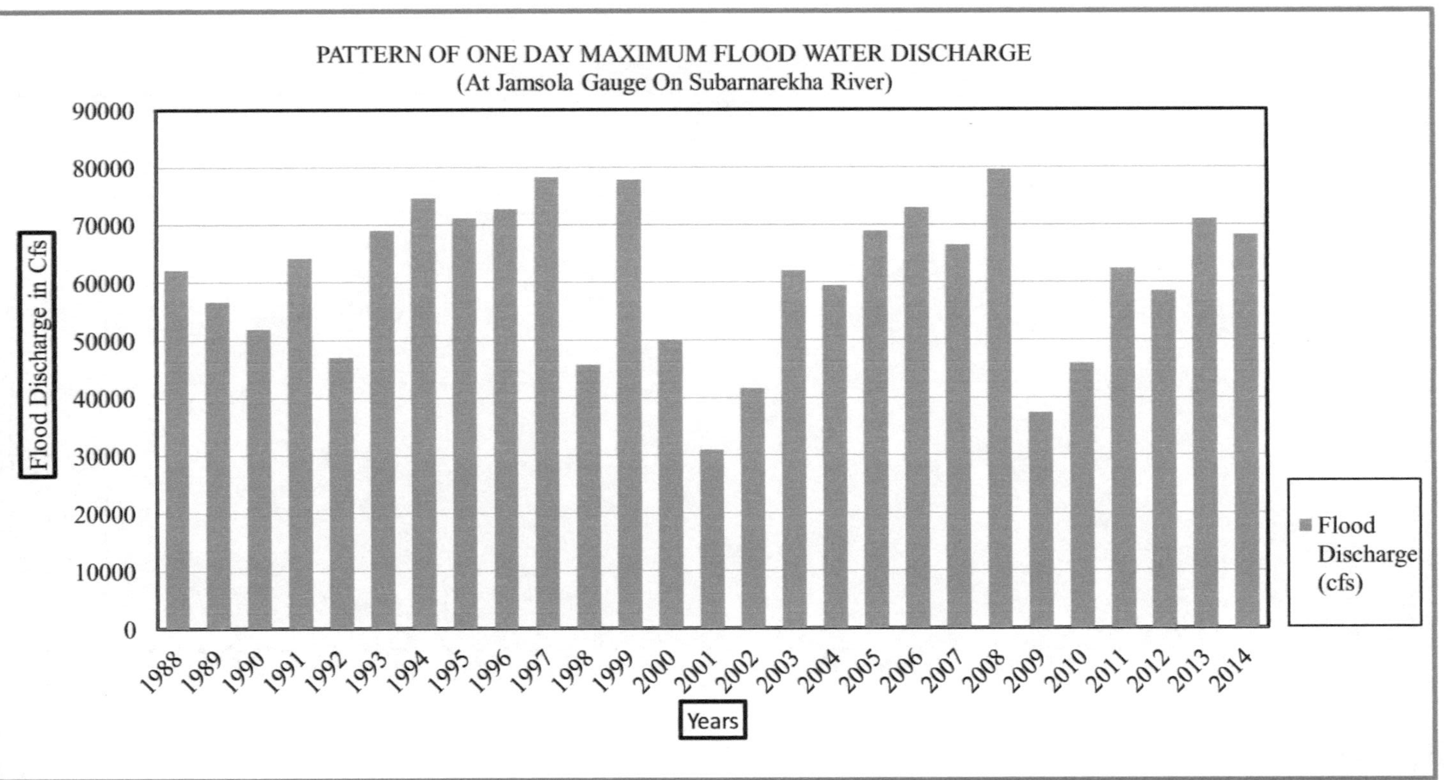

Fig. 3.5

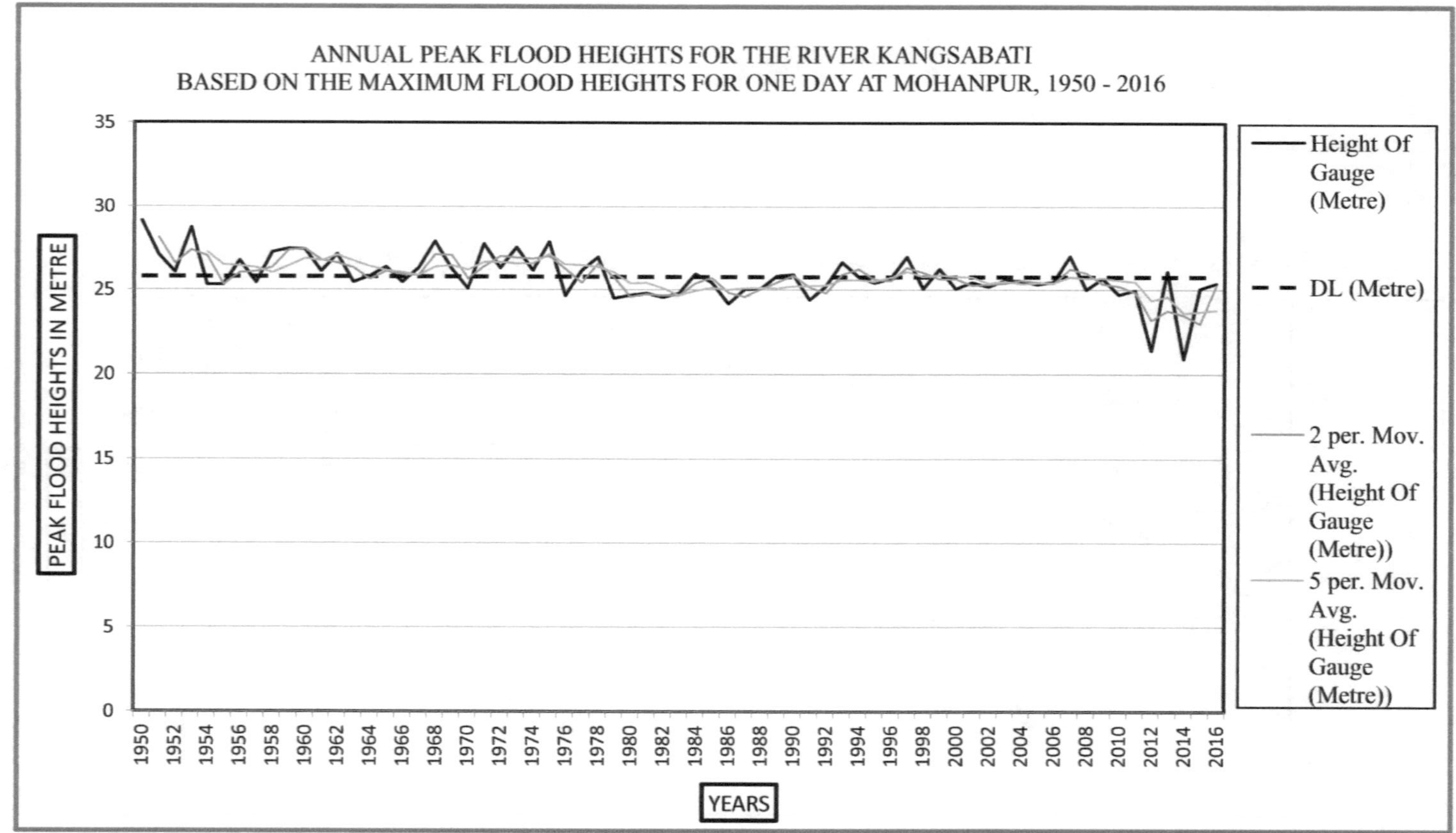



**Fig. 3.6**

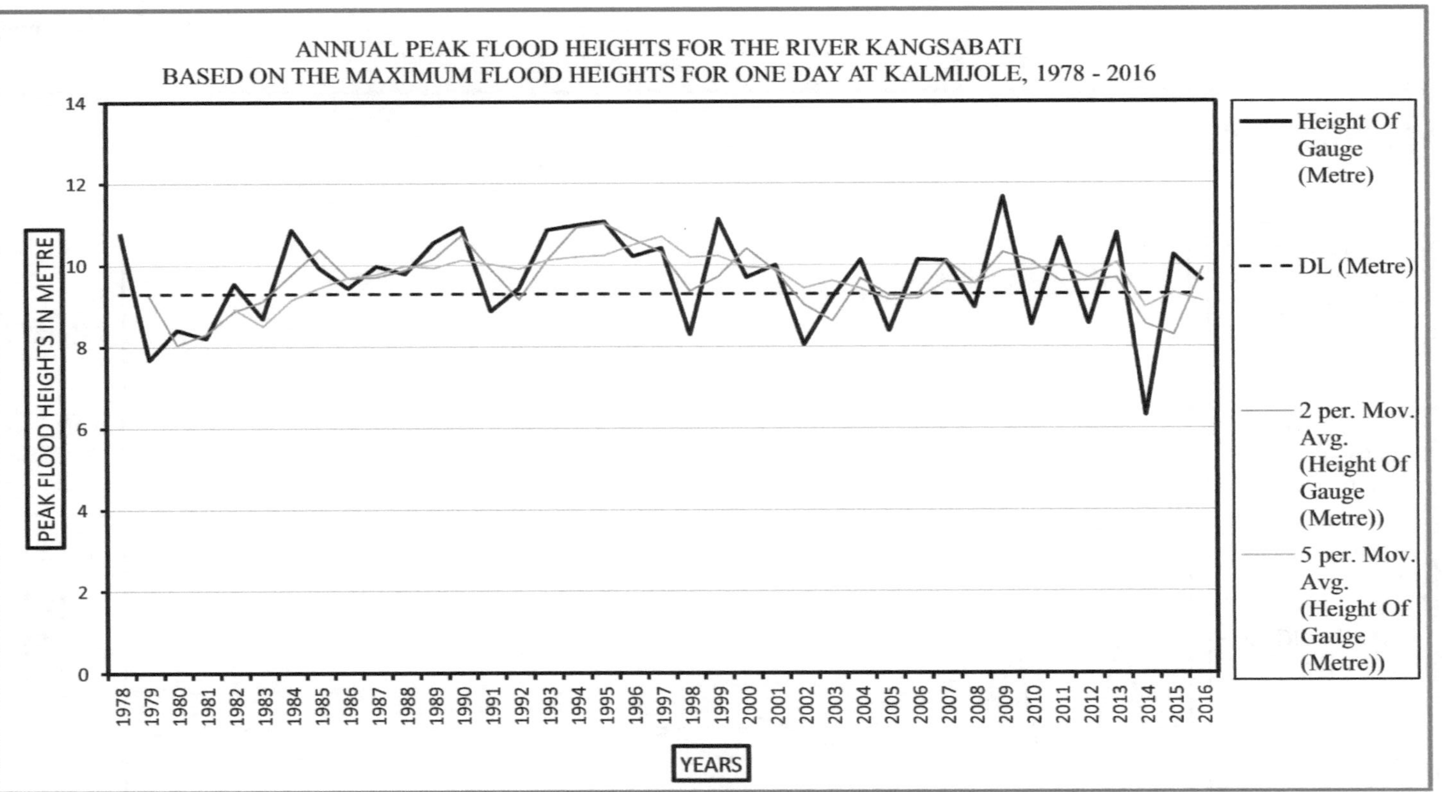


**Fig. 3.7**

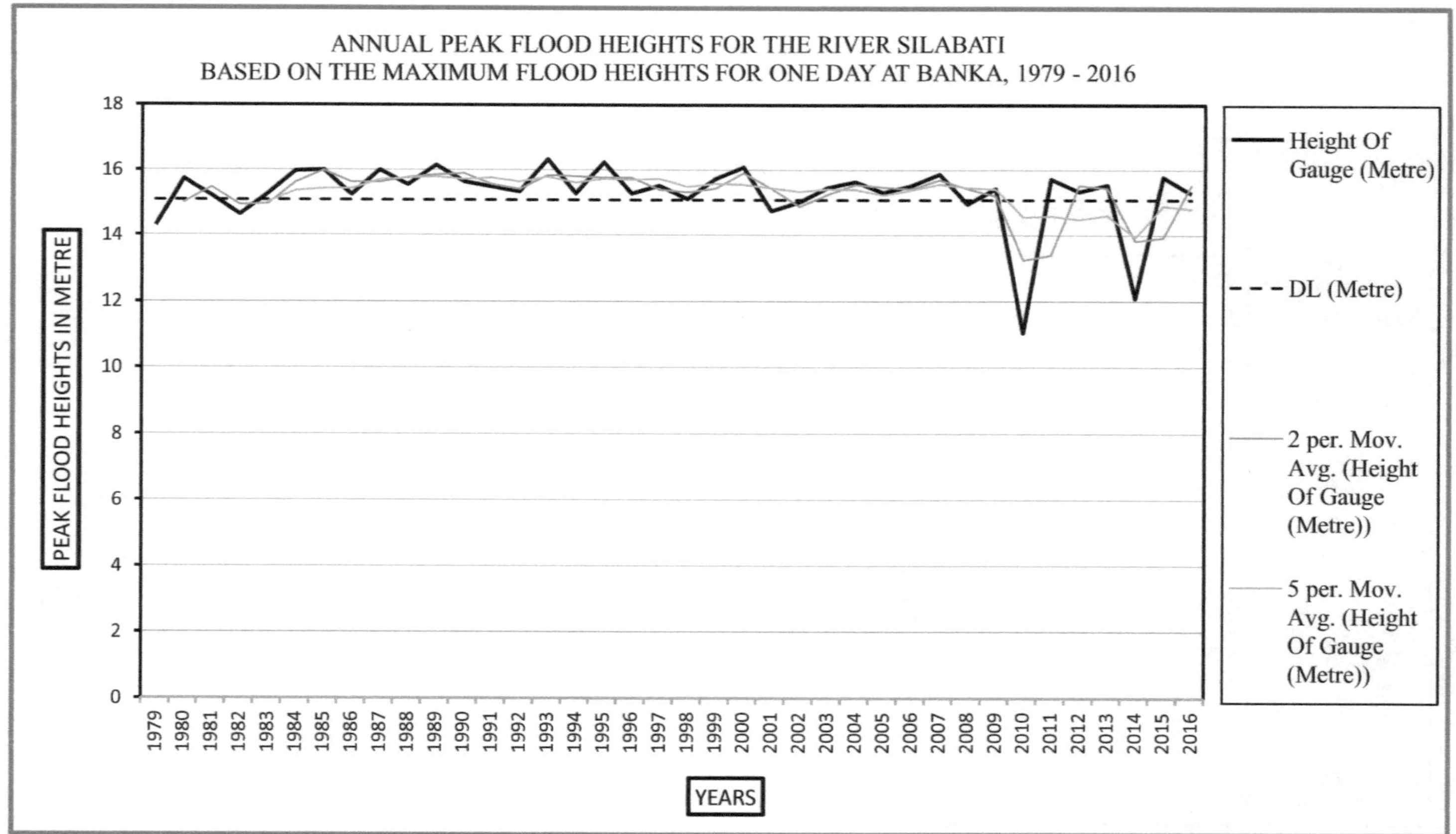


Fig. 3.8

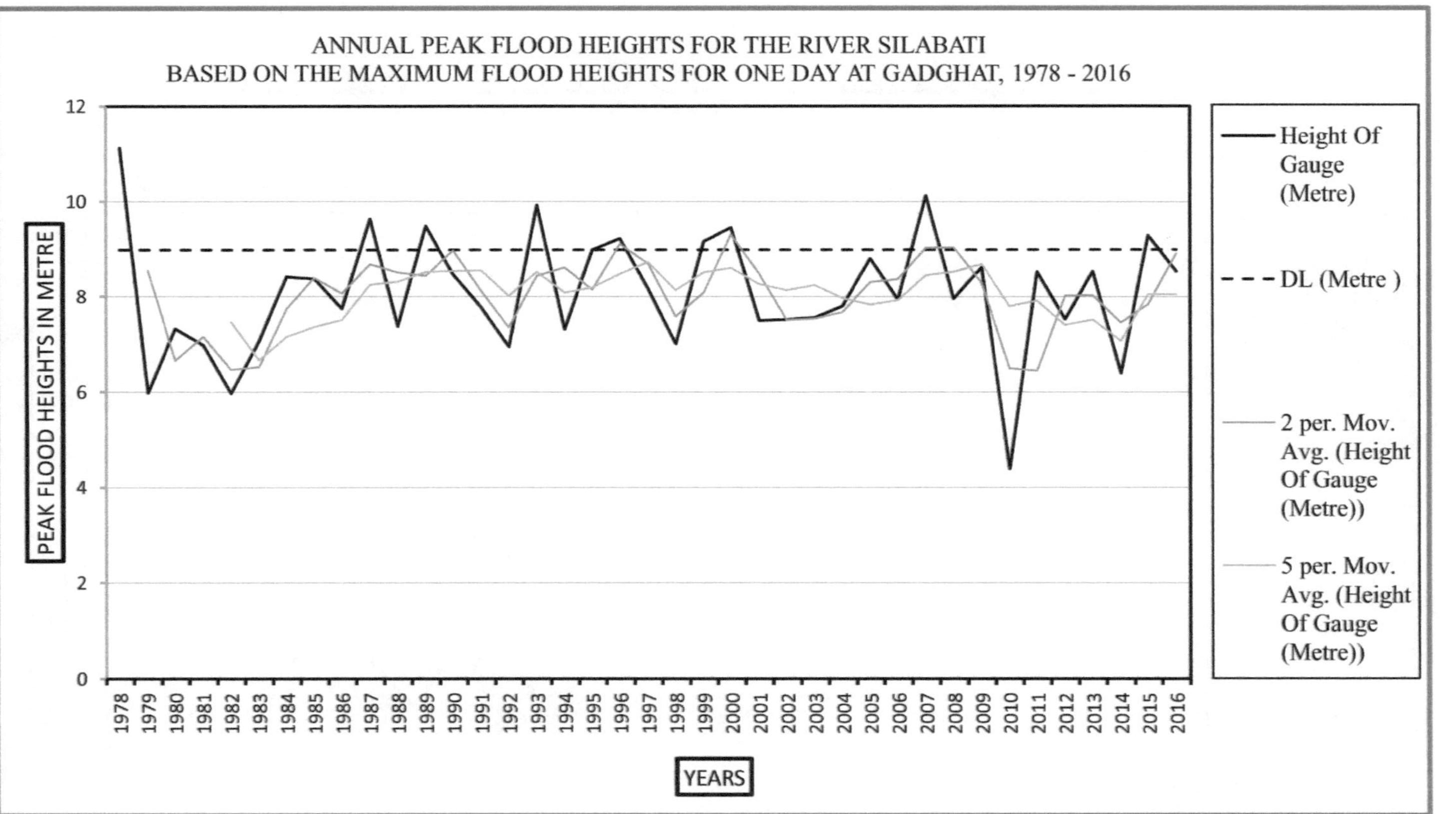


Fig. 3.9

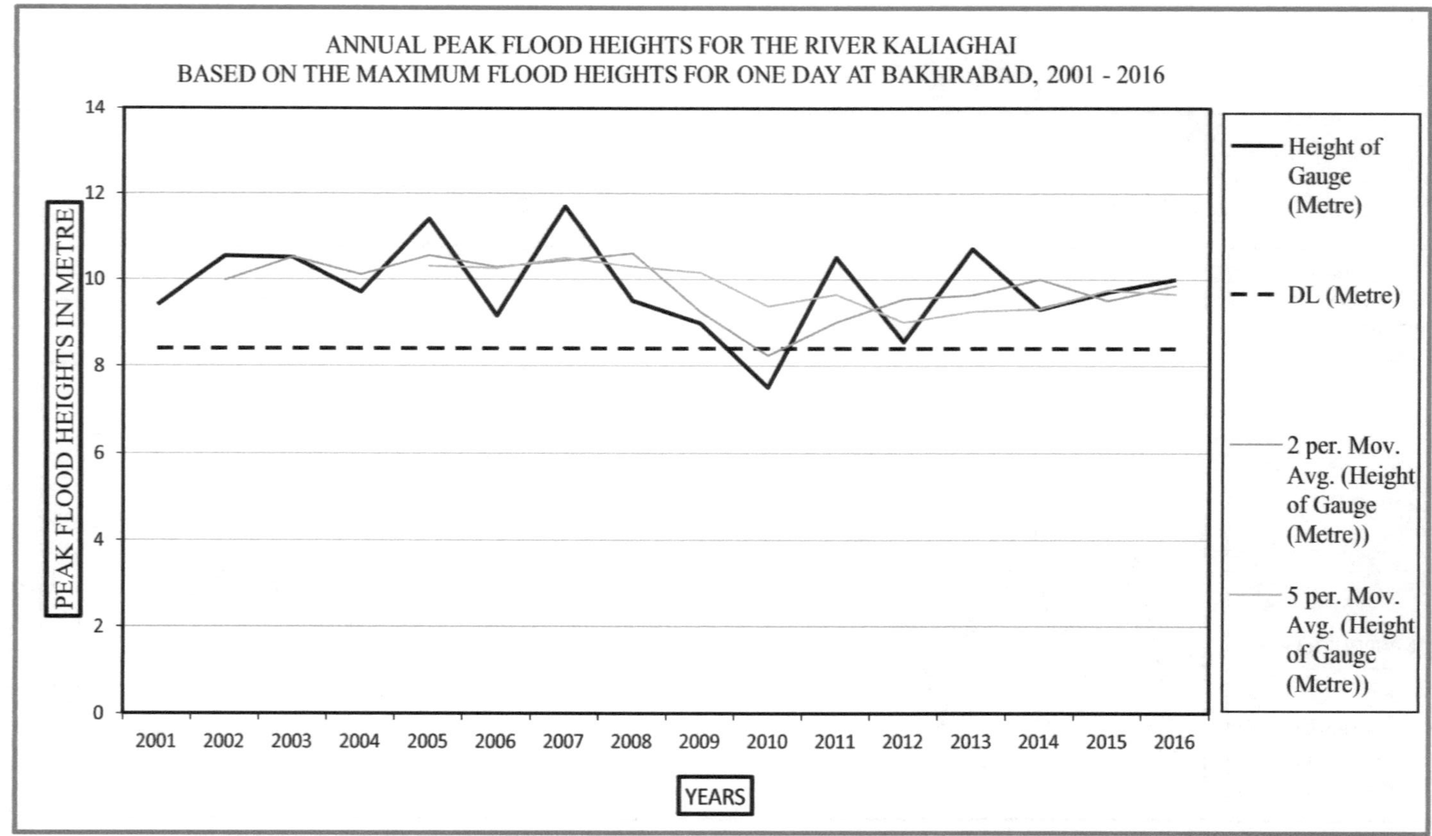


**Fig. 3.10**

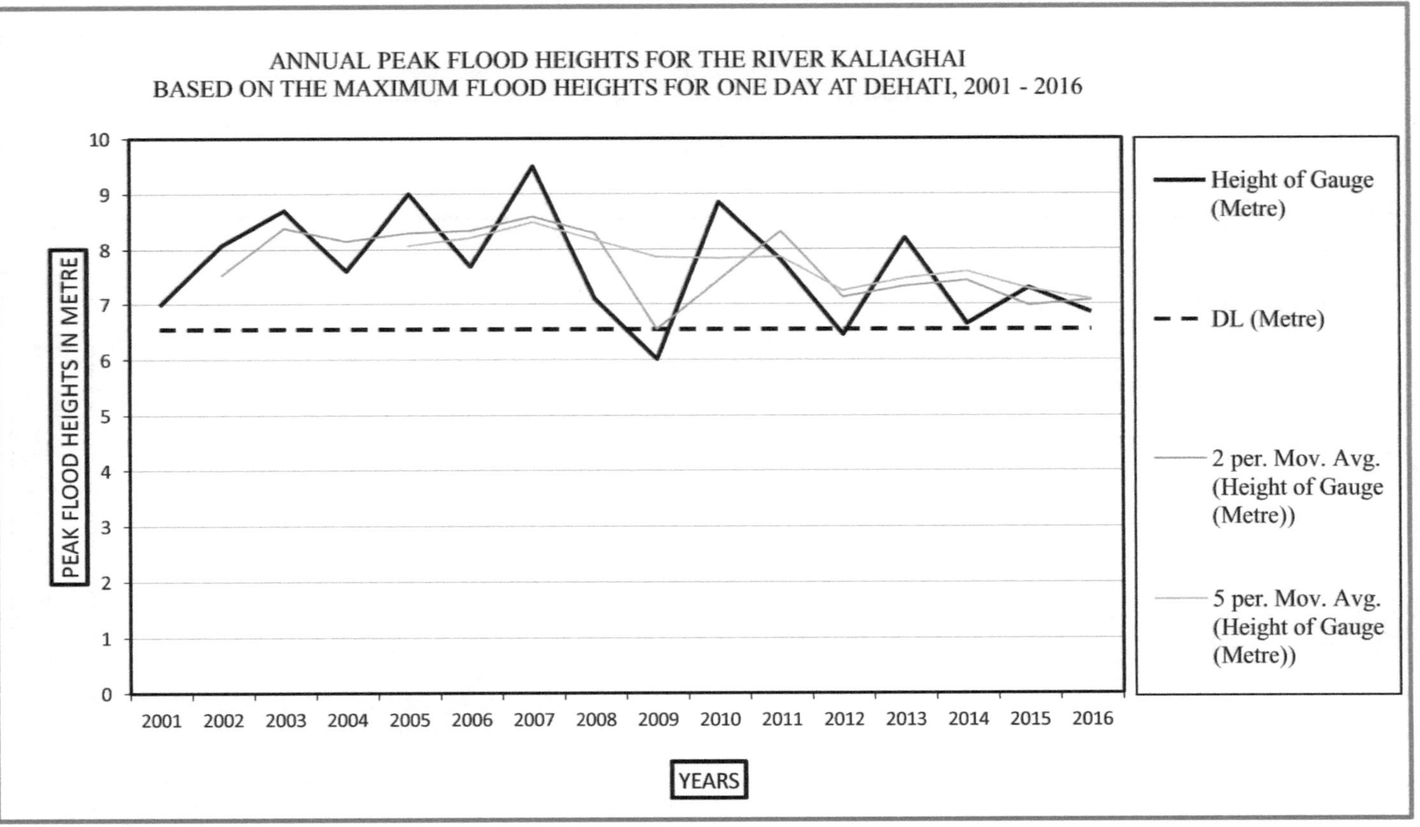


Fig. 3.11

ANNUAL PEAK FLOOD HEIGHTS FOR THE RIVER SUBARNAREKHA
BASED ON THE MAXIMUM FLOOD HEIGHTS FOR ONE DAY AT ASUI-DHRAMPUR, 2005 - 2016
PEAK FLOOD HEIGHTS IN METRE
YEARS
Height of Gauge (Metre)
DL (Metre)
2 per. Mov. Avg. (Height of Gauge (Metre))
5 per. Mov. Avg. (Height of Gauge (Metre))

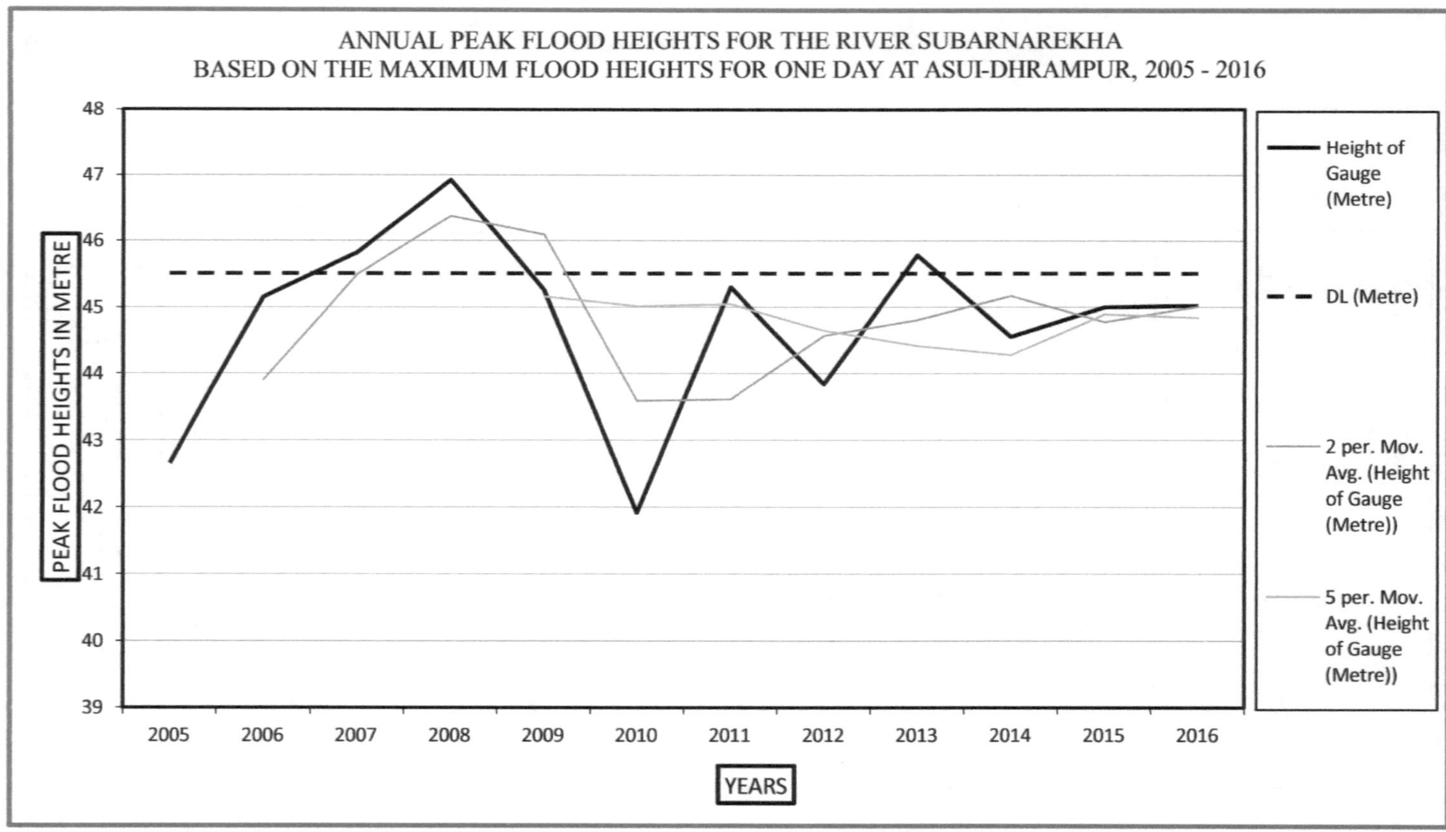

**Fig. 3.12**

Frequency of Flood during Monsoon'2013
River: COSSYE     Gauge Station: Mohanpur     District: Paschim Medinipur
Gauge Level     PDL     DL     EDL
EDL = 26.36 mGTS
DL = 25.75 mGTS
PDL = 25.14 mGTS
Gauge Level in mGTS
Date

Frequency of Flood during Monsoon'2013
River: SHILABATI     Gauge Station: Banka     District: Paschim Medinipur
Gauge Level
PDL
DL
EDL
EDL = 15.69 mGTS
DL = 15.02 mGTS
PDL = 14.35 mGTS
Gauge Level in mGTS
Date

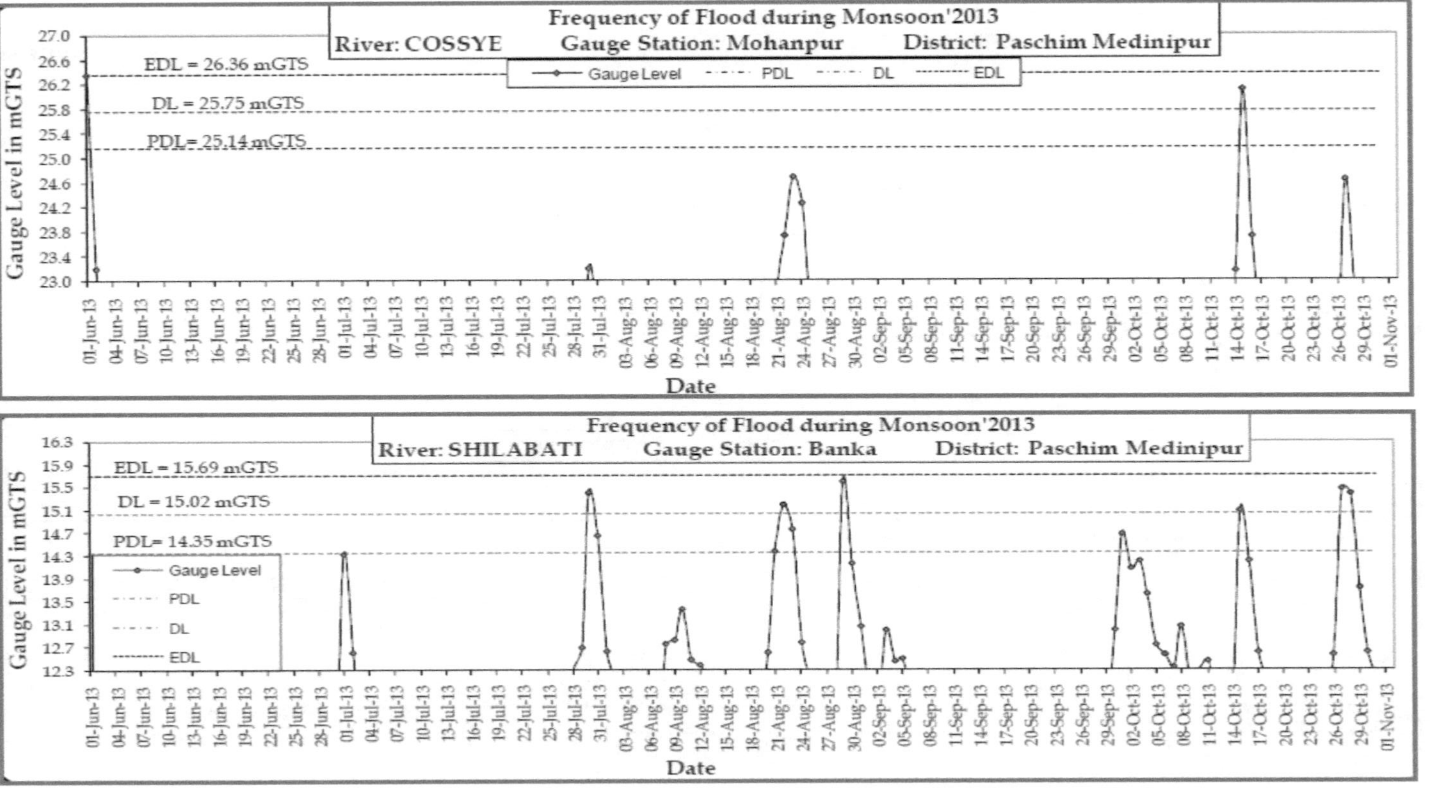

**Fig. 3.13**

Frequency of Flood during Monsoon'2013
River : KALIAGHAI     Gauge Station: Bakhrabad     District: Paschim Medinipur
Gauge Level     PDL     DL     EDL
Gauge Level in mGTS
EDL = 8.85 mGTS
DL = 8.40 mGTS
PDL = 7.95 mGTS
Date
Frequency of Flood during Monsoon'2013
River : SUBARNAREKHA     Gauge Station: Gopibullavpur     District: Paschim Medinipur
Gauge Level     PDL     DL     EDL
Gauge Level in mGTS
EDL = 46.50 mGTS
DL = 45.50 mGTS
PDL = 44.50 mGTS
Date

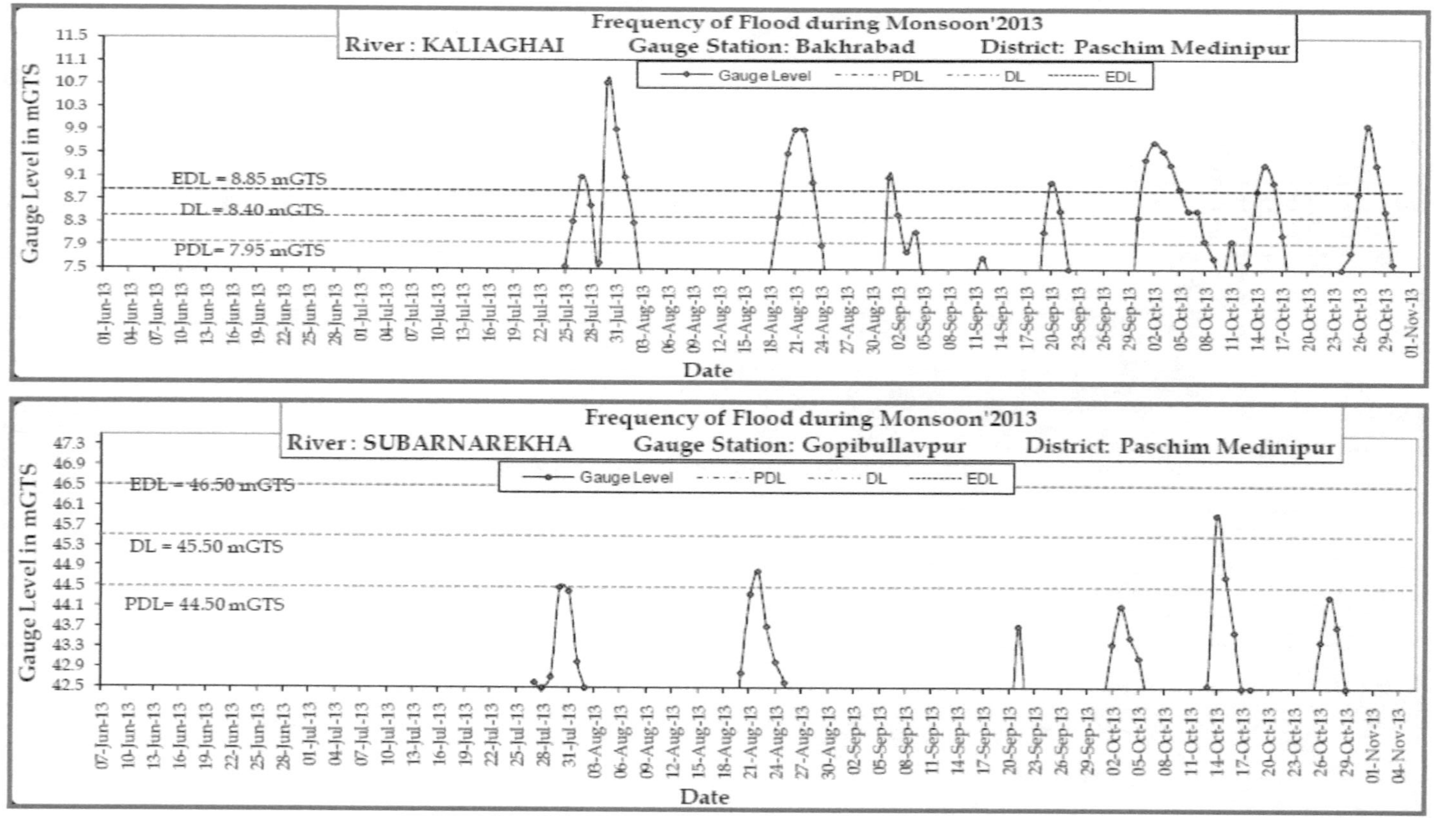

**Fig. 3.14**

### 3.1.2 Nature of Peak Flood

There is a wide range of methodology employed in analysing floods. The majority of these methods are related to and employed in the water discharge data. Chow has given stress on the study of floods based on water discharge data (1964, ch. 25, p. 6). But my study area has very limited of discharge data. Moreover, discharge data are found to exercise only a small role in the pattern and process of human occupancies. On the other hand, the study area has some data base of water levels. Since the water levels influence more on the human occupation under inundation. Here attempts have been made to analysis floods by taking water levels data. Chow also suggested to analysis flood with water level data at the absence of water discharge data (1964, ch. 25, p. 6).

For the analysis of nature of peak discharge, empirical methods have been applied because of non-availability of gauged discharge data. Various methods adopted for determining peak discharge have shown widely varying results even in the same river (See Table 3.3). For this anomaly the researcher has attached his field experiences with the rainfall, discharge and flow conditions of the rivers while estimating some hydrological situations for the study area.

Flood frequency analysis technique is applied in all the gauged river basins. Because of shortage of discharge data, only the water levels data have been used by the researcher to estimate relative frequencies and peak floods at different recurrent intervals of floods. The relative frequencies are estimated by using Weibull's plotting position formula stated by -

$$P\ (X \geq x) = \frac{M}{N+1} \tag{i}$$

Where, P (X≥ x) is the probability of exceedance of a given flood, m is the rank of the event arranged in descending order and N is the total number of events of flood occurrences. Another significance of the Weibull's method is the determination of return period or recurrent interval of a particular flood occurrence. The recurrent interval or return period T in years is calculated by adopting the formula –

$$T = \frac{N+1}{M} \tag{ii}$$

Where, T indicates that within T years, certain floods may be equalled or exceeded once on average.

The River respective delta heads Gauge reading has been taken to analysis the floods frequency. Usually an arbitrary elevation has been established based on the experience at the delta heads which are usually called as the danger level of the flood and when the river discharge exceeds that danger level, the river is said to be in 'flooding' (Table 3.1).

■ **Table 3.1: Flood stages of the Rivers at their Delta heads**

| Rivers | Reading Station | Danger Level in Metres |
| --- | --- | --- |
| Kangsabati | Mohanpur | 25.75 |
| Silabati | Gadghat | 8.99 |
| Kaliaghai | Bakhrabad | 8.4 |
| Subarnarekha | Asui – Dharampur | 45.50 |

The Kangsabati River has been experienced 31 high floods on the basis of gauge reading at Mohanpur in 65 years of interval and the probability of the occurrence of floods i.e. the average return time of a flood of particular intensity has been calculated with the division of total years of record by the total number of floods of that intensity. The time period so obtained gives the probability value i.e. after an interval of that period a flood of that intensity or more is likely to occur. Thus, the probability of occurrence of high floods in Kangsabati River is 2.13 years. In Silabati River has experienced 10 high magnitude floods in 38 years of interval and the probability of occurrence of high floods is 3.9 years. In Kaliaghai River has experienced 14 high magnitude floods in 15 years of interval and the probability of occurrence of high floods is 1.14 years. And in Subarnarekha River has experienced 3 high magnitude of floods in 11 years interval and the probability of occurrence is 4 years (See Table 3.2).

The estimated values of peak discharges (See Table 3.3) by empirical methods are found to be hazardous. They vary from 1782 Cumecs to 11337 Cumecs for Kangsabati River. As in the case of the Kangsabati, the Dickens and Ryves value for peak discharge may be accepted. The Dickens and Ryves value for peak discharge may be accepted for other three rivers namely; Silabati, Kaliaghai and Subarnarekha. The annual peak flood series for 1950 to 2016 of the Kangsabati River (See Table 3.4) shows its highest peak which conforms to a recurrence interval of 68 years with a probability of 1.47 percent. The lowest peak conforms to a recurrent interval of 1.01 years with a probability of 98.53 percent. In case of Silabati River highest peak which conforms to a recurrence interval 40 years with a probability of 2.5 percent and the lowest peak conforms to a recurrent interval of 1.03 years with a probability of 97.5 percent. The annual peak flood series for 2001 to 2016 of the Kaliaghai River shows its highest peak which conforms to a recurrence interval of 17 years with a probability of 5.88 percent and the lowest peak conform to a recurrent interval 1.06 years with a probability of 94.12 percent. And the another one, the River Subarnarekha shows its highest peak which conforms to a recurrent interval of 13 years with a probability of 7.69 percent and the lowest peak conforms to a recurrent interval of 1.08 years with a probability of 92.31 percent.

■ **Table 3.2: High Flood Frequencies and Their Recurrence Interval**

| River | Total Time Span | Number of High Flood Events | Recurrence Interval of High Magnitude Flood Events |
|---|---|---|---|
| Kangsabati | 1950-2015 = 65 years | 31 (High Magnitude Floods) | 65+1/31 = 2.13 (one each in 2.13 years) |
| Silabati | 1978-2016 = 38 years | 10 (High Magnitude Floods) | 38+1/10 = 3.9 (one each in 3.9 years) |
| Kaliaghai | 2001-2016 = 15 years | 14 (High Magnitude Floods) | 15+1/14 = 1.14 (one each in 1.14 years) |
| Sub-arnarekha | 2005-2016 = 11 years | 3 (High Magnitude Floods) | 11+1/3 = 4 (one each in 4 years) |

*Source: Irrigation and Waterways Department, Govt. of West Bengal. (Data processed by the Researcher).*

■ **Table 3.3: Peak Flood or Q (in Cumecs) Determination of Different Rivers**

| Methods Adopted By | Empirical Formulae | The Kangsabati (A = 8369 km²) | The Silabati (A = 4088 km²) | The Kaliaghai (A = 1913 km²) | The Subarnarekha (A = 18951 km²) | Remarks |
|---|---|---|---|---|---|---|
| **Dickens (1865)** | $Q_p = C_D A^{3/4}$ | 3354 | 1960 | 1109 | 6192 | When Dickens Cnstant, $C_D = 6$ |
| **Ryves (1884)** | $Q_p = C_R A^{2/3}$ | 1782 | 1103 | 663 | 3081 | When RyvesCnstant, $C_R = 8.5$ |
| **Inglish (1930)** | $Q_p =$ | 11337 | 6819 | 4378 | 5871 | - |

$Q_p$ = Discharge in Cumecs, A = Catchment Area of the River

■ **Table 3.4:** Estimation of Relative Frequencies of Water Levels (1950 – 2016), River: Kangsabati, Gauge Site: Mohanpur

| Year | Peak Water Levels (Metre) | Rank (m) | Recurrence Interval (T = N+1/m) | Probability (P = m/N+1) | Probabilityin Percentage |
|---|---|---|---|---|---|
| 1950 | 29.13 | 1 | 68 | 0.0147 | 1.47 |
| 1953 | 28.7 | 2 | 34 | 0.0294 | 2.94 |
| 1968 | 27.88 | 3 | 22.67 | 0.0441 | 4.41 |
| 1975 | 27.85 | 4 | 17 | 0.0588 | 5.88 |
| 1971 | 27.72 | 5 | 13.6 | 0.0745 | 7.45 |
| 1973 | 27.54 | 6 | 11.33 | 0.0882 | 8.82 |
| 1959 | 27.45 | 7 | 9.71 | 0.1029 | 10.29 |
| 1960 | 27.42 | 8 | 8.5 | 0.1176 | 11.76 |
| 1958 | 27.24 | 9 | 7.56 | 0.1324 | 13.24 |
| 1962 | 27.12 | 10 | 6.8 | 0.1471 | 14.71 |
| 1951 | 27.08 | 11 | 6.18 | 0.1618 | 16.18 |
| 2007 | 27 | 12 | 5.67 | 0.1765 | 17.65 |
| 1997 | 26.98 | 13 | 5.23 | 0.1912 | 19.12 |
| 1978 | 26.94 | 14 | 4.86 | 0.2059 | 20.59 |
| 1956 | 26.72 | 15 | 4.53 | 0.2206 | 22.06 |
| 1993 | 26.64 | 16 | 4.25 | 0.2353 | 23.53 |
| 1965 | 26.35 | 17 | 4 | 0.25 | 25 |
| 1967 | 26.29 | 18 | 3.78 | 0.2647 | 26.47 |
| 1972 | 26.29 | 19 | 3.58 | 0.2794 | 27.94 |
| 1969 | 26.23 | 20 | 3.4 | 0.2941 | 29.41 |
| 1999 | 26.22 | 21 | 3.24 | 0.3088 | 30.88 |
| 1977 | 26.15 | 22 | 3.09 | 0.3235 | 32.35 |
| 1974 | 26.14 | 23 | 2.96 | 0.3382 | 33.82 |
| 2013 | 26.1 | 24 | 2.83 | 0.3529 | 35.29 |
| 1961 | 26.08 | 25 | 2.72 | 0.3676 | 36.76 |
| 1952 | 26.02 | 26 | 2.62 | 0.3824 | 38.24 |
| 1984 | 25.95 | 27 | 2.52 | 0.3971 | 39.71 |
| 1990 | 25.9 | 28 | 2.43 | 0.4118 | 41.18 |
| 1989 | 25.81 | 29 | 2.34 | 0.4265 | 42.65 |
| 1964 | 25.8 | 30 | 2.27 | 0.4412 | 44.12 |
| 1994 | 25.8 | 31 | 2.19 | 0.4559 | 45.59 |
| 2009 | 25.68 | 32 | 2.13 | 0.4706 | 47.06 |
| 1996 | 25.66 | 33 | 2.06 | 0.4853 | 48.53 |

| Year | Peak Water Levels (Metre) | Rank (m) | Recurrence Interval (T = N+1/m) | Probability (P = m/N+1) | Probability in Percentage |
|---|---|---|---|---|---|
| 2003 | 25.56 | 34 | 2 | 0.5 | 50 |
| 2004 | 25.54 | 35 | 1.94 | 0.5147 | 51.47 |
| 2006 | 25.46 | 36 | 1.89 | 0.5294 | 52.94 |
| 1985 | 25.45 | 37 | 1.84 | 0.5441 | 54.41 |
| 1963 | 25.44 | 38 | 1.79 | 0.5588 | 55.88 |
| 1966 | 25.44 | 39 | 1.74 | 0.5735 | 57.35 |
| 2001 | 25.44 | 40 | 1.7 | 0.5882 | 58.82 |
| 1957 | 25.41 | 41 | 1.66 | 0.6029 | 60.29 |
| 1995 | 25.41 | 42 | 1.62 | 0.6176 | 61.76 |
| 2016 | 25.38 | 43 | 1.58 | 0.6324 | 63.24 |
| 2005 | 25.32 | 44 | 1.55 | 0.647 | 64.7 |
| 1954 | 25.28 | 45 | 1.51 | 0.6618 | 66.18 |
| 1955 | 25.28 | 46 | 1.48 | 0.6765 | 67.65 |
| 1992 | 25.2 | 47 | 1.45 | 0.6912 | 69.12 |
| 2002 | 25.18 | 48 | 1.42 | 0.7059 | 70.59 |
| 1970 | 25.07 | 49 | 1.39 | 0.7206 | 72.06 |
| 1998 | 25.06 | 50 | 1.36 | 0.7353 | 73.53 |
| 2000 | 25.06 | 51 | 1.33 | 0.75 | 75 |
| 2015 | 25.06 | 52 | 1.31 | 0.7647 | 76.47 |
| 1988 | 25.05 | 53 | 1.28 | 0.7794 | 77.94 |
| 1987 | 25.02 | 54 | 1.26 | 0.7941 | 79.41 |
| 2008 | 25 | 55 | 1.24 | 0.8088 | 80.88 |
| 2011 | 24.98 | 56 | 1.21 | 0.8235 | 82.35 |
| 1981 | 24.78 | 57 | 1.19 | 0.8382 | 83.82 |
| 1983 | 24.78 | 58 | 1.17 | 0.8529 | 85.29 |
| 2010 | 24.7 | 59 | 1.15 | 0.8676 | 86.76 |
| 1980 | 24.68 | 60 | 1.13 | 0.8824 | 88.24 |
| 1976 | 24.64 | 61 | 1.11 | 0.8971 | 89.71 |
| 1982 | 24.57 | 62 | 1.1 | 0.9176 | 91.76 |
| 1979 | 24.5 | 63 | 1.08 | 0.9264 | 92.64 |
| 1991 | 24.4 | 64 | 1.06 | 0.9411 | 94.11 |
| 1986 | 24.17 | 65 | 1.05 | 0.9559 | 95.59 |
| 2012 | 21.42 | 66 | 1.03 | 0.9706 | 97.06 |
| 2014 | 20.92 | 67 | 1.01 | 0.9853 | 98.53 |

*Source: Irrigation and Waterways Department, Govt. of West Bengal. (Data processed by the Researcher).*

**■ Table 3.5:** Estimation of Relative Frequencies of Water Levels (1978 – 2016), River: Silabati, Gauge Site: Gadghat

| Years | Height Of Gauge (Metre) | Rank (m) | Recurrence Interval (T = N+1/m) | Probability (P = m/N+1) | Probability in Percentage |
|---|---|---|---|---|---|
| 1978 | 11.12 | 1 | 40 | 0.025 | 2.5 |
| 2007 | 10.12 | 2 | 20 | 0.05 | 5 |
| 1993 | 9.93 | 3 | 13.33 | 0.075 | 7.5 |
| 1987 | 9.64 | 4 | 10 | 0.1 | 10 |
| 1989 | 9.49 | 5 | 8 | 0.125 | 12.5 |
| 2000 | 9.46 | 6 | 6.67 | 0.15 | 15 |
| 2015 | 9.29 | 7 | 5.71 | 0.175 | 17.5 |
| 1996 | 9.23 | 8 | 5 | 0.2 | 20 |
| 1999 | 9.17 | 9 | 4.44 | 0.225 | 22.5 |
| 1995 | 8.99 | 10 | 4 | 0.25 | 25 |
| 2005 | 8.8 | 11 | 3.64 | 0.275 | 27.5 |
| 2009 | 8.62 | 12 | 3.33 | 0.3 | 30 |
| 2013 | 8.53 | 13 | 3.08 | 0.325 | 32.5 |
| 2016 | 8.53 | 14 | 2.86 | 0.35 | 35 |
| 2011 | 8.52 | 15 | 2.67 | 0.375 | 37.5 |
| 1990 | 8.47 | 16 | 2.5 | 0.4 | 40 |
| 1984 | 8.42 | 17 | 2.35 | 0.425 | 42.5 |
| 1985 | 8.38 | 18 | 2.22 | 0.45 | 45 |
| 1997 | 8.17 | 19 | 2.11 | 0.475 | 47.5 |
| 2008 | 7.96 | 20 | 2 | 0.5 | 50 |
| 2006 | 7.94 | 21 | 1.9 | 0.525 | 52.5 |
| 2004 | 7.8 | 22 | 1.81 | 0.55 | 55 |
| 1991 | 7.77 | 23 | 1.74 | 0.575 | 57.5 |
| 1986 | 7.74 | 24 | 1.67 | 0.6 | 60 |
| 2003 | 7.56 | 25 | 1.6 | 0.625 | 62.5 |
| 2012 | 7.53 | 26 | 1.54 | 0.65 | 65 |
| 2002 | 7.52 | 27 | 1.48 | 0.675 | 67.5 |
| 2001 | 7.5 | 28 | 1.43 | 0.7 | 70 |
| 1988 | 7.38 | 29 | 1.38 | 0.725 | 72.5 |
| 1980 | 7.33 | 30 | 1.33 | 0.75 | 75 |
| 1994 | 7.31 | 31 | 1.29 | 0.775 | 77.5 |
| 1983 | 7.07 | 32 | 1.25 | 0.8 | 80 |
| 1998 | 7.01 | 33 | 1.21 | 0.825 | 82.5 |
| 1981 | 6.98 | 34 | 1.18 | 0.85 | 85 |

| Years | Height Of Gauge (Metre) | Rank (m) | Recurrence Interval (T = N+1/m) | Probability (P = m/N+1) | Probability in Percentage |
|---|---|---|---|---|---|
| 1992 | 6.95 | 35 | 1.14 | 0.875 | 87.5 |
| 2014 | 6.4 | 36 | 1.11 | 0.9 | 90 |
| 1979 | 5.98 | 37 | 1.08 | 0.925 | 92.5 |
| 1982 | 5.97 | 38 | 1.05 | 0.95 | 95 |
| 2010 | 4.39 | 39 | 1.03 | 0.975 | 97.5 |

*Source: Irrigation and Waterways Department, Govt. of West Bengal. (Data processed by the Researcher).*

■ **Table 3.6:** Estimation of Relative Frequencies of Water Levels (2001 – 2016), River: Kaliaghai, Gauge Site: Bakhrabad

| Years | Height of Gauge (Metre) | Rank (m) | Recurrence Interval (T = N+1/m) | Probability (P = m/N+1) | Probability in Percentage |
|---|---|---|---|---|---|
| 2007 | 9.5 | 1 | 17 | 0.0588 | 5.88 |
| 2005 | 9 | 2 | 8.5 | 0.1176 | 11.76 |
| 2010 | 8.85 | 3 | 5.67 | 0.1765 | 17.65 |
| 2003 | 8.7 | 4 | 4.25 | 0.2353 | 23.53 |
| 2013 | 8.2 | 5 | 3.4 | 0.2941 | 29.41 |
| 2002 | 8.08 | 6 | 2.83 | 0.3529 | 35.29 |
| 2011 | 7.8 | 7 | 2.43 | 0.4118 | 41.18 |
| 2006 | 7.68 | 8 | 2.13 | 0.4706 | 47.06 |
| 2004 | 7.6 | 9 | 1.89 | 0.5294 | 52.94 |
| 2015 | 7.3 | 10 | 1.7 | 0.5882 | 58.82 |
| 2008 | 7.1 | 11 | 1.55 | 0.6471 | 64.71 |
| 2001 | 6.98 | 12 | 1.42 | 0.7059 | 70.59 |
| 2016 | 6.85 | 13 | 1.31 | 0.7647 | 76.47 |
| 2014 | 6.65 | 14 | 1.21 | 0.8235 | 82.35 |
| 2012 | 6.45 | 15 | 1.13 | 0.8824 | 88.24 |
| 2009 | 6.01 | 16 | 1.06 | 0.9412 | 94.12 |

*Source: Irrigation and Waterways Department, Govt. of West Bengal. (Data processed by the Researcher).*

■ **Table 3.7:** Estimation of Relative Frequencies of Water Levels (2005 – 2016), River: Subarnarekha, Gauge Site: Asui – Dhrampur

| Years | Height of Gauge (Metre) | Rank (m) | Recurrence Interval (T = N+1/m) | Probability (P = m/N+1) | Probability in Percentage |
|---|---|---|---|---|---|
| 2008 | 46.92 | 1 | 13 | 0.0769 | 7.69 |
| 2007 | 45.82 | 2 | 6.5 | 0.1538 | 15.38 |
| 2013 | 45.78 | 3 | 4.33 | 0.2308 | 23.08 |

Contd…

| Years | Height of Gauge (Metre) | Rank (m) | Recurrence Interval (T = N+1/m) | Probability (P = m/N+1) | Probability in Percentage |
|---|---|---|---|---|---|
| 2011 | 45.3 | 4 | 3.25 | 0.3077 | 30.77 |
| 2009 | 45.26 | 5 | 2.6 | 0.3846 | 38.46 |
| 2006 | 45.15 | 6 | 2.17 | 0.4615 | 46.15 |
| 2016 | 45.02 | 7 | 1.86 | 0.5385 | 53.85 |
| 2015 | 45 | 8 | 1.63 | 0.6154 | 61.54 |
| 2014 | 44.56 | 9 | 1.44 | 0.6923 | 69.23 |
| 2012 | 43.84 | 10 | 1.3 | 0.7692 | 76.92 |
| 2005 | 42.66 | 11 | 1.18 | 0.8462 | 84.62 |
| 2010 | 41.92 | 12 | 1.08 | 0.9231 | 92.31 |

*Source: Irrigation and Waterways Department, Govt. of West Bengal. (Data processed by the Researcher).*

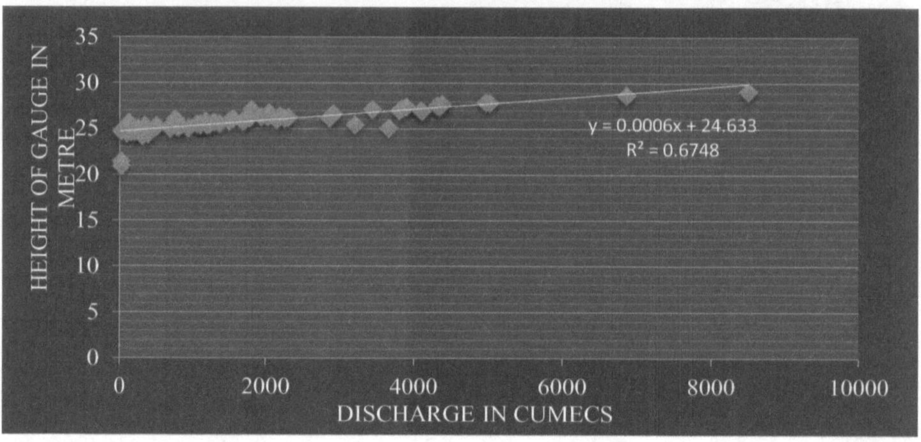


**Fig. 3.15:** Showing the relationship between nature of Peak Water Level and Discharge of Kangsabati River at Mohanpur Station.

## 3.2 Zoning of Flood Prone Areas

Proper delineation of flood prone areas is an important step to the areas that are most liable to flood. With accurate identification of the hazard zones meticulous management strategy and precautionary measures can be taken in the high-risk zone of flood to sustain environmental stability of the area. The primary concept of delineation of flood prone areas is to regulate the land use in the flood prone areas to restrict damage potential and also mitigate the negative effects of floods on people and economy. In a regulated way flood prone area are required to be developed. Because, in one hand it is ensure that existing hazard and flood damage potential do not increase and the other hand new developmental works are not subjected to serious damaged. Perspective of this view, the demarcation and identification of flood prone areas belonging to different frequencies of inundation on a large-scale map seem to have great importance.

In the beginning of the nineteenth century attempts were made to draw inundations map in different parts of the world. Such inundation maps were found in the United States Geological Survey Reports. A new series of flood inundation maps known as Hydrologic Investigation Atlas were published by USGS in 1959. However, flood hazard mapping and zoning techniques United States owe to origin and development to the pioneering works of several individuals including Ellis (1969), Wolman (1971) and Dingman (1975). India being is of the most flood prone countries of the world, the need for flood inundation mapping as well as flood plain zoning is most essential for disaster preparedness and mitigation of floods. It is, however to be noted that the pace of research in this area of vital human concern is rather slow in the country. Paschim Medinipur district is also affected by flood in every year, yet no attempt has so far been made to study or to map the flood intensifying zones of the district.

The adopted methodology of this study is shown in figure no. 3.16, which shows the flowchart for the development of flood hazard map as well as flood prone zoning. The various steps are involved in the following manner as follows. Firstly, the flood inundation map from 2007 to 2016 has been collected from the National Remote Sensing Centre (NRSC), Bhuvan, an Indian Geo-Platform of the Indian Space Research Organisation (ISRO). River Peak Water Level (PWL) data have been collected from the Irrigation and Waterways Department of West Bengal. Secondly, for demarcation of the river catchment area, Digital Elevation Model (DEM) has been derived from Bhuvan. Thirdly, To determine the flood-affected frequency map, flood inundation maps from 2007 to 2016 has been used (see the 'Flood frequency analysis' Section 3.2.3) and to determine the flood water depth map, DEM and PWL of the major rivers has been used (see the 'Flood water depth analysis' Section 3.2.4). Finally, the flood hazard map has been developed by considering both the flood-affected frequency map and flood water depth map (see the 'Flood hazard map preparation' Section 3.2.5). Then the final flood hazard map combined with housing and population data to calculate the flood exposure for these two elements.

### 3.2.1 Flood Frequency Analysis

Different hydrological variables, such as flood frequency, depth of flooding, rate of water level rises, water velocity, and physical exposure of land and sediments loads are influencing flood hazards of a particular area. Two hydraulic components i.e. flood frequency and flood water depth has been considered in this study for the evaluation and determination of potential flood hazard areas. The concept of flood affected frequency has been adopted from Islam and Sado, 2000 (see Fig. 3.17). Nine-year images have been classified into water and non-water areas and superimposed together to generate a flood affected frequency map (see Table 3.8). Firstly, the classified image of 2007, 2008 and 2009 has been associated to formulate an individual flood frequency map. The process continues for the rest of the year. By this procedure a three-flood extent map has been prepared. And this three-flood frequency map lumped together to formulate a flood affected frequency map (see Fig. 3.18).

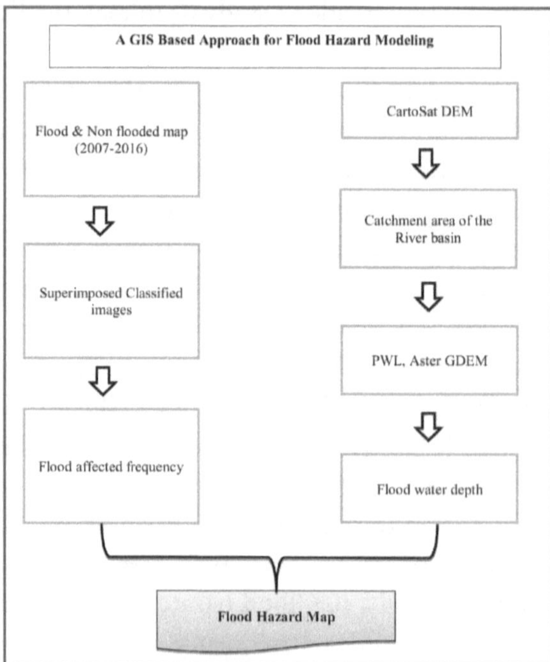


**Fig. 3.16:** A GIS based computational protocol for flood hazard mapping.

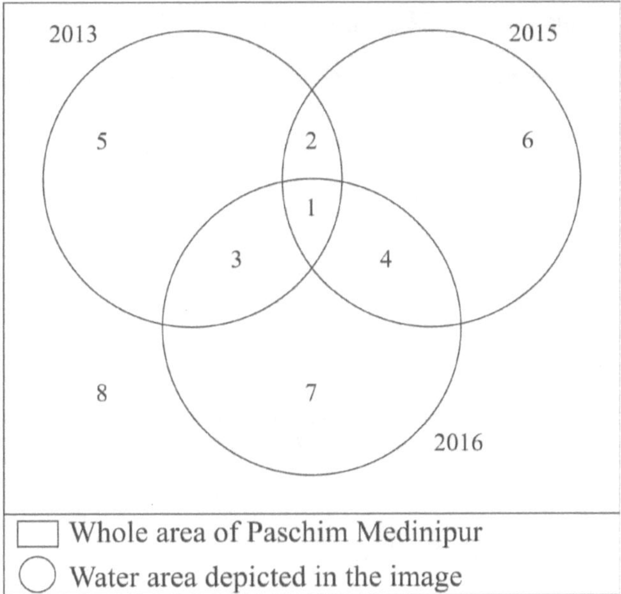


**Fig. 3.17:** Concept of flood affected frequency (Adopted from Islam and Sado, 2000).

The inundated area that found in all of the images considered the highly affected areas and therefore, it is a potentially high damage zone. The common inundated areas that appeared into two and one of the three maps have been accounted medium to low damages areas respectively. If any of the images inundate area is not found than that is classified as a non-flooded area (see Fig. 3.17). The final flood affected frequency map has been reclassified again into four categories according to the severity of inundation, assembling to flood rankings class 1, class 2, class 3 and class 4 as no- flood, low, medium and highly hazardous areas respectively (see Table 3.8).

The flood affected frequency map has been revealed that around 12% of the study area in a high hazard zone that is subject to regular inundation. Around 80% of the study area in a non-flood category which is not subjected by the river waters and around 8% of the area has been subjected to medium to low flood categories.

**■ Table 3.8: Classification of flood affected frequency**

| Sl. No | Map 1 | Map 2 | Map 3 | Area in sq.km | % of the area | Assignment of class |
|---|---|---|---|---|---|---|
| 1 | W | W | W | 1063.94 | 11.36 | 4 |
| 2 | NW | W | W | 265.35 | 2.83 | 3 |
| 3 | W | NW | W | 115.68 | 1.26 | 3 |
| 4 | NW | W | W | 185.25 | 1.98 | 3 |
| 5 | W | NW | NW | 53.16 | 0.57 | 2 |
| 6 | NW | W | NW | 112.73 | 1.20 | 2 |
| 7 | NW | NW | W | 68.49 | 0.73 | 2 |
| 8 | NW | NW | NW | 7499 | 80.09 | 1 |

Map 1 comprises classified maps of 2007, 2008 and 2009; Map 2 represents 2011, 2012 and 2013; Map 3 represents 2014, 2015 and 2016. W= Water, NW= Non Water.

### 3.2.2 Flood Water Depth Analysis

For developed the series of flood water depth maps, DEM and Peak Water Level data of the major rivers has been used. These flood depth maps has reclassified into four categories i.e. no water, shallow, medium and deep. A rule based approached have been used in the model builder utility of Arc GIS to derive the flood water depth map of the study area. If, in a single image deep flood observed and a medium flood is observed in at least one of the other images, then it has been regarded as deep; if it found medium in two images, then it has been considered medium; if it found shallow in two images, then it has been considered shallow. After that remaining areas are considered as a non-flooded area (Fig. 3.18).

Flood depth maps revealed that around 1025 sq.km area occupied deep flood depth categories and medium, shallow, non-flood area occupied 2.26%, 1.21%, 85% respectively (see Table 3.9). Here, the depth maps developed only basis of land condition during the creation of the elevation model of the study area.

**■ Table 3.9:** Area occupied by each category of floodwater depth

| Depth category | Area in sq.km | % of the area |
| --- | --- | --- |
| No water | 8014.25 | 85.59 |
| Shallow | 113.07 | 1.21 |
| Medium | 211.77 | 2.26 |
| Deep | 1024.60 | 10.94 |

### 3.2.3 Development of the Flood Hazard Map

Geospatial techniques, particularly RS, has shown great potential for hazard assessment (McKean et al. 1991), the big challenge is the lack of generally accepted methods forproducing hazard maps (Rhoads 1986). The final hazard map has been derived from combined to the flood affected frequency map and flood depth maps. If a cell represents non-flooded in both maps, then it was considered a non-hazard zone. If a cell represents low flooded areas in flood affected frequency map and shallow flood water depth in flood water depth maps then it is subjected to low hazard zone. If a cell represents medium flooded areas in flood affected frequency map and medium flood water depth in flood water depth maps then it is subjected to medium hazard zone. And then if a cell represents deep flood water in flood water depth maps and high flood areas in flood affected frequency map than it is treated by high hazard zone.

Based on hazard intensity, again the flood hazard map has been reclassified into four categories corresponding to class 1, class 2, class 3 and class 4 as no-hazard, low hazard, medium hazard and high hazard zone respectively (see Fig. 3.24). The final flood hazard map intersected with population and housing data of 2011 census, to estimate the exposure of these two components to flood hazard. Table 3.10 represents the distribution of population in different flood hazard zone and Table 3.11 revealed the distribution of housing unit in different flood hazard zone.

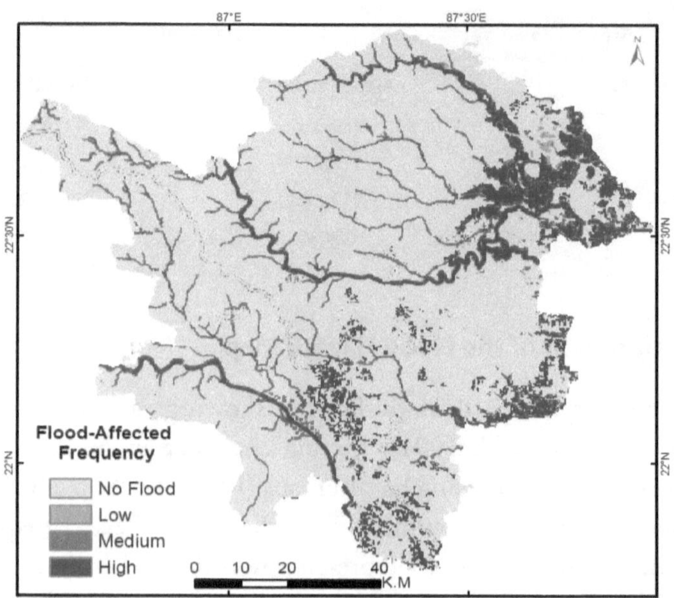


**Fig. 3.18:** Flood affected frequency.

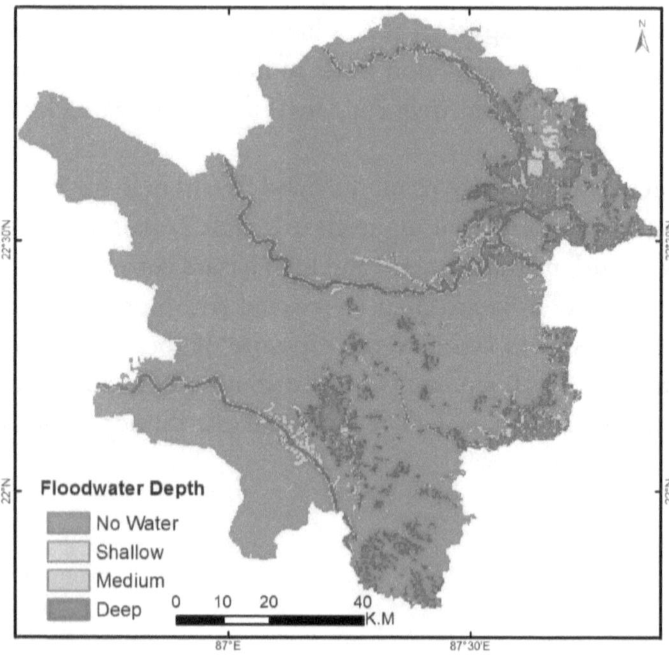


**Fig. 3.19:** Flood water depth.

**■ Table 3.10:** Exposure of the population to flood hazards

| Hazard Zone | Population (%) | Female (%) | Children (%) |
|---|---|---|---|
| High | 24 | 21 | 23 |
| Medium | 6.35 | 11 | 9.53 |
| Low | 22.13 | 24.74 | 22.75 |
| No Hazard | 47.52 | 43.53 | 44.72 |

**■ Table 3.11:** Exposure of Human Settlement in different flood hazard zone

| Hazard Zone | Katcha Houses (%) | Semi-pucca Houses (%) | Pucca Houses (%) |
|---|---|---|---|
| High | 16.51 | 13.54 | 8.19 |
| Medium | 11.15 | 8.48 | 7.52 |
| Low | 23.63 | 20.36 | 18 |
| No Hazard | 48.71 | 57.62 | 66.29 |

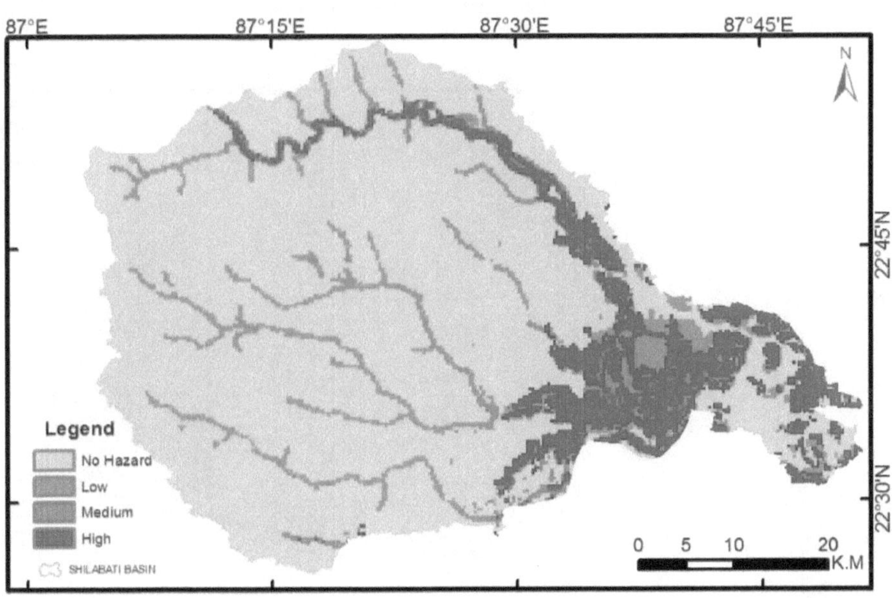


**Fig. 3.20:** Flood hazard map of Silabati Catchment in Paschim Medinipur District.

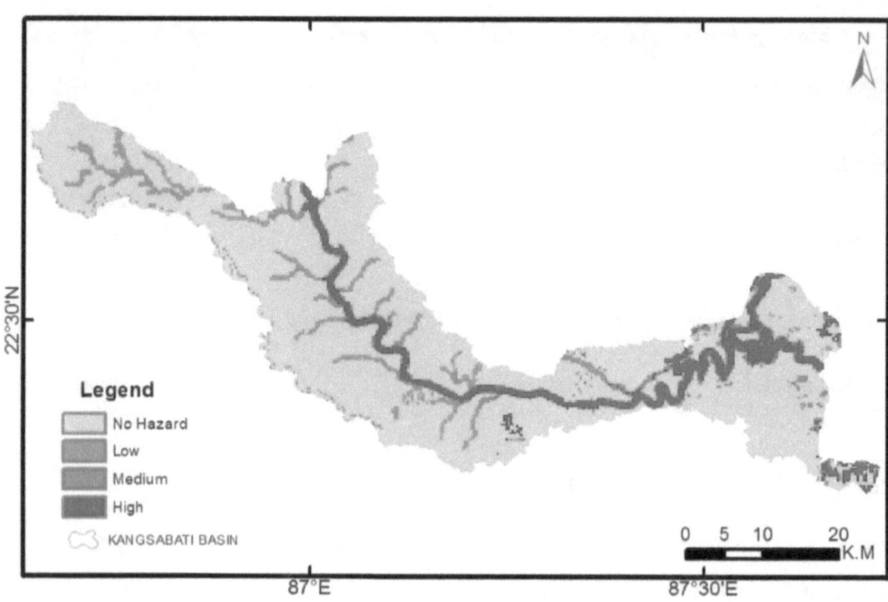


**Fig. 3.21:** Flood hazard map of Kangsabati Catchment in Paschim Medinipur District.

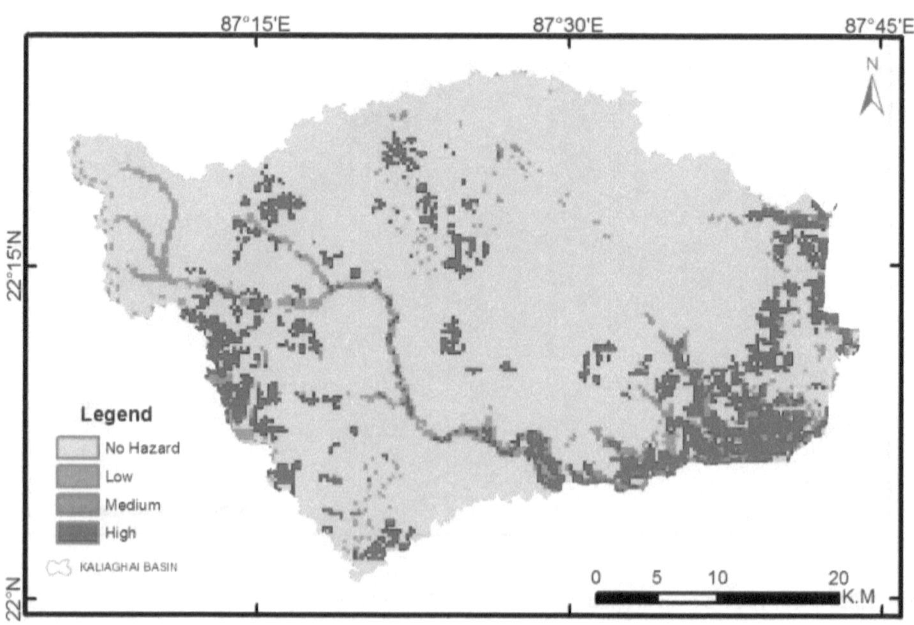


**Fig. 3.22:** Flood hazard map of Kaliaghai Catchment in Paschim Medinipur District.

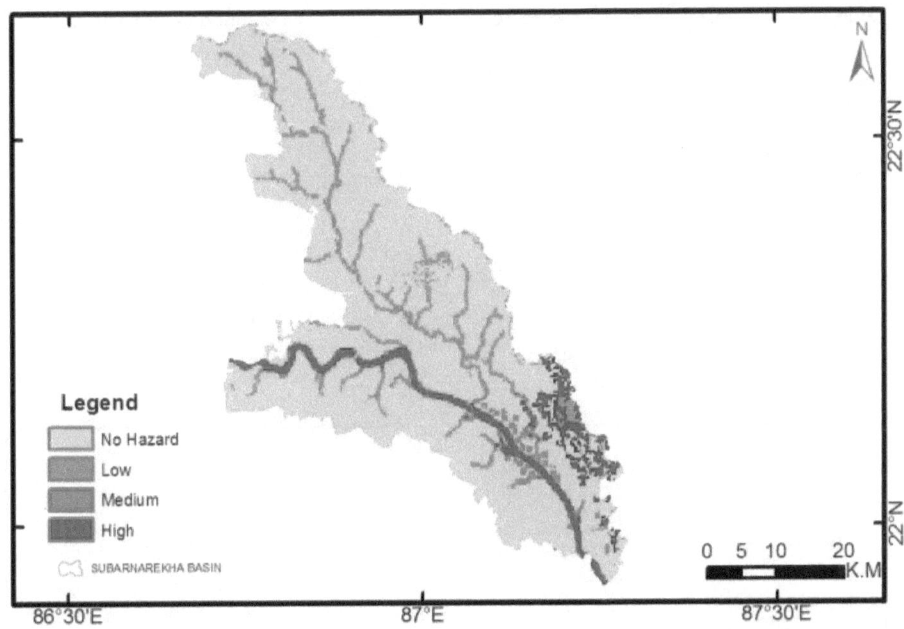



**Fig. 3.23:**  Flood hazard map of SubarnarekhaCatchment in Paschim Medinipur District.

**■ Table 3.12:  Catchment-wise different flood affected area**

| Name | Hazard Zone | Affected Area (Sq.Km) |
|---|---|---|
| Kaliaghai | | |
| | No Hazard | 1375.71506966000 |
| | Low | 69.67509318830 |
| | Medium | 24.98806735580 |
| | High | 203.52481868300 |
| | Total | 1673.90304888710 |
| Kangsabati | | |
| | No Hazard | 1332.58596256000 |
| | Low | 117.73146585800 |
| | Medium | 68.81252244250 |
| | High | 148.75791790400 |
| | Total | 1667.88786876450 |
| Subarnarekha | | |
| | No Hazard | 1512.78406028000 |
| | Low | 149.53886102400 |

Contd…

| Name | Hazard Zone | Affected Area (Sq.Km) |
|---|---|---|
| | Medium | 69.46175673590 |
| | High | 118.50048219100 |
| | Total | 1850.28516023090 |
| Silabati | | |
| | No Hazard | 2153.17958182000 |
| | Low | 220.28478782300 |
| | Medium | 65.44897202360 |
| | High | 313.59554883200 |
| | Total | 2752.50889049860 |

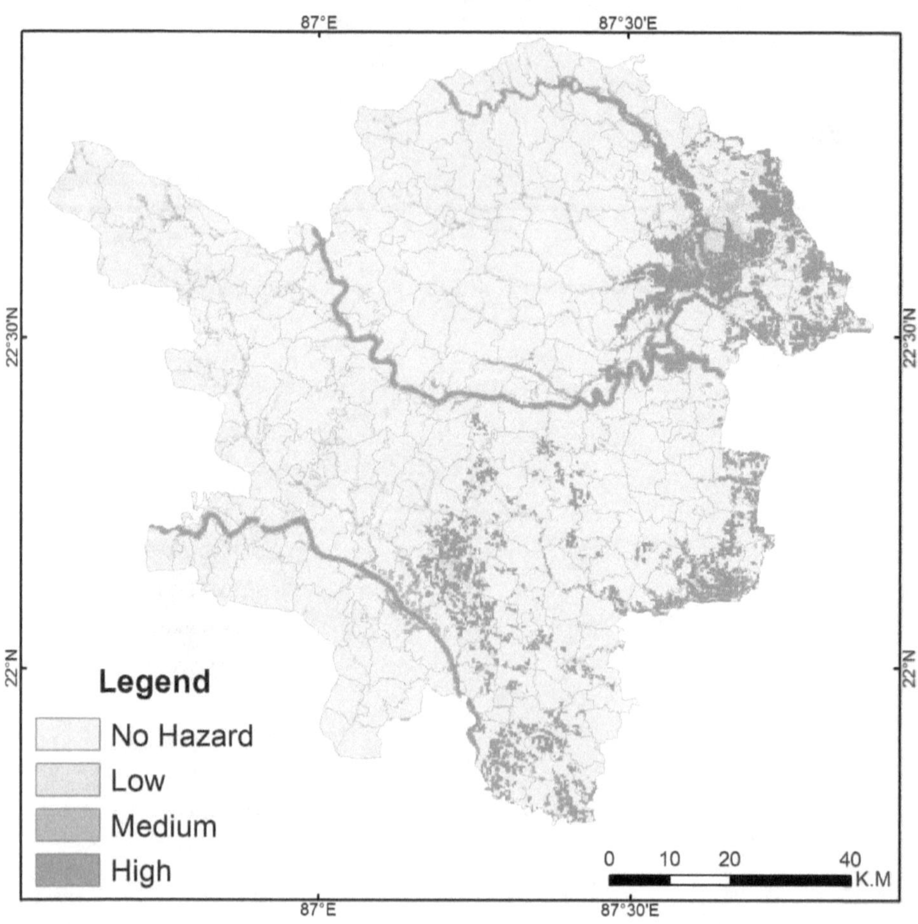


**Fig. 3.24:** Flood hazard map at Panchayat level obtained from flood affected frequency and flood water depth together.

The exposure analysis revealed that 24% population to the total population in the study area has been exposed to high flood hazard zone and 6.35%, 22.13%, 47.52% population in the study area has been exposed to medium, low, no hazards zone respectively. Similarly, 21% female population and 23% child population exposed to high flood hazard zones. Around 35.74% female population and 32.28% child population exposed low to medium hazard zones. Almost 43.53% female population and 44.72% child population has been exposed to no hazard zones. In addition to the housing types almost 16.51% Katcha, 15.54% Semi-pucca and 10.19% Pucca houses has been exposed to high hazard zones. Around 34.78% Katcha, 26.84 Semi-pucca, 25.52% Pucca houses exposed to medium to low hazard zones. Analysis clearly indicates that floods remain a significant threat to the people in PaschimMedinipur. As observed in PaschimMedinipur district people setup their settlement on the flood plains and many brick kiln industries also setup on the floodplains which destroy the stiffness of the river embankment. Therefore, consequently the flood hazard increased rapidly. That is why to ameliorate the flood induced damage, the derived flood hazard map worthless. In developing countries, where exact information is seriously lacking, such hazard maps are extremely useful for saving the lives and property of millions of people, particularly marginal groups.

## 3.3 Impacts of Flood on People and Economy

Man's affinity for flood plain has a long history. Though the flood hazards are playing adverse impact on many aspects of human occupance, yet the concentration of the people in flood hazard zones of advance countries or even third world countries is not decreasing. In third world countries like India which are economically and technologically backward to control the problem like flood or unable to render better means of adjustments to the people suffer more. The damages caused by floods have direct and indirect effects on socio-economic life of the people dwelling in the flood prone areas. In different ways floods mainly cause damage to agricultural lands. Floods also damage the houses of people. Grazing lands and fodder crops also damage and thereby cattle population and livestock reduce. Besides these, some indirect damages are also associated with floods. These indirect damages are generally associated with health and general welfare. Normal public health services are subject to greater pressure in the face of disruption of transportation and utilities specially water and shelter and hence adversely affect health condition. A good number of works have been carried out in India on this line. Works of Mukhopadhyaya (1968), Kayasth and Yadava (1977) and Barthakur (2000) are highly worth mentioning. Flood being are of the most serious problems, cause huge loss of property and other kinds of belongings of people in Paschim Medinipr district especially in the south and south-eastern portion of the district. In the district of Paschim Medinipur, the reverine areas being under excessive supply of water due to heavy rains, cause floods which badly affect human settlement, occupation etc. The frequently occurring high floods, rivers bank erosion, channel shifting in many parts of the district, especially in the active flood plain areas people are not be able to adjust with the floods. The flood frequency occurrence and the vulnerability of flood hazards have been discussed in chapter III and VI respectively. This chapter reveals that loss of property and life; disruption of socio-economic activity including transport and communication; damage of agricultural land and finally loss of agricultural crops. The variability of flood damage in both space and time reflects a large number of influencing factors like land use, characteristics of flood water, i.e. depth, velocity, duration and damage reducing actions taken up in the flooded area. But, however, it must emphasise that flood damages are highly variable and often extremely difficult to estimate (Panda, 1989).

Though the district lies under recurrent floods, lacks in reliable flood damage data. It is worth mentioning that the Rastriya Brah Ayog head issued guidelines in 1981 for collecting flood damage data at the village and block levels by the State Revenue Department with the co-operation with the Irrigation Department, Flood Control Department, Public Works Department and Agricultural Department. The concerned departments are mainly responsible for collection of flood damage data under the following major heads: (i) affected area, (ii) affected villages, (iii) affected population, (iv) human life lost, (v) affected houses, (vi) loss of cattle population, (vii) damage of crop area, (viii) damage of crop in terms of rupees and (ix) damage of public utilities.

The researcher collected data regarding flood damage from the Department of Disaster Management, District Magistrate Office, Paschim Medinipur. The flood damages are assessed by the respective District collectors in the affected areas collected their subordinate officers at the block level. They assess the damage done to crops, breaches to the embankments and lines of transport, loss of life and property. This is mainly done to assess the extent of distress of the people and area and plan the relief. The damage done to the public properties are assessed by their respective officers and reported to their department which is given in the Table – 4.1 to reveal the flood damage of the last eight years. It has been observed that the present assessment of damage neither gives a complete picture nor their data mutually exclusive. There is a substantial error between block level, district level and state level damage data. It has been revealed major omissions. Hence, the flood damage data supplied by the Government have their own limitations.

### 3.3.1 Flood Damage Analysis as per Report

The damage caused by floods during the period 2008 – 2016 has been presented in Table 3.13. The table reveals that maximum damaged occurred in the year 2008, 2009, 2013 and 2015. The damage caused by floods in these four years brought immense misery to the people of the district. The highest population affected by heavy rain and flood water discharge from different dam in the year of 2015 and it has been estimated approximately 35 lakhs as per report of the Disaster Management Department supersedes all other damage recorded of flood. In 2015, the flood damage occurred over 3200 Sq.Km. of area and 90374 hectors of crops area were damaged. It has been estimated that 56214 houses fully and 211411 houses partly damaged by the 2015 flood. It also estimated that 11267 villages were affected and 13 persons died and 11 cattle population also died. Hence, the damage occurs in several forms. The agricultural lands with standing paddy plants remain completely submerged under water for several days in low lying areas. Human habitation and crops are washed away by strong currents causing numerous breaches across the roads and embankments. Communication links get dislocated and damaged. The researcher extensively visited different places of the district to have a picture of the catastrophic flood of 2015. Some people who had experiences to witness several floods in the district like to opine that such flood did not occur in the district for last decade. Some scene of devastation of this catastrophic flood is presented in plate 3.1, 3.2, 3.3 and 3.4.

The Sarberia II GP has been highest population affected GP during flood seasons among all in last five years data, then the Narajole and Nandanpur I respectively. All those GP are highly affected because the Meandering characteristics of the river channel. Debra, Sabong and Keshpur blocks are highly population affected blocks in last five years data and it has been estimated

373442, 276018 and 258019 population has been affected respectively (see Table 4.3). The two years and five years moving average of GP wise population affected data (see Fig.4.1) also reveal an apparent upward trend. It has been observed that unlike other kinds of damages, the population affected has an increasing tendency. This is because of the increasing trend of population or may probably be due to more and more of the flood plains brought under human use and gradual rise of the river's beds due to siltation.

The number of houses damaged and areas affected in the district for the period 2008 – 2016 are presented in graphical form in Figure 4.4 and 4.7. It is observed that maximum area has been affected by flood in the year 2013, but in the year 2015 showing the maximum damages of houses. The Figure 4.4, 4.5 and 4.6 reveals that the damage patterns in terms of number of affected villages, number of houses damages and population affected are in the rising trend. It has been observed that maximum number (57) of human lives lost in the year of 2008, although it has also been depicted that most population affected flood year is 2015. It is observed that maximum cattle loss occurred by flood in the year 2008, whereas in the year 2016 has been observed the minimum cattle loss by flood. Table 4.1 also reveals that road and electricity damages only associated with high flood years. In 2015, 135 HT, 161 LT electric polls and 52 km. morrum road has been damaged. Hence, it is clearly signifying that the damage pattern in Paschim Medinipur District directly associated with flood characteristics in respected years, not having any similar trend.

■ Table: 3.13 Different kinds of flood damages in Paschim Medinipur District during 2008 – 2016

| Period of Occurrence | Nature (Cause) of calamity | No. of villages affected | Area affected (approx. Sq.km.) | Crop area affected (hec.) | Population affected (approx.) | Houses of damage | Loss of human life | Cattle loss | Road and electricity damaged |
|---|---|---|---|---|---|---|---|---|---|
| 9.8.2016 to 7.9.2016 | Flood water discharge | 265 | 75 | 6574 | 14000 | F- 157 P- 2126 | 5 | - | - |
| 3.5.2016 | Storm with thunder shower | 244 | 60 | - | 9300 | F- 232 P- 562 | 2 | - | - |
| 28.7.2015 to 17.8.2015 | Heavy rain & flood water discharge from different dam | 11267 | 3200 | 90374 | 35 lakh | F- 56214 P- 211411 | 13 | 11 | 135 HT & 161 LT electric polls, 52 km morrum road |
| 18.2.2015 to 1.2.2015 | Hailstorm | 212 | 60 | 10280 | 9000 | F- 22 P- 303 | - | - | - |
| 13.10.2013 to 1.11.2013 | Heavy rain & flood water discharge from different dam | 5922 | 1700 | 56783 | 9.5 lakh | F- 23544 P- 66084 | 16 | 148 | - |
| 19.8.2013 to 8.9.2013 | Do | 3163 | 900 | 58922 | 8.0 lakh | F- 6303 P- 39744 | 10 | | 15 km road |
| 27.7.2013 to 7.8.2013 | Do | 2641 | 750 | 34723 | 4.0 lakh | F- 3032 P- 21296 | 4 | 9 | - |
| 23.9.2011 to 28.9.2011 | Release of flood water & inundation | 24 | 7 | NA | 5500 | F- 210 P- 1255 | - | - | - |
| 24.5.2009 to 25.05.2009 | Cyclone AILA | 3973 | 1800 | NA | 6.3 lakh | F- 23497 P- 64960 | - | 246 | Morrum Rd – 52 km, Kutcha Rd- 33km. |
| 16.6.2008 to 4.9.2008 | Flood | 6410 | 1800 | 60153 | 16.5 lakh | F- 87357 P- 96212 | 57 | 3584 | |

Source: Disaster Management Department, Paschim Medinipur, 2017.

■ **Table: 3.14GP wise no. of affected population based on last 5 years data**

| Name of vulnerable GP | No. of population affected |
| --- | --- |
| Narajole | 31779 |
| Rajnagar | 28890 |
| Nandanpur I | 31640 |
| Nandanpur II | 29212 |
| Sarberia I | 28551 |
| Sarberia II | 32159 |
| 2 No. Kamalpur | 19484 |
| 3 No. Ranichwak | 11264 |
| 6 No. Benai | 18154 |
| 10 No. Palaspai | 14501 |
| 13 No. Jotghanashyam | 23452 |
| 14 No. Dudhkumra | 22610 |
| Sultanpur (1 no.) | 23229 |
| Dirghagram (3 no.) | 16491 |
| Mansuka (4 no.) | 11329 |
| Birsingha (5 no.) | 25331 |
| Mohanpur (6 no.) | 30830 |
| Dewanchak 1 (7 no.) | 17717 |
| Dewanchak 2 (8 no.) | 16394 |
| Ajabnagar 1 (9 no.) | 17728 |
| Ajabnagar 2 (10 no.) | 15585 |
| Manoharpur 1 (11 no.) | 1559 |
| Manoharpur 2 (11 no.) | 13855 |
| Irapala | 13161 |
| Mohanpur – I (5 No.) | 13236 |
| Mohanpur – II (6 No.) | 13884 |
| 3 No. Mangrul | 22128 |
| 4 No. Mainikundu | 26420 |

*Source: Disaster Management Action Plan, 2016.*

■ **Table 3.15:** No. of affected population with health establishments based on last 5 years data

| Sl. No | Name of affected Block | No. of affected GP | No. of affected population | Health establishments likely to be affected | | | |
|---|---|---|---|---|---|---|---|
| | | | | RH | BPHC | PHC | SC |
| 1 | Keshpur | 11 | 258019 | 0 | 0 | 1 | 12 |
| 2 | Medinipur Sadar | 5 | 119082 | 0 | 0 | 1 | 5 |
| 3 | KGP-I | 2 | 68121 | 0 | 0 | 0 | 0 |
| 4 | KGP-II | 2 | 49125 | 0 | 0 | 0 | 0 |
| 5 | Keshiary | 5 | 20296 | 0 | 0 | 0 | 4 |
| 6 | Narayangarh | 8 | 172132 | 0 | 0 | 0 | 15 |
| 7 | Datan – I | 4 | 75225 | 0 | 0 | 1 | 12 |
| 8 | Datan-II | 2 | 46571 | 0 | 0 | 0 | 0 |
| 9 | Mohanpur | 1 | 21950 | 0 | 0 | 0 | 1 |
| 10 | Debra | 9 | 373442 | 0 | 0 | 0 | 6 |
| 11 | Sabang | 13 | 276018 | 0 | 0 | 1 | 21 |
| 12 | Daspur-I | 6 | 182231 | 0 | 0 | 0 | 8 |
| 13 | Daspur-II | 6 | 109465 | 0 | 0 | 1 | 34 |
| 14 | Ghatal | 12 | 217209 | 0 | 0 | 1 | 28 |
| 15 | Chandrakona-I | 4 | 75668 | 0 | 0 | 0 | 8 |
| 16 | Chandrakona-II | 5 | 7247 | 0 | 0 | 0 | 8 |
| 17 | Ghatal Municipality | 13 ward | 38000 | 0 | 0 | 0 | 0 |

*Source: Disaster Management Action Plan, 2016.*

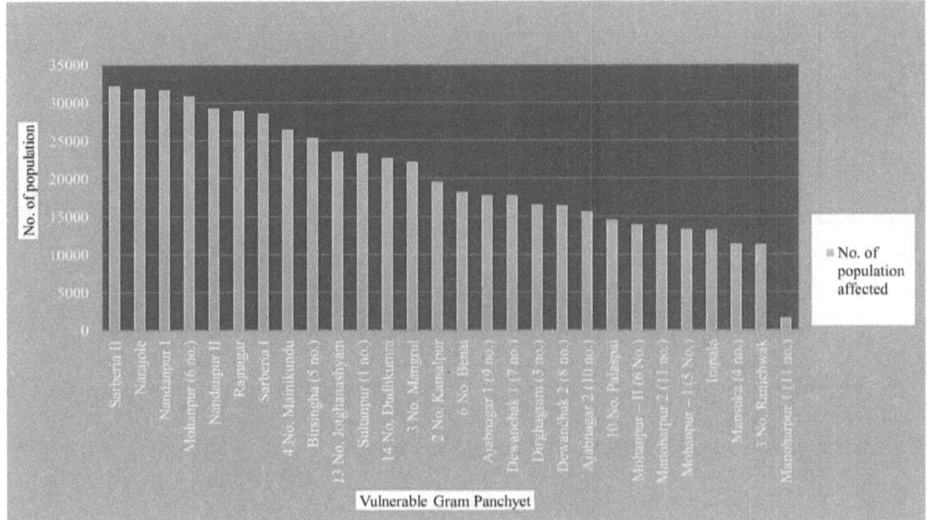


**Fig. 3.25:** Last five years GP wise affected population during the time of flood season.

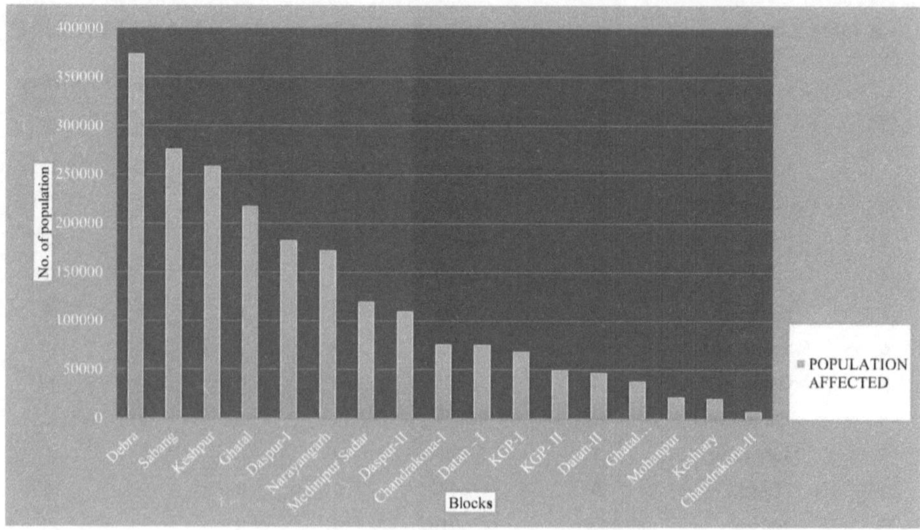


**Fig. 3.26:**  Last five years Block wise affected population during the time of flood season.

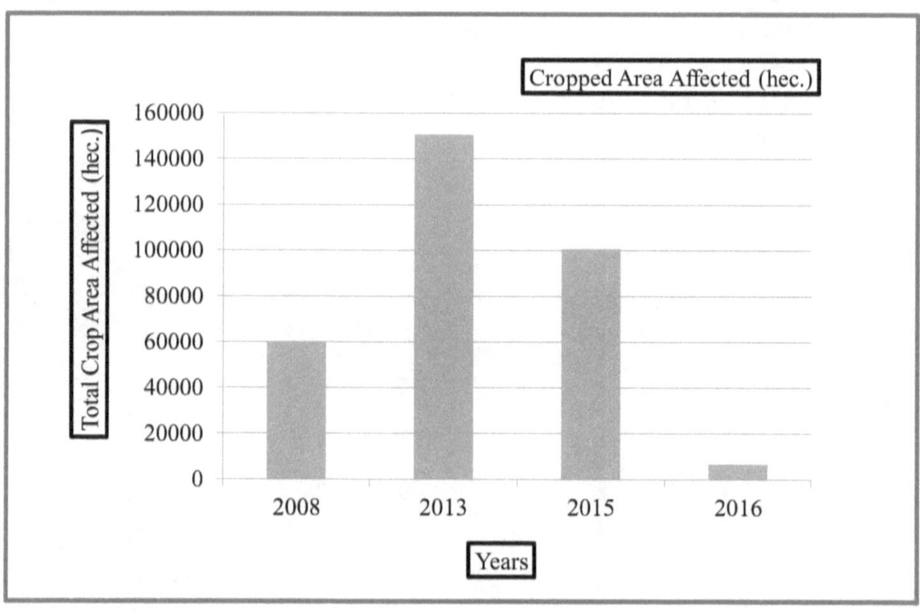


**Fig. 3.27:**  Crop area affected during some selected flood years.

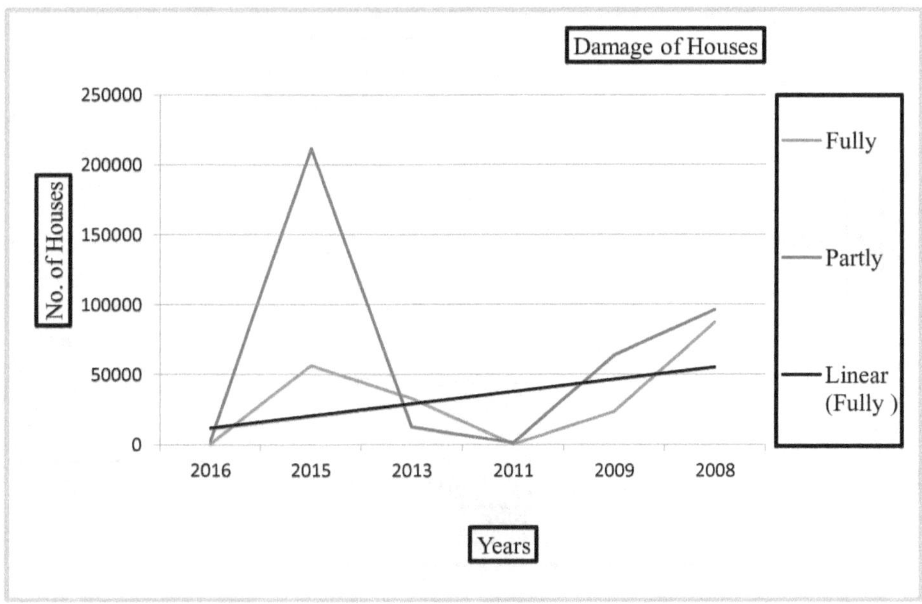


**Fig. 3.28:** Damage of houses during some selected flood years.

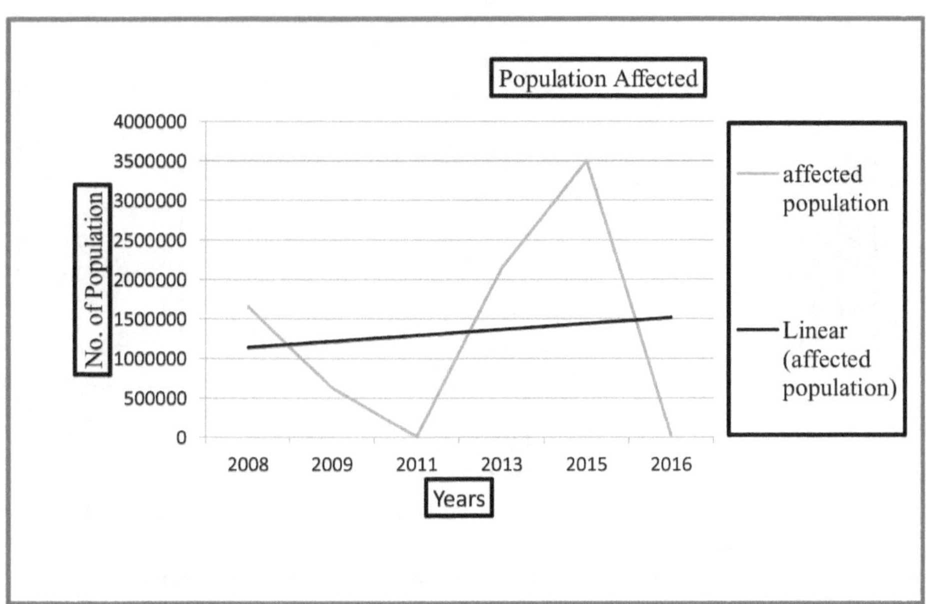


**Fig. 3.29:** Number of Population affected in Paschim Medinipur District due to flood during 2008 – 2016.

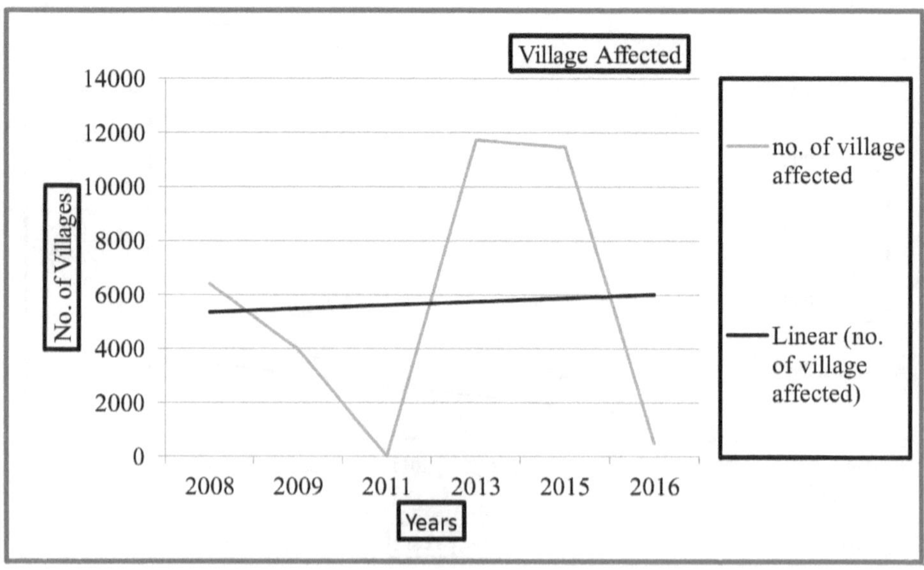


**Fig. 3.30:** Number of Village affected in Paschim Medinipur District due to flood during 2008 – 2016.

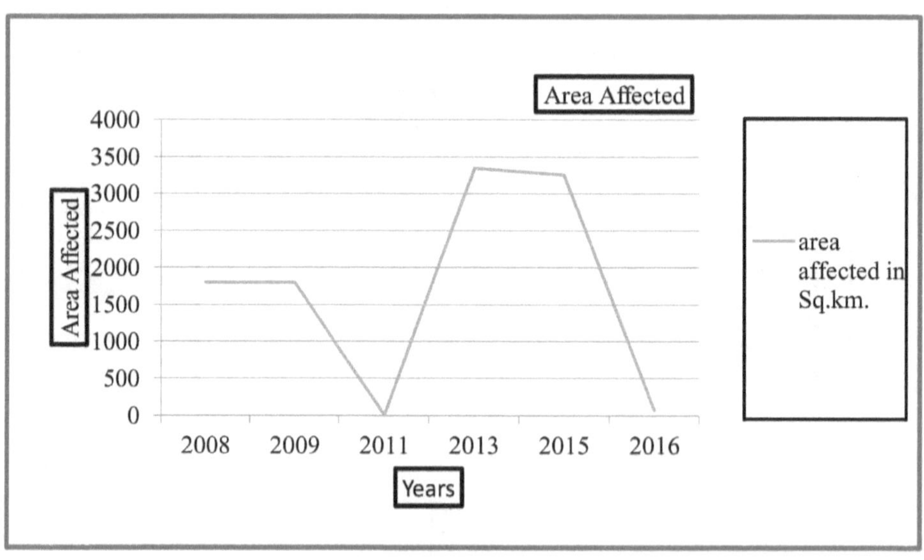


**Fig. 3.31:** Area affected in Paschim Medinipur District due to flood during 2008 – 2016.

**Plate 3.1:** Submerged agricultural land at Nij Narajole Gram Panchyet at Silabati and Kangsabati interfluves.

**Plate 3.2:** Damage of standing crops at Sankrail Block in Subarnarekha catchment.

**Plate 3.3:** Ravages of 2015 Flood. A Ex Zamindars Bundh washed out and floating the village in Lowada GP.

**Plate 3.4:** Flood inundations in Ghatal Town in the year of 2017.

**Plate 3.5:** A scene of river bank erosion and captured agricultural field at Boita village in Kangsabati River.

**Plate 3.6:** A scene of river channel shifting and reducing the crop production in Subarnarekha River.

**Plate 3.7:** A scene of pucca houses totally collapsed by flood water in the year of 2017.

# FACTORS ASSOCIATED WITH FLOODING AND FLOOD INTENSIFYING CONDITION

Catchment Characteristics: Subarnarekha Catchment – Kangsabati Catchment – Kaliaghai Catchment – Silabati Catchment, Geological and Geomorphological Characteristics,

Morphometric Characteristics: Basin Shape and Elongation Ratio – Drainage Density and Texture of Topography–Stream Network and Bifurcation Ratio – Longitudinal Profile and Gradient of Flow – Dimension of Channels, Meteorological Characteristics: Rainfall in the Catchment Basins – Intensity of Rainfall in the period preceding the floods, Hydrological Characteristics: Ground Water, Other variable Catchment Basin Characteristics: Soil Type, Land Use.

Flood result from a number of basic factors of which the most important are climatological in nature. An understanding of flood situation requires information about climatological, hydrological and geomorphological which are responsible for floods. As heavy and prolonged is the universal cause of floods, so morphometric and hydrological characteristics of the basin also important factors to form a situation like flood. These situations may be grouped into basin network and channel characteristics some of which are stable and some others are more unstable (see Table 4.1).

Among the stable basin characteristics, basin area and drainage density are probably the most important factors which determine the total volume of stream flow, generated by a given catchment wide precipitation from the river basin. The drainage patterns whose effects are closely related to that of bifurcation ratio and basin shape also belongs to this category. Generally, the dendritic drainage patterns are associated with sharp high magnitude flood peaks at the basin outlet; while in trellised drainage patterns permit the evacuation of flood flows from the downstream tributaries before the flood water from the upstream tributaries have arrived at the outlet. This result in a more muted flood response (Ward, 1978). The river discharge is a function of width, depth and velocity and velocity depends on hydraulic radius, channel slope and bed roughness and above all meander length. Thus, the channel geometry is also equally important for flooding. Besides, there are numerous variable characteristics of the basin and the networks whose effects on flood hydrograph are often complex. Some of these important secondary characteristics result from the complex interaction between climate, geology, soil type, vegetation cover and land use. This determines the water storage capacity of soil and sub-surface layers with low storage potential often result in rapid and intensified flooding while high infiltration rate of soil allows the bulk of precipitation to be absorbed through percolation and thereby reduces catchment flood response. Thus, keepingin view of the above-mentioned factors, in this chapter a brief review has been made of the various causes and intensifying conditions of flood in the different rivers of Paschim Medinipur district. This chapter highlights the catchment basin characteristics and their bearing of floods. Inter-relationship of the catchment basin characteristics with that of flooding has been attempted to establish the causal relationship. For those relationships a spatial and non-spatial data set used which are following.

## 4.1 Catchment Characteristics

### 4.1.1 The Subarnarekha Catchment

The Subarnarekha catchment is a long strip of land, wide in its upper part and narrow in the lower part. It lies between 85°8′ E to 87°32′ E and from 21°15′ N to23°34′ N. It drains a large portion of the districts of Ranchi, Manbhum, Singbhum, Paschim Medinipur, Mayurbhanj and Balasore. The total catchment area of the river is 18951 Sq.Km. Comprising of 13590 Sq.Km in Bihar, 2160 Sq.Km in West Bengal and 3201 Sq.Km in Odisha. After a course of about 500 K.M the river falls into the Bay of Bengal. Owing to the hilly character of its catchment area, the Subarnarekha is subjected to sudden floods of short duration.

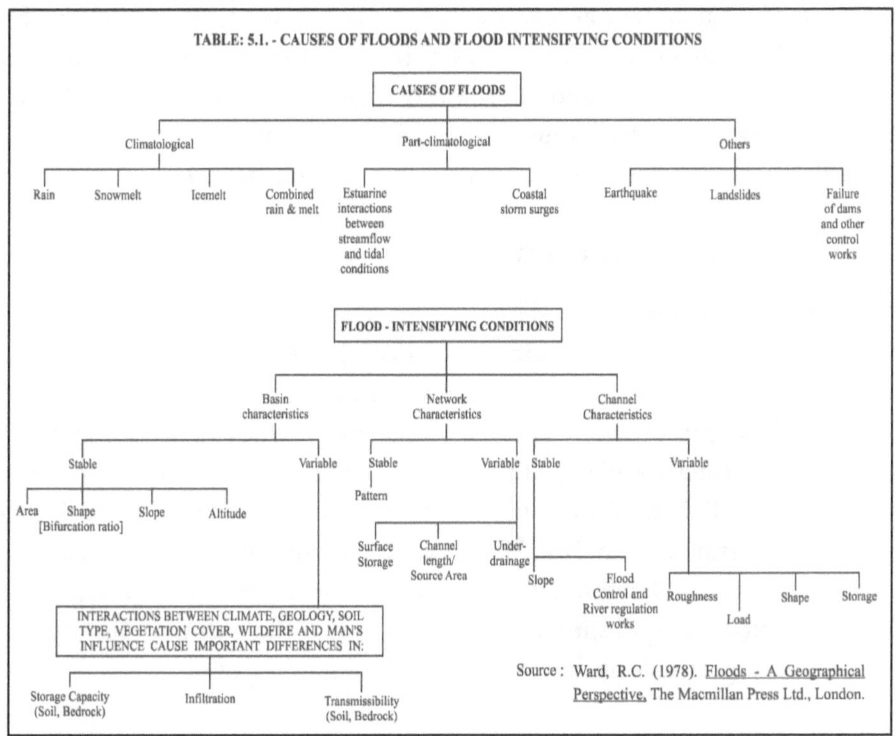



■ **Table 4.2:** Spatial and Non-Spatial data set

| Data | Scale/Resolution | Source |
|---|---|---|
| ASTER GDEM (Elevation, Slope, Drainage Density) | 30 m. | NASA and METI |
| Geomorphology | 1:50k | NGLM |
| Hydro-Geology | 1:50000 | CGWB & GSI |
| Soil | 1:2,50,000 | NBSS & LUP |
| Ground Water | - | CGWB |

## 4.1.2 The Kangsabati Catchment

The Kangsabati catchment is a long fragmented of land, wide in its upper part and very narrow (0.065 km) in the lower part of the study area. The total catchment area of the river is 8369 sq.km. It lies between 86° E to 88° E and 23° N. It drains a large portion of the districts of Purulia, Bankura, Paschim Medinipur and Purba Medinipur. After a course of about 465.23 K.M the rivers fall into the Hooghly River. The river has been dammed near Mukutmonipur 3 K.M upstream of its mouth for irrigation and flood control purposes. The catchment area of the river at the dam site 3626 Sq.Km. The floods in the Kangsabati river are flashy in nature because the uncontrolled catchment below the dam and may be very high when there is a rainfall in the Bankura or Paschim Medinipur district. The situation further worsens when it synchronizes with the release of water from Kangasabati Dam.

### 4.1.3 The Kaliaghai Catchment

The kaliaghai catchment is a short strip of land, very parochial in its origin area and very spacious in its middle portion and its outfall also very parochial. So, it is an irregular shape of basin. It lies between 22° 6′ 40″ N to 87° 27′ 46″ E. The total length of the river is 121 kms and in study area its length 106 kms. The total catchment area of the river is 2145 sq.km. the upper reach from Dudhkundi to Bakrabad measuring 568.75 sq.km. is of steep slope 1.4 m/km (District Annual Plan 2015-16, Paschim Medinipur). These carchments have undergone rapid deforestation making the land surface bare of vegetation which has initiated rapid surface run-off and maximum output of surface run-off which brings floods in the lower reach during heavy rain.

### 4.1.4 The Silabati Catchment

The upper part of the Silabati catchment long narrow strip and in study area its almost rounded shape. It lies between 23° 15′ N to 23° 24′ N and 86° 28′ E to 86° 48′ E. The total catchment of the river is 4088 Sq.Km. It drains a large portion of the Bankura and Paschim Medinipur district and smaller portion of the Puruliya district and it drains on the towns of Taldangra (Bankura), Garbeta, Chandrakona, Goaltore, Salboni, Khirpai, Banka, Ghatal and Daspur (Paschim Medinipur). The total length of the river is 207 K.M and in study area its length about 112 K.M.

■ Table 4.3: Catchment Characteristics

| River | Total length in K.M | Length in said District (K.M) | Total catchment area in Sq.Km | Catchment area in said District (Sq.Km) |
|---|---|---|---|---|
| 1 | 2 | 3 | 4 | 5 |
| Kangsabati | 372.58 | 143.87 | 8369 | 2172.48 |
| Silabati | 207 | 112 | 4088 | 2032.64 |
| Kaliaghai | 121 | 106 | 1913 | 1725.54 |
| Subarnarekha | 395 | 87.86 | 18951 | 2160 |

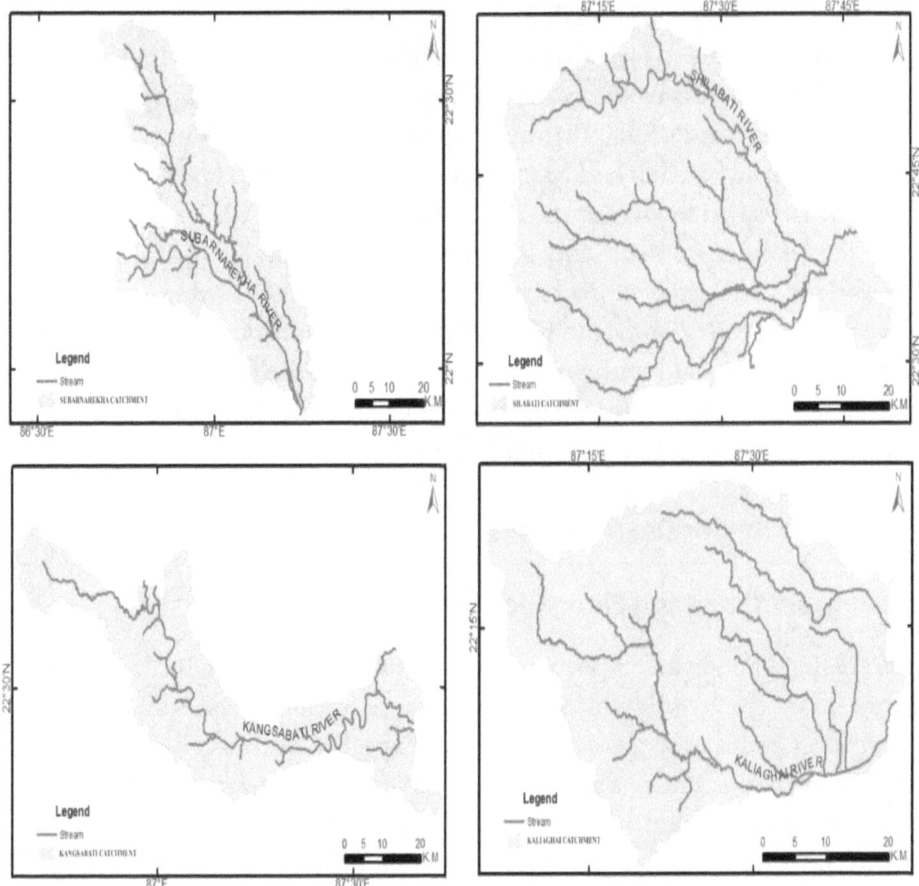

**Fig. 4.1:** Major River catchments of Paschim Medinipur District.

## 4.2 Geological and Geomorphological Characteristics

Geologically most part of the catchment basins of the rivers are formed of Quaternary sediment and older alluvial of Pleistocene to lower Holocene age although Subarnarekha basin is formed by igneous and metamorphic rocks of the Archaean age with flood plain deposits. A detail geomorphic and geologic account of the catchment basins, their important tributaries, their extension over the physiographic provinces, sections and their geological outcrops are given in the Table 4.4 and 4.5.

The Subarnarekha flows over the eastern part of the Ranchi Plateau over the Archaean and pre-cambrian formations and mineral bearing metamorphic of Singbhum. In Paschim Medinipur District the Subarnarekha flows over the Gopiballavpur upland over Holocene flood plain formations. River Kangsabati and Silabati flows over the eastern adjacent areas of Chhotonagpur Plateau over the plateau of Purulia, Plateau fringe fans in Bankura, Medinipur laterite terrace, Garbeta badland and Medinipur formations of Pleistocene to Miocene age. The Kaliaghai flows over the rolling topography of Chhotonagpur Plateau over the Jhargram upland and Paradeltaic fan surfaces of Purba Medinipur formations of Pleistocene to lower Holocene periods. All these river basins have a rugged topography and high relief in upper portion of the basins which limits infiltration rate to the minimum and contribute for a high run off rate that enters into Medinipur plain through the channel before draining to the Bay of Bengal, causing serious flood havocs.

## 4.3 Morphometric Characteristics

### 4.3.1 Basin Shape and Elongation Ratio

The basin shape is an important morphometric parameter in the geometry of the channel network which in turn has a serious impact on the flood. The elongation ratio, as a measure of basin shape has been worked out for the catchment basins under the study (see Table 5.6). Elongation ratio is one of the main areal properties of basin. Areal properties express the overall plan form and dimensions of the basin. The Elongation Ratio ($R_e$) defines by Schumm (1956) as the ratio of the diameter of a circle with the same area as that of the basin to the maximum basin length:

$$R_e = D_c/L_b \tag{4.1}$$

Where, $D_c$ is diameter of the circle with the same area as that of the basin and $L_b$ is the maximum basin length. The value of $R_e$ approaches 1.0 as the shape of a drainage basin approaches to a circle. The ratio varies from 0.6 to 1.0 over a wide variety of climatic and geologic regimes. Typical values are close to 1.0 for regions of very low relief and are between 0.6 and 0.8 for regions of strong relief and steep ground slope.

■ **Table 4.4:** Geological and Geomorphological Characteristics of the Catchment Basins

| Catchment Basin | Important Tributaries | Coverage of the Basin | | Age | Geological Formation | Rock Type | Nature and Characteristics of landforms assemblages |
|---|---|---|---|---|---|---|---|
| | | Physiographic Province | Physiographic Section | | | | |
| 1 | 2 | 3 | 4 | 5 | 6 | 7 | |
| Kangsabati | Taraphini, Bhairab- Banki, Kumari, Patloi | Chhotonagpur Plateau | Purulia Plateau, Plateau fringe fans in Bankura, Midnapore Laterite Terrace, Midnapore fans. | Pleistocene, Pleistocene to lower Holocene, Miocene to Pliocene and Holocene | Lalgarh formation, Sijua formation, Bhairab Banki formation, Panskura formationand Present day flood plain deposits. | Quaternary sediment with sand, silt and clay. | Vast pediplain with high and lows, immense soil erosion forming a badlands topography; Flat terrain with scattered exposure; Soft unconsolidated sediments, low slope, flood proneness confined to flood plain areas; Landforms of Sijua formation are on higher ground and devoid of any flood or water logging hazard. |
| Kaliaghai | Kapaleswa-ri, Baghai | Rolling topography of adjacent areas of the Chhotonagpur Plateau | Upland of Jhargram division, Paradeltaic fan surfaces of Purba Medinipur | Pleistocene, Pleistocene to lower Holocene and Holocene. | Lalgarh formation, Sijua formation and present day flood plain deposits. | Sedimentary With unconsolidatedsand, silt and clay. | Vast pediplain with high and lows, immense soil erosion forming a badlands topography; Soft unconsolidated sediments, low slope, flood proneness confined to flood plain areas; Landforms of Sijua formation are on higher ground and devoid of any flood or water logging hazard. |

*Source: After Kolkata Geological Quadrangle Maps of G.S.I, 2007.*

**■ Table 4.5: Geological and Geomorphological Characteristics of the Catchment Basins**

| Catchment Basin | Important Tributaries | Coverage of the Basin | | Age | Geological Formation | Rock Type | Nature and Characteristics of landforms assemblages |
| | | Physiographic Province | Physiographic Section | | | | |
| 1 | 2 | 3 | 4 | 5 | 6 | | 7 |
| Silabati | Jaipanda, Ketia, Tamal, Kubai, Parang, Donai, Katan. | Eastern adjacent areas of Chhotonagpur Plateau. | Purulia Plateau, Plateau fringe fans in Bankura, Garbeta Badland, Midnapore formations. | Pleistocene, Pleistocene to lower Holocene and Holocene. | Lalgarh formation, Sijua formation, Panskura formation. | Older alluvial, Quartz, Phyllite, Granite Pebbles | Vast pediplain with high and lows, immense soil erosion forming a badlands topography; Soft unconsolidated sediments, low slope, flood proneness confined to flood plain areas; Landforms of Sijua formation are on higher ground and devoid of any flood or water logging hazard. |
| subarnarekha | Kanchi, Jamira, Burhabala-ng, Dulung. | Chhotonagpur Plateau. | Ranchi Plateau, Dalma Volcanics, Singbhum Group, Gopiballavpur Upland. | Archaean & Lower Pre-Cambrian, Palaeoproterozoic, Meso Proterozoic and Holocene flood plain. | Lalgarh formation, Sijua formation, Panskura formation and Present day flood plain deposits. | Igneous and Metamorphic with Garnet – Staurolite Schist, Carbon Phylite, Pyroclastics, Kuilapal Granite, Quartz- Tourmaline rocks. | Hard, layered, high to medium slope, flaky characterised by Singbhum group; Hard and high slope of Dalma volcanics; In meso proterozoic characterised by hard, foliated, easily weathered and high to medium slope with high run off. |

*Source: After Kolkata Geological Quadrangle Maps of G.S.I, 2007.*

■ **Table 4.6:** Morphometric Characteristics of the major river catchment

| Catchment Basin | Catchment Area (Sq.Km) in District | Total stream length (K.M) in District | Drainage Density (Sq.Km) | Bifurcation Ratio | Elongation Ratio |
|---|---|---|---|---|---|
| 1 | 2 | 3 | 4 | 5 | 6 |
| Kangsabati | 2172.48 | 994.24989 | 0.458 | 4.58 | 0.55 |
| Silabati | 2032.64 | 890.76261 | 0.438 | 4.83 | 0.58 |
| Kaliaghai | 1725.54 | 824.179125 | 0.478 | 3.29 | 0.80 |
| Subarnarekha | 2160 | 795.51672 | 0.368 | 3.17 | 0.51 |

The Elongation Ratio of all four river basins have values ranging from 0.50 to 0.80, the Subarnarekha River has lowest ratio of 0.51 preceded by the Kangsabati with 0.55 and Silabati with 0.58. The other one river has the elongation ratio of 0.80. Thus, this elongation ratio indicates the extreme climate, geologic regimes, strong relief and steep ground slopes of the catchment basins where the reduction of divides is still progress with headword erosion and consequent extension of the actively eroding channels at their upper reaches.

## 4.3.2 Drainage Density and Texture of Topography

The catchment basin is hydrologically important because it directly affects the run-off but the relationship of total stream length to basin area is one of the most sensitive and variable morphometric parameters which controls the texture of the landscape dissection and the spacing of streams (Chorley, 1969). Drainage density is defined as the ratio of the total stream length within a catchment basin to total basin area projected over a planimetric surface (Strahler, 1969). It is the total stream length per unit area of the basin. Drainage density exhibits a very wide range of values and is commonly believed to reflect the operation of the complex factors controlling surface run-off. The common values of density range from 3 to 4 Sq.Km. in highly resistant igneous rock surface or on hard sand stones revealing thereby coarse texture to 200-256 Sq.Km in badlands areas revealing a super fine texture (Strahler, 1969). The lower drainage density values for all the four catchment basins of Paschim Medinipur ranging from 0.3 to 0.5 indicates a coarse texture which can be attributed to the hard and resistant surface rock types which becomes the controlling factor in the development of the streams of lower orders.

### 4.3.3 Stream Network and Bifurcation Ratio

Besides basin catchment area and basin shape, a more direct influence on the general form of the unit hydrograph is exerted by the "Bifurcation Ratio" of the stream network. It shows little variation in homogenous bedrocks from one area to another. But where structural effects cause basin elongation, this value may increase appreciably. The effects of such distortions upon maximum flood discharge, assuming precipitation and controls to be same throughout, the high bifurcation ratio would yield a low but extended peak flow whereas the rotund basin with low bifurcation ratio would produce a sharp peak. Thus it is an important control over the "peakedness" of the run-off hydrograph (Chow, 1964).

The streams of all the four drainage basins are ordered based on the most popular stream ordering system of Strahler where the smallest fingertip tributaries are designated as order 1$^{st}$ and the joining of the two streams of first order form a stream segment of the 2$^{nd}$ order and so on. So that the trunk stream gets the highest order (Strahler, 1969). The total numbers of stream segments are counted and the bifurcation ratio is calculated by the division of the number of stream segments of the given order to the number of segments of the next higher order, i.e.

$$R_b = Nu/N\,(u+1) \tag{4.2}$$

Where, $R_b$ is Bifurcation ratio and $N_u$ is the number of stream of order 'U'. It has been established that in a region of uniform climate and rock type, this bifurcation ratio tends to remain constant in different drainage basins. It varies between 3.0 to 5.0 for watersheds where the geologic structure does not distort the drainage pattern. The theoretical minimum possible value of 2.0 is rarely found under natural conditions. Because the bifurcation ratio is a dimensionless property and because drainage system in homogenous materials tends to display geometrical similarity, it is not surprising that the ratios show only a small variation from region to region. But abnormally high bifurcation ratios might be expected in regions of steeply dipping rock strata where narrow strike valleys are confined between hogback ridges (Strahler. 1971).

The present study reveals that the bifurcation ratios of all the stream networks of the river basins range between 3.17 to 4.83. The high bifurcation for the Kangsabati and Silabati can be attributed the elongated course for a long distance confined with plateau and plateau fringe areas of Purulia and Bankura. For the Subarnarekha and Kaliaghai catchments, the bifurcation ratio shows only small variation from 3.17 to 3.29 displaying a geometrical similarity with nearly homogeneous type of network development without much of structural control. Thus, the floods in the Kangsabati and Silabati show very peculiar characters, which damage much more compared to those of the Subarnarekha and the Kaliaghai.

### 4.3.4 Longitudinal Profile and Gradient of Flow

The channel gradient or longitudinal profile represents fall in bed elevation with distance down channel (Panda, 89). Being a ratio between the stream bed elevation and length, the stream gradient is related to the hydraulic variables, namely; discharge, channel length and bed materials size. Gradient is to state that difference in elevation (ED) divided by the horizontal distance (HD) between two points. The gradient of the trunk stream has a significant effect on the flood discharge with steep gradient favouring quick disposal of flood water and reducing basin lag. The longitudinal profiles have been drawn for the trunk streams of Paschim Medinipur District i.e. the Kangsabati, Kaliaghai, Silabati and Subarnarekha to observe the nature of gradients available for the disposal of flood water. The Fig. 4.2, 4.3, 4.4, 4.5 reveals the nature of the long profiles which have been drawn from the WRIS Web GIS, with altitude plotted against the horizontal distance along the course of the river. The profiles of Kangsabati River reveal that the mean gradient is lowest at the study area i.e. 1 in 2949 and the highest at upper part of the study area i.e. 1 in 665 (see Fig. 4.3). So, profiles also reveal that the steep gradient in upper part of the study area is able to discharge the rainfall quickly to the study area and the flood water cannot be removed quickly from the study area due to lower gradient. Again, when excessive dam discharge water come to the lower reach of the river, the hydraulic pressure of the river increased enormously and breaks the embankment of the river or water starts piling up and inundates large areas. This river has a considerable portion of the catchment in the hilly terrain and a portion of the basin at the mouth is in the flood plains. Next comes to Silabati and Subarnarekha which has a mean gradient at upper part of the study area 1 in 275 and

1 in 964 respectively (see Fig. 4.4: & 4.5). The gradient is sufficient enough to dispose the flood water from the upper catchments to the flood plains and coastal plains within 24 hours of the rainfall. Besides, the all three rivers Kaliaghai also flooded during Monsoon period due to heavy and prolonged rainfall. It is the only river whose origin in study area and its mean gradient is 1 in 1289 (see Fig. 4.2). It has been observed that because of the lower gradient the flood water takes long time to dispose.

The acute break in the longitudinal profile of the Plateau Rivers at the junction of the two contrasting slopes of steep plateau and flat plain is responsible for creating inundation. Due to this acute break, rivers cannot carry both silt and water at the same rate. Silts get deposited and choke the channel and thus, water spreads in the lower plain region, causing floods.

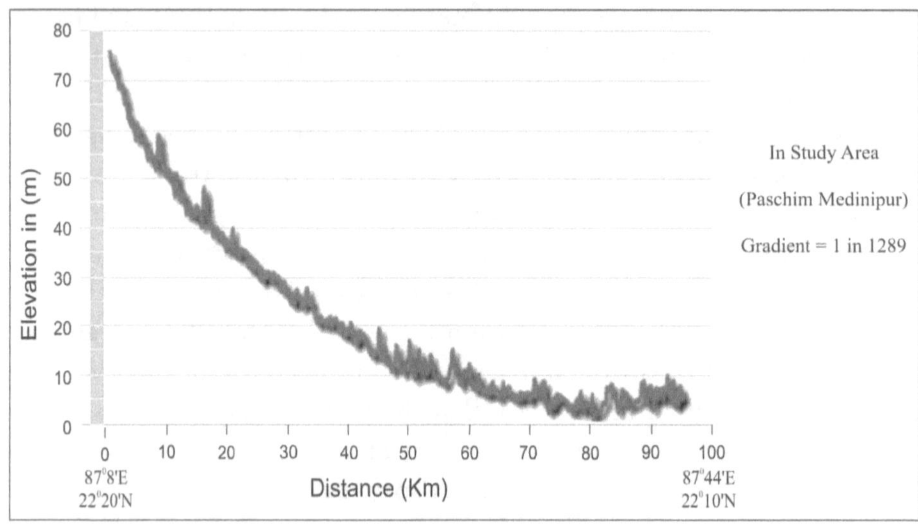


**Fig. 4.2:** Longitudinal Profiles of the River Kaliaghai.

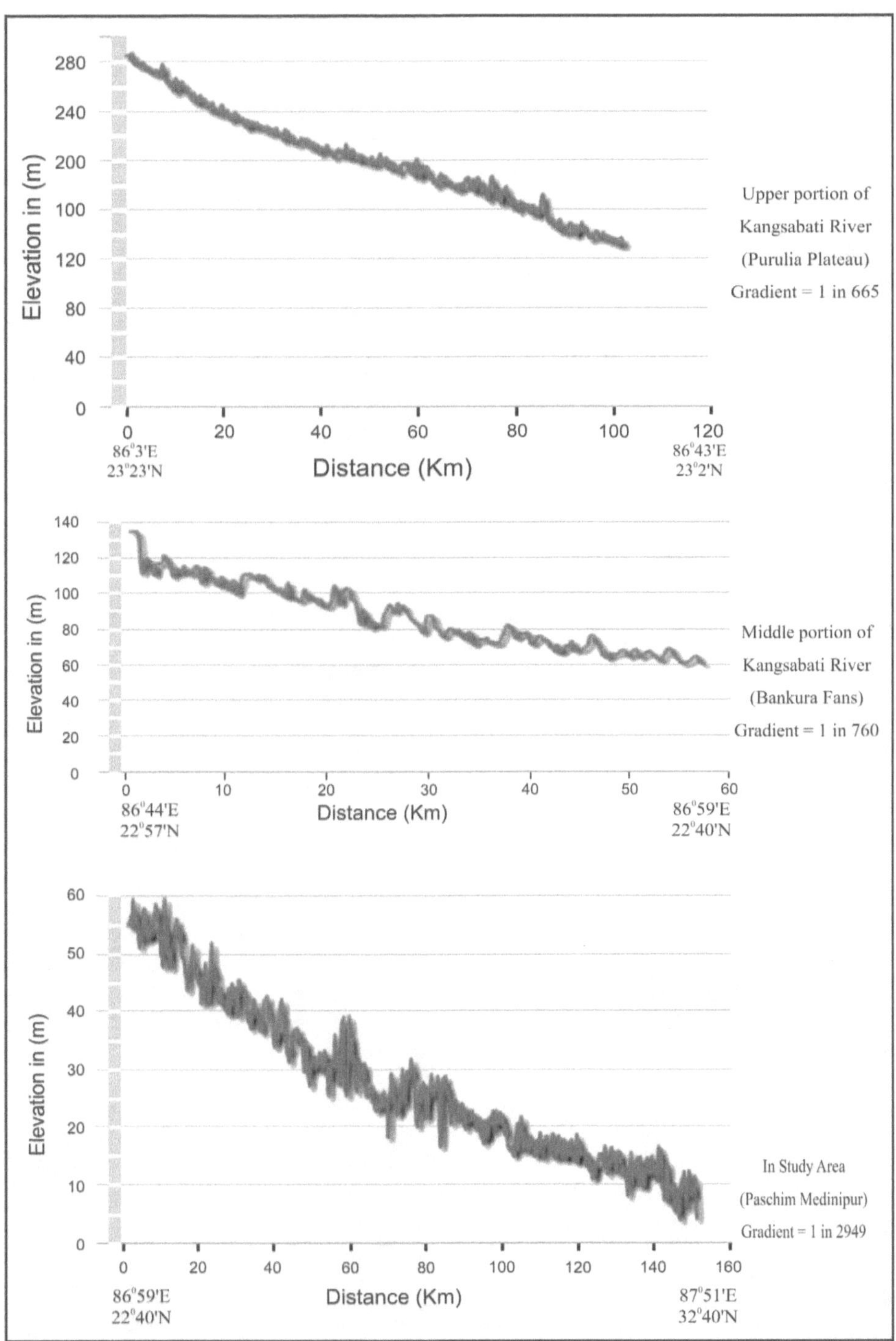


**Fig. 4.3:** Longitudinal Profiles of the River Kangsabati.

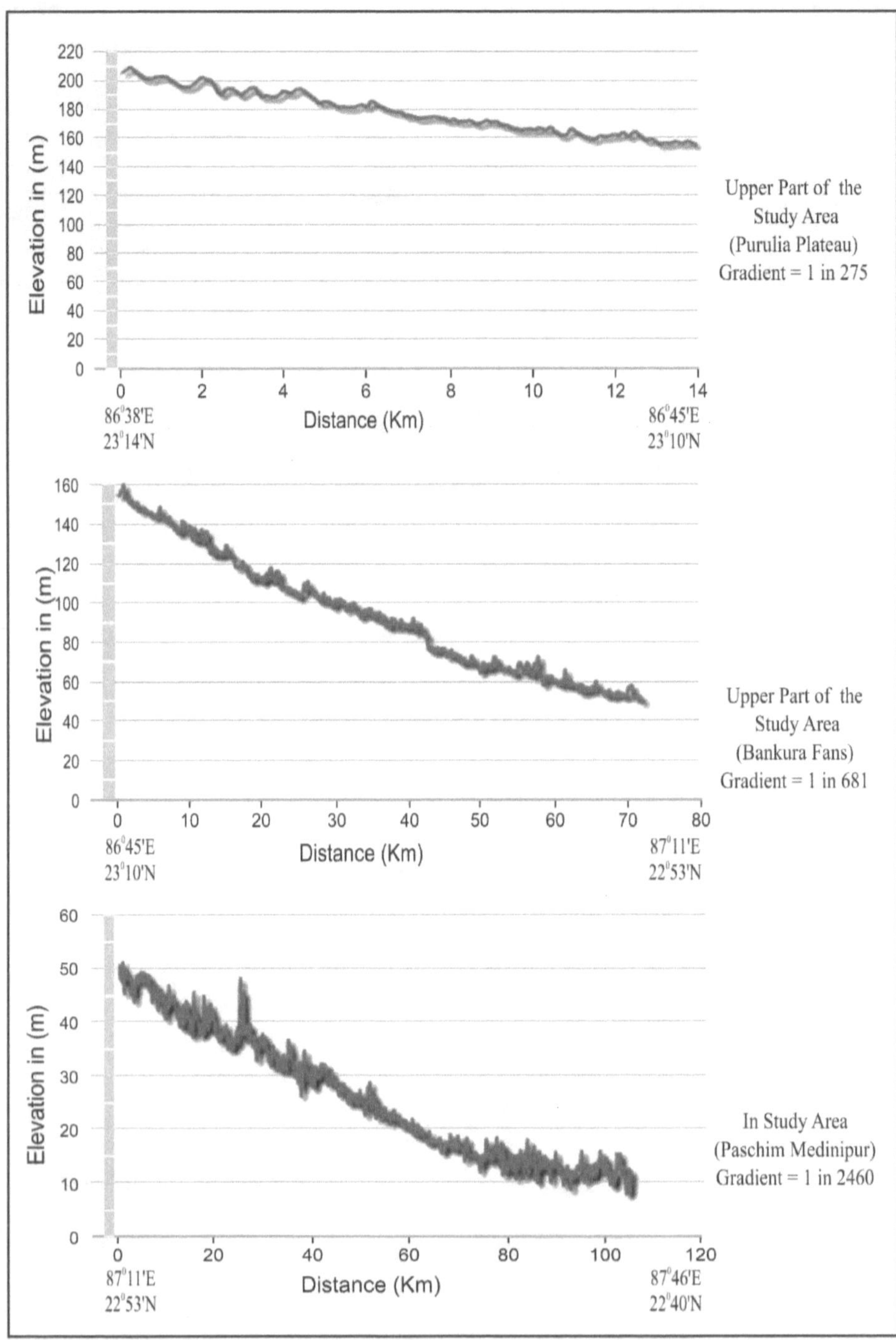



**Fig. 4.4:** Longitudinal Profiles of the River Silabati.

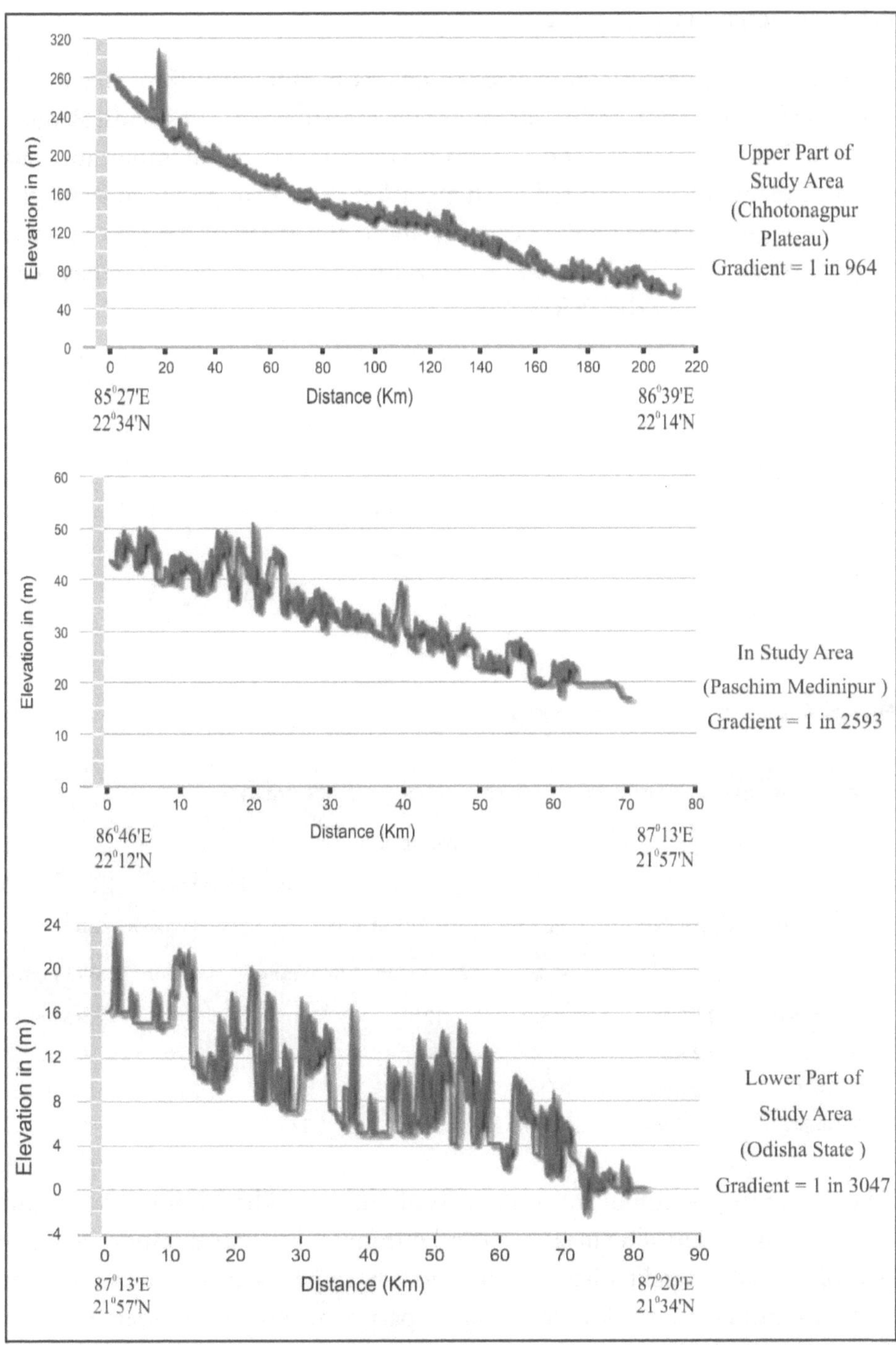


**Fig. 4.5:** Longitudinal Profiles of the River Subarnarekha.

### 4.3.5 Dimensions of Channel

Measurement of channel dimensions, such as bankful elevation, maximum depth and flood prone width are important measurements of floods. Among of them flood prone width and bankful elevation is very much important. The flood prone width is measured at an elevation that corresponds to twice the maximum depth of the bankful channel and is the width of the river at flood flows (Rosgen, 1996). The flood prone width and bankful elevation has been derived directly from the WRIS Web GIS.

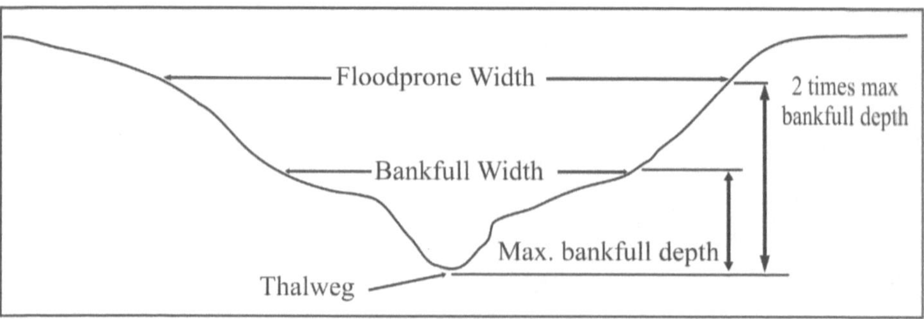


**Fig. 4.6:** Channel dimensions – Cross Section view.

■ **Table 4.7:** Flood Prone Width and Bankful Elevation of different river

| River | Channel Dimensions | | | | | |
|---|---|---|---|---|---|---|
| | Flood Prone Width | | Bankful Elevation | | | |
| | Upper Part of Study Area | Lower Part of Study Area | Upper part | | Lower part | |
| | | | Maximum | Minimum | Maximum | Minimum |
| Subarnarekha | 2.8 K.M | 1.6 K.M | 12 m. | 2 m. | 6 m. | 0.5 m. |
| Kangsabati | 1.2 K.M | 0.07 K.M | 6 m. | 0.5 m. | 0.5 m | 0.4 m. |
| Silabati | .32 K.M | 0.05 K.M | 5 m. | 1m. | 2 m. | 0.5 m. |
| Kaliaghai | 0.1 K.M | 0.2 K.M | 1 m. | 0.2 m. | 3.5 m. | 0.2 m. |

The flood prone width of the upper part of Subarnarekha River is 2.8 km and lower part is 1.6 km. The maximum and minimum bankful elevation in upper part of the Subarnarekha River 12 m. and 2m. respectively and the maximum and minimum bankful elevation in lower part 6 m. and.5 m. Respectively (see Fig. 4.10). Both the channel dimensions in lower portion of the study area are much lower than the upper portion. So, when high flood waters come to the lower reach of the river the flood water piling up due to lower bankful height and flood prone width, and inundates large areas. The other three rivers namely; Kangsabati, Silabati and Kaliaghai carrying the same channel dimension nature like Subarnarekha River. So, whenever maximum flood water comes, the lower portion of the river has been automatically flooded.

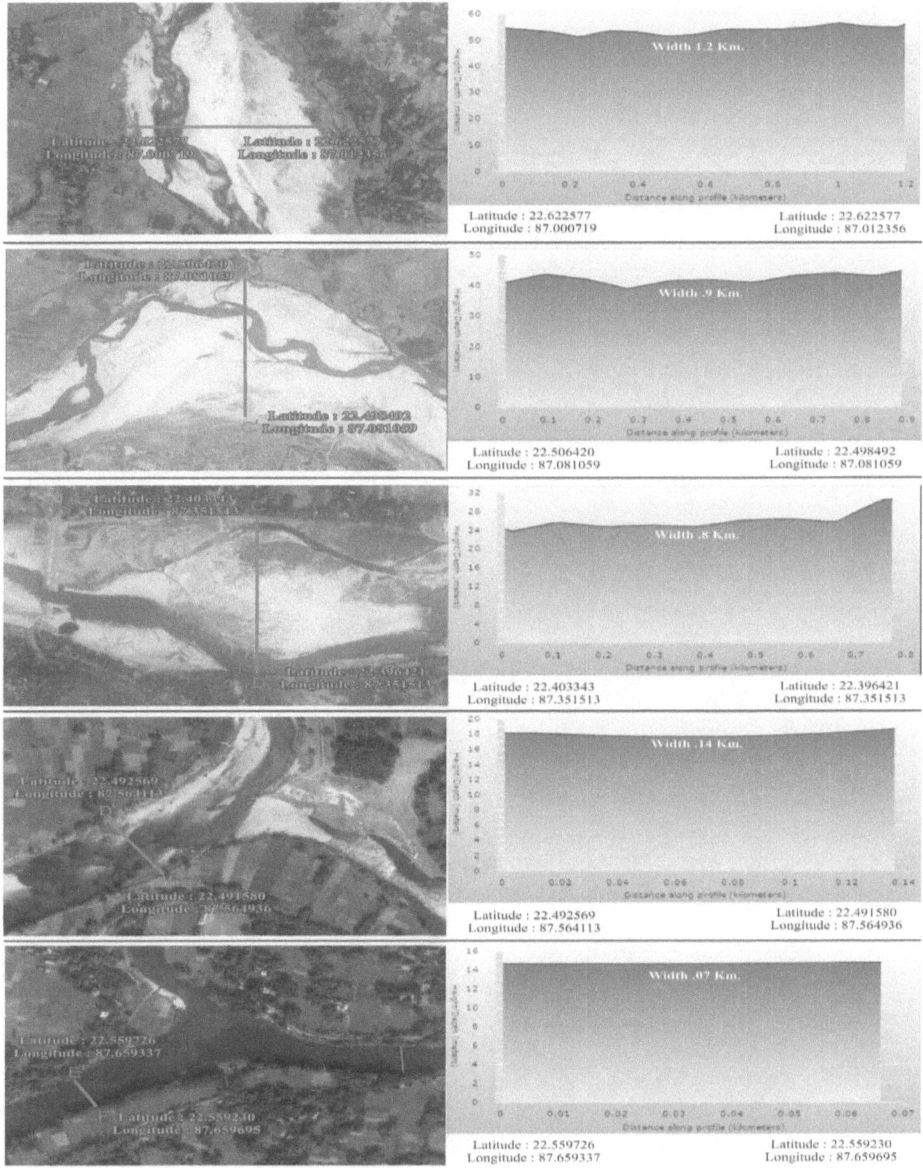



**Fig. 4.7:** Flood Prone Width of Kangsabati Catchment.

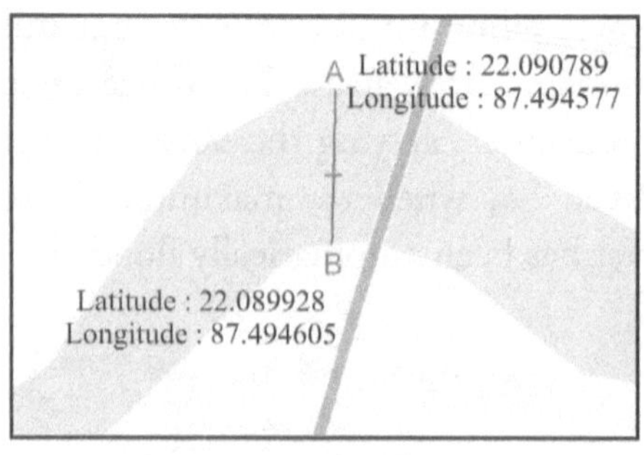



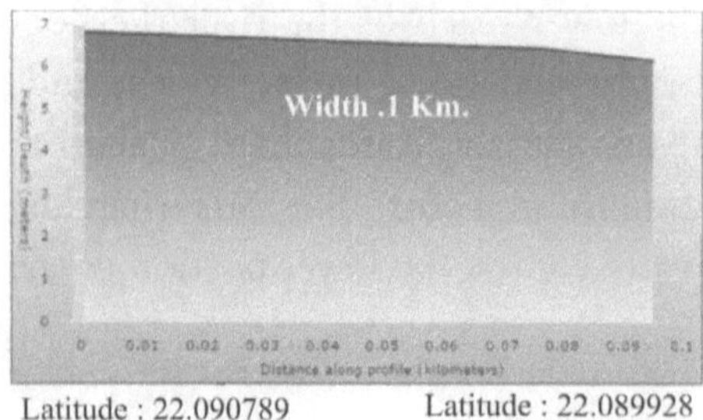



Latitude : 22.090789        Latitude : 22.089928
Longitude : 87.494577       Longitude : 87.494605

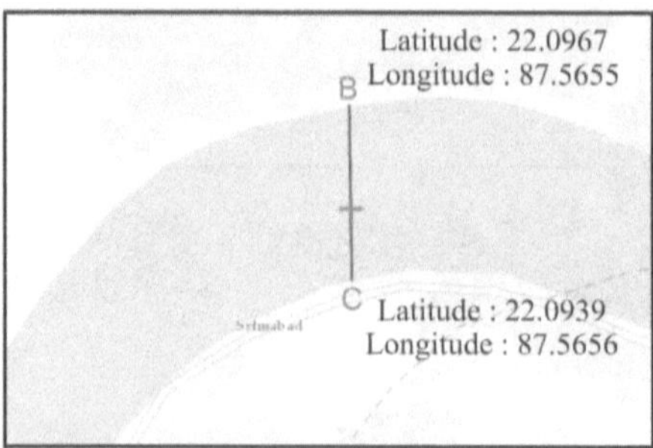



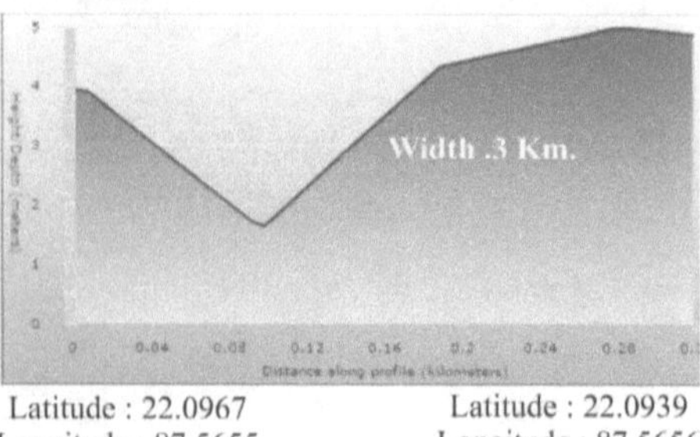



Latitude : 22.0967          Latitude : 22.0939
Longitude : 87.5655         Longitude : 87.5656

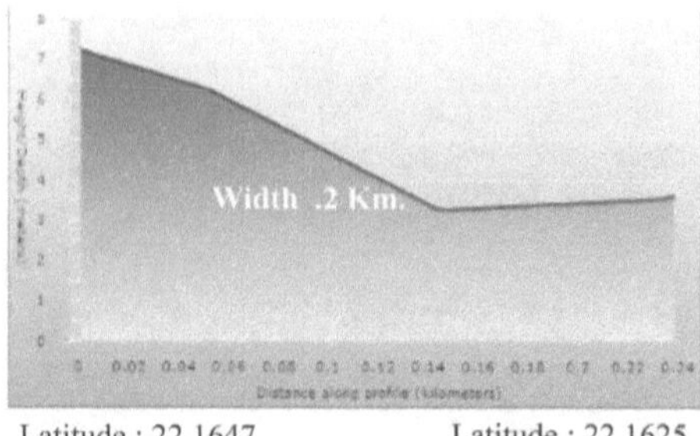



Latitude : 22.1647          Latitude : 22.1625
Longitude : 87.8217         Longitude : 87.8218

**Fig. 4.8:** Flood Prone Width of Kaliaghai Catchment.

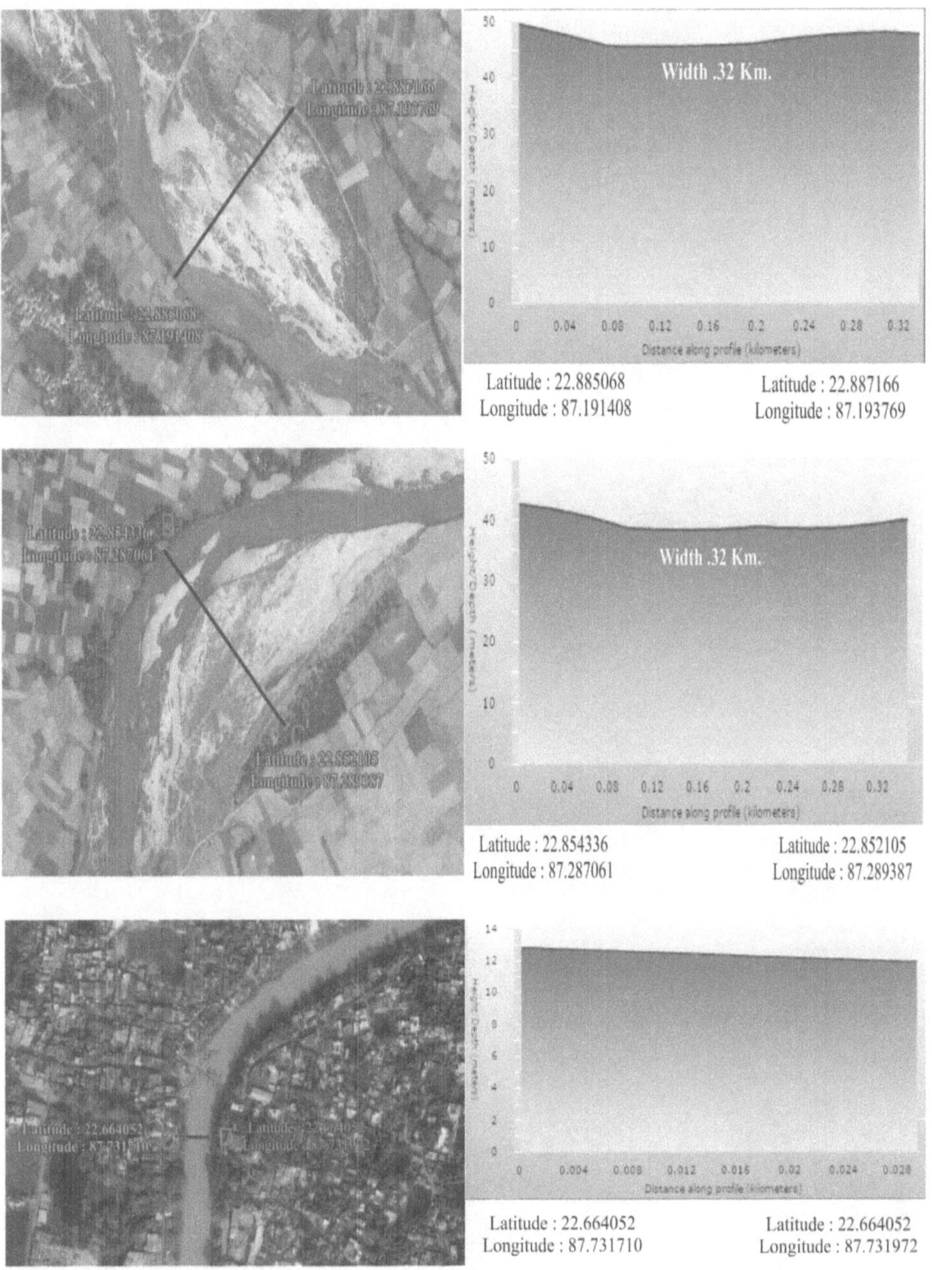


Latitude : 22.885068     Latitude : 22.887166
Longitude : 87.191408     Longitude : 87.193769

Latitude : 22.854336     Latitude : 22.852105
Longitude : 87.287061     Longitude : 87.289387

Latitude : 22.664052     Latitude : 22.664052
Longitude : 87.731710     Longitude : 87.731972

**Fig. 4.9:** Flood Prone Width of Silabati Catchment.

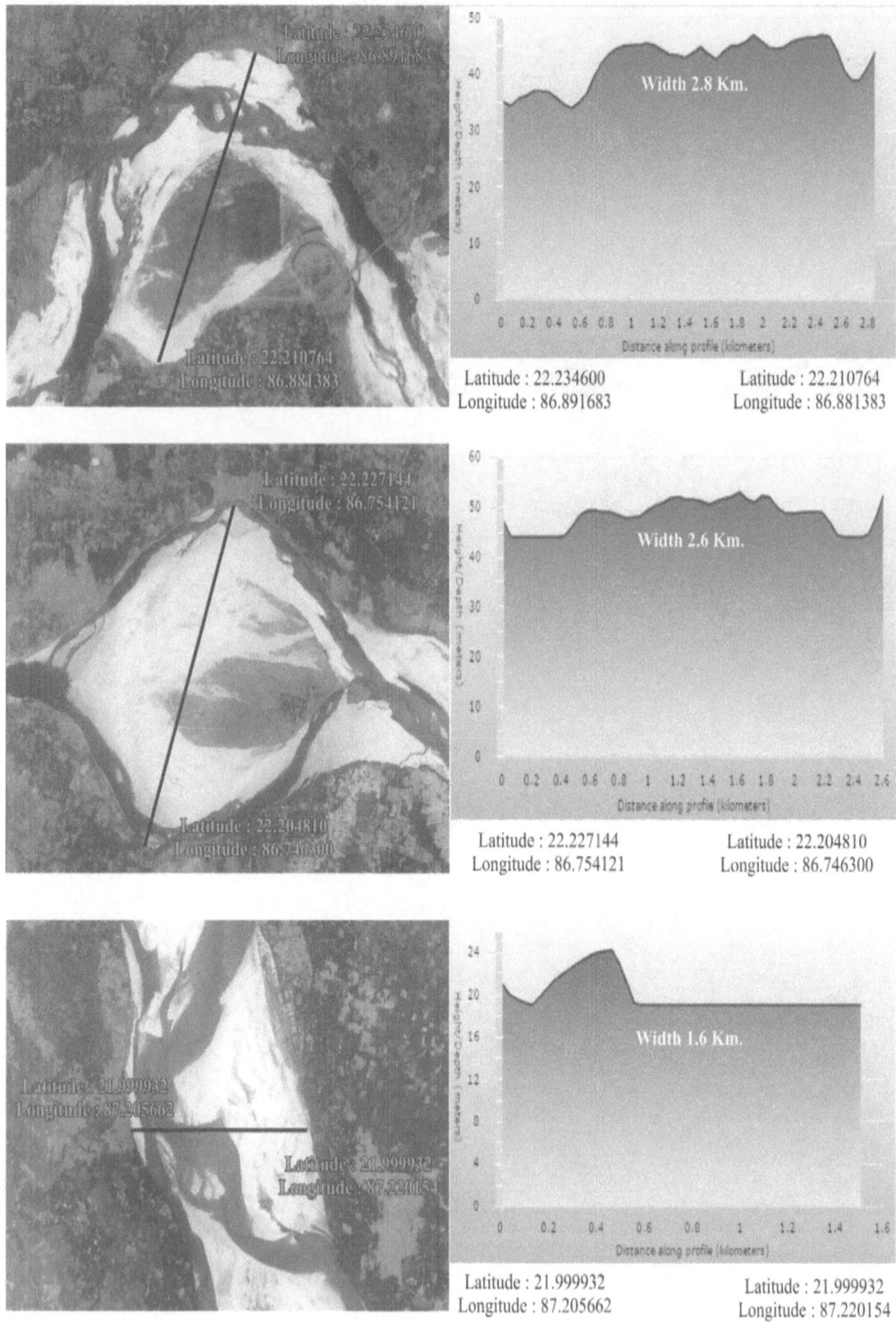



**Fig. 4.10:** Flood Prone Width of Subarnarekha Catchment.

## 4.4 Meteorological Characteristics

### 4.4.1 Rainfall in the Catchment Basins

The primary cause of flood in the Medinipur Plain region is the huge amount of water brought to the Medinipur Plain through South-east flowing rivers with excessively heavy and prolonged rainfall in their catchment areas inside or outside the District or State. This is further intensified by the obstruction of the flood flow by the rising tide. Ghatal is one of the most vulnerable flood prone areas in Paschim Medinipur District which is affected by this way. A relationship has been worked out among the rainfall departure from the normal with the natural calamities like floods, droughts and cyclones (See Table 4.8) through field interview, height of gauge level, amount of rainfall occurs and author field perception. It is revealed out from the data that very negative departures seem to be associated with drought conditions whereas both the positive and negative departures are associated with floods. This implies that the floods have occurred even if the rainfall is low over the district but high in the other district or stage on in the specific catchments and subsequently flood is taken place in its plain region. And formation of cyclone over the head of Bay of Bengal is also responsible for creating flood situation.

The catchment basins of the major rivers of Paschim Medinipur district enjoy climate of the hot and humid conditions having nearly 150 cm average annual rainfall. There are, however, local variations in rainfall and temperatures from the Western to South-Eastern part of the district and also the catchment basins. The winter's months of November, December, January and February are almost dry. Occasional sowers with thunders quall occur in the hot summer months of March to June. The South-West monsoon breaks in the 2nd or 3rd week of June and continues up to the 1st week of October. Most of the rainfall in the catchment as well as in the study area occur between the mid of June to mid of October i.e. during the period of the South-West monsoon. The rainfall in this period accounts for 75 to 80 percent of the total rainfall (See Table 4.9). During the transitional period of this monsoon season, a series of tropical cyclones formed over the Bay of Bengal Coast. Its affect fall on the catchment basins and bringing heavy rainfall which becomes the cause of flood havoc and drainage congestion. If very deep depression occurs over the Jharkhand Plateau, then also occurs flood by the additional dam discharge water from Massanjore, Mithon and Galudhi. The constraints imposed by this precipitation are of two folds i.e. firstly the rainfall is concentrated relatively over a short period (June to September) and secondly at both ends of monsoon, there are periods of highly variable precipitation. Almost in every year 85 to 90% run-off occurs during monsoon period (see Table 4.9). Some of the year has been exceptional because of cyclonic storms. So, the monsoon period from middle of June to middle of October are most important from the point of view of floods because the amount and distribution of precipitation in the catchments during this period determine the nature and intensity of the floods.

■ **Table 4.8:** Rainfall and Associated Natural Calamity in Paschim Medinipur District

| Year | Normal Rainfall(mm) | Actual Rainfall(mm) | Departure from | | Natural calamity |
|---|---|---|---|---|---|
| | | | (mm) | (In%) | |
| 1 | 2 | 3 | 4 | 5 | 6 |
| 1956 | 1538 | 1892.6 | 354.6 | 23.06 | Flood |
| 1957 | 1538 | 1171.7 | -366.3 | -23.82 | |
| 1958 | 1538 | 1352.3 | -185.7 | -12.07 | |
| 1959 | 1538 | 1720.8 | 182.8 | 11.89 | Flood |
| 1960 | 1538 | 1404.6 | -133.4 | -8.67 | Flood |
| 1961 | 1538 | 1847.0 | 309.0 | 20.9 | Flood |
| 1962 | 1538 | 1419.0 | -119.0 | -7.74 | Flood |
| 1963 | 1538 | 1411.0 | -127.0 | -8.26 | |
| 1964 | 1538 | 1091.9 | -446.1 | -29.01 | Drought |
| 1965 | 1538 | 937.9 | -600.1 | -39.02 | Drought |
| 1966 | 1538 | 1254.1 | -283.9 | -18.46 | Drought |
| 1967 | 1538 | 1626.0 | 88.0 | 5.72 | |
| 1968 | 1538 | 1393.9 | -144.1 | -9.37 | |
| 1969 | 1538 | 1554.0 | 16.0 | 1.04 | |
| 1970 | 1538 | 1277.7 | -260.3 | -16.92 | |
| 1971 | 1538 | 2399.5 | 861.5 | 56.01 | Flood |
| 1972 | 1538 | 1686.4 | 148.4 | 9.64 | |
| 1973 | 1538 | 1545.3 | 7.3 | 0.47 | |
| 1974 | 1538 | 1722.5 | 184.5 | 12.0 | |
| 1975 | 1538 | 1382.7 | -155.3 | -10.10 | |
| 1976 | 1538 | 1045.7 | -492.3 | -32.01 | |
| 1977 | 1538 | 1601.3 | 63.3 | 4.12 | |
| 1978 | 1538 | 2146.3 | 608.3 | 39.55 | Flood |
| 1979 | 1538 | 1068.3 | -469.7 | -30.54 | |

| Year | Normal Rainfall(mm) | Actual Rainfall(mm) | Departure from | | Natural calamity |
|---|---|---|---|---|---|
| | | | (mm) | (In%) | |
| 1980 | 1538 | 1422.0 | -116.0 | -7.54 | |
| 1981 | 1538 | 1842.1 | 304.1 | 19.77 | |
| 1982 | 1538 | 1454.8 | -83.2 | -5.41 | |
| 1983 | 1538 | 1146.0 | -392 | -25.49 | |
| 1984 | 1538 | 1989.4 | 451.4 | 29.35 | Flood |
| 1985 | 1538 | 1575.5 | 37.5 | 2.44 | Cyclone, Flood |
| 1986 | 1538 | 1752.6 | 214.6 | 13.95 | Flood |
| 1987 | 1538 | 1626.6 | 88.6 | 5.76 | |
| 1988 | 1538 | 1596.0 | 58.0 | 3.77 | |
| 1989 | 1538 | 1805.5 | 267.5 | 17.39 | |
| 1990 | 1538 | 2336.0 | 798.0 | 51.89 | Flood |
| 1991 | 1538 | 1543.0 | 5.0 | 0.33 | |
| 1992 | 1538 | 1352.6 | -185.4 | -12.05 | |
| 1993 | 1538 | 2262.8 | 724.8 | 47.13 | Flood |
| 1994 | 1538 | 1807.4 | 269.4 | 17.52 | |
| 1995 | 1538 | 1715.6 | 177.6 | 11.55 | |
| 1996 | 1538 | 1520.4 | -17.6 | -1.14 | |
| 1997 | 1538 | 1709.3 | 171.3 | 11.14 | Flood |
| 1998 | 1538 | 1301.5 | -236.5 | -15.38 | |
| 1999 | 1538 | 1956.9 | 418.9 | 27.24 | Flood |
| 2000 | 1538 | 1293.9 | -244.1 | -15.87 | |
| 2001 | 1538 | 1615.3 | 77.3 | 5.03 | |
| 2002 | 1538 | 1758.9 | 220.9 | 14.36 | |
| 2003 | 1538 | 1542.9 | 4.9 | 0.32 | |
| 2004 | 1538 | 1366.1 | -171.9 | -11.18 | |
| 2005 | 1538 | 1396.3 | -141.7 | -9.21 | |
| 2006 | 1538 | 1530.9 | -7.1 | -0.46 | |
| 2007 | 1538 | 2227.7 | 689.7 | 44.84 | Flood |
| 2008 | 1538 | 2160.2 | 622.2 | 40.66 | Flood |
| 2009 | 1538 | 1283.3 | -254.7 | -16.56 | Cyclone Aila |
| 2010 | 1538 | 1075.2 | -462.8 | -30.09 | Agri. Drought |
| 2011 | 1538 | 1645.0 | 107.0 | 6.96 | Flood |
| 2012 | 1538 | 1330.0 | -208.0 | -13.52 | Nil |
| 2013 | 1538 | 2331.26 | 793.26 | 51.58 | Flood |
| 2014 | 1538 | 1122.1 | -415.9 | -27.04 | Nil |
| 2015 | 1538 | 1875.0 | 337.0 | 21.9 | Flood |

Contd…

■ **Table 4.9:** Mean Normal Rainfall (mm) in the Catchment Basins from 1956 – 2015

| Catchment Basins | Mean Normal Rainfall (mm) | | | | | Monsoon Rainfall in% to total Rainfall | Annual Run-off (2000 – 2016) |
|---|---|---|---|---|---|---|---|
| | Dec - Feb | March - May | June – Sep | Oct - Nov | Annual | | |
| Kangsabati | 38.93 | 212.23 | 1184.16 | 122.49 | 1557.81 | 76.01 | 73.38 |
| Silabati | 50.68 | 272.99 | 1443.82 | 156.76 | 1924.25 | 75.03 | 93.14 |
| Kaliaghai | 35.62 | 225.78 | 1184.78 | 108.79 | 1554.97 | 76.20 | 84.12 |
| Subarnarekha | 29.18 | 179.57 | 1205.23 | 152.00 | 1565.98 | 76.96 | 90.82 |

*Source: Medinipur Irrigation and Waterways office (Data processed by the Researcher).*

Besides these no. of rainy days received in an area is an important factor to determine the flood condition. According to Indian Meteorological Department (IMD), a rainy day has defined as a day with rainfall of 2.5 mm or more rainfall. Following these criteria, numbers of rainy days have been calculated for each of the monsoon month from 1956 to 2015 period for the station of Medinipur. It has been shown that in last 59 years most of the rainfall occurs in the monsoon period which enhances the flood situation at this particular period.

## 4.4.2 Intensity of Rainfall in the period preceding the Floods

It is not the annual total rainfall that matters for the flood situation but the heavy and prolonged rainfall in the catchment basins with the cyclones contribute towards the surface run-off and attainment of the flood stage (Panda, 1989). Hence, the intensity of rainfall in the period preceding the floods is most significant. The analysis of the rainfall records in the catchment basins of the rivers and their corresponding flood stage has been shown for selected floods in the Table 4.11, 4.12, 4.13 and 4.14. From the entire above Table, it can be noticed that the precipitation in the catchments preceding the flood is effective and this effective period is 5 days for the Kangsabati, Silabati, Subarnarekha and 3 days for the Kaliaghai. For the analysis of that two flood (see Table 4.11) the water of the river Subarnarekha has touched Danger Level (D.L) is 45.50 m. at about 10.30 A.M on 06.07.2007 and reached maximum level 45.82 at 2 P.M on same day.

In the year of 2008 the water of River Subarnarekha has crossed Extreme Danger Level (E.D.L) is 46.50 m. at about 46.92 m. at 7.00 P.M on 18.06.2008, rainfall recorded to 18.06.2008 is 595 mm. Water level reduced below Danger

Level is 45.50 m. on 26.06.2008 is 44.22 m. For the River of Kangsabati, Silabati and Kaliaghai 2015 floods have been analysed. The water level of Kangsabati River has touched 30.07.2015 is 9.29 m. and crossed the Extreme Danger Level on 03.08.2015 is 9.90 m. and water level reduced below Danger Level is 8.87 m. on 06.08.2015(see Table 4.12). The water level of Silabati River crossed the Extreme Danger Level on 03.08.2015 and the water level dropped below Danger Level (D.L) on 07.08.2015 (see Table 4.13). The water level of River Kaliaghai has crossed D.L is 8.40 m. on 26.07.2015 and crossed E.D.L is 8.85 m. on 29.07.2015. The water level dropped below E.D.L on 04.08.2015 and dropped below D.L on 05.08.2015(see Table 4.14). Hence, the short and long duration floods reveal that long duration floods were preceded by much heavier rainfall than short duration floods.

It has also been observed for the River Kangsabati, Silabati and Subarnarekha that the heavy rainfall of about 5 – 9 cm per day for five consecutive days leads to a flooding stage in their lower reach. But, however, for the Kaliaghai, because of the smaller size of their catchments, rainfall of 2 cm per day for three consecutive days can lead to the flood stage in the lower reach of Kaliaghai Catchment. Before the arrival of flood water in the Kangsabati, Kaliaghai and Subarnarekha catchments the flood water comes earlier through their distributaries depending upon the nature of rainfall in their respective catchments. Thus, before the arrival of flood water in the catchments the other drainage channels filled up with the rain during heavy rainfall in monsoon period.

■ **Table 4.10: Frequency of Rainy Days in annual and in different Season**

| Year | Annual | | Pre Monsoon (March to May) | | Monsoon (June to September) | | Post Monsoon (October to November) | | Winter (December to February) | |
|---|---|---|---|---|---|---|---|---|---|---|
| | Rainfall in mm | Rainy Days (Days/Year) | Rainfall in mm | Rainy Days (Days/Year) | Rainfall in mm | Rainy Days (Days/Year) | Rainfall in mm | Rainy Days (Days/Year) | Rainfall in mm | Rainy Days (Days/Year) |
| 1956 | 1892.6 | 112 | 381 | 21 | 1351.78 | 75 | 159.76 | 16 | 0.00 | 0 |
| 1957 | 1171.7 | 76 | 12.7 | 9 | 1026.1 | 53 | 15.7 | 9 | 171.4 | 5 |
| 1958 | 1352.3 | 83 | 166.3 | 13 | 1122.7 | 59 | 107.5 | 9 | 5.8 | 2 |
| 1959 | 1720.8 | 104 | 144.1 | 11 | 1196.2 | 75 | 323.1 | 13 | 57.4 | 5 |
| 1960 | 1404 | 85 | 168.4 | 12 | 1090 | 56 | 146.2 | 7 | 0.00 | 0 |
| 1961 | 1847 | 101 | 73.7 | 6 | 1374.1 | 74 | 329 | 13 | 70.2 | 8 |
| 1962 | 1419 | 90 | 171.3 | 19 | 1054.3 | 61 | 181.8 | 9 | 11.6 | 1 |

Contd...

| Year | Annual | | Pre Monsoon (March to May) | | Monsoon (June to September) | | Post Monsoon (October to November) | | Winter (December to February) | |
|---|---|---|---|---|---|---|---|---|---|---|
| | Rainfall in mm | Rainy Days (Days/Year) | Rainfall in mm | Rainy Days (Days/Year) | Rainfall in mm | Rainy Days (Days/Year) | Rainfall in mm | Rainy Days (Days/Year) | Rainfall in mm | Rainy Days (Days/Year) |
| 1963 | 1411.2 | 90 | 177.1 | 18 | 1111 | 62 | 109.5 | 9 | 13.6 | 1 |
| 1964 | 1091.9 | 79 | 65.2 | 6 | 921.9 | 65 | 104.8 | 8 | 0.00 | 0 |
| 1965 | 937.9 | 85 | 73.9 | 11 | 799 | 66 | 42 | 4 | 23 | 3 |
| 1966 | 1254.1 | 85 | 73.6 | 10 | 974 | 61 | 163 | 10 | 43.5 | 4 |
| 1967 | 1626 | 97 | 214.1 | 18 | 1289.6 | 73 | 12.5 | 3 | 109.8 | 3 |
| 1968 | 1393.9 | 82 | 10.4 | 3 | 1207.7 | 66 | 166.4 | 11 | 9.4 | 2 |
| 1969 | 1554 | 90 | 291.2 | 14 | 1232 | 70 | 25.4 | 5 | 7.4 | 1 |
| 1970 | 1277.7 | 91 | 164 | 16 | 1006.1 | 61 | 94.2 | 11 | 13.4 | 3 |
| 1971 | 2399.5 | 108 | 437 | 23 | 1516 | 69 | 404.4 | 14 | 11.4 | 2 |
| 1972 | 1686.4 | 80 | 62.1 | 9 | 1592.9 | 67 | 31 | 3 | 0.4 | 1 |
| 1973 | 1545.3 | 115 | 153.6 | 19 | 1019.1 | 69 | 342 | 21 | 30.6 | 6 |
| 1974 | 1722.5 | 96 | 208.5 | 18 | 1359.8 | 69 | 154.2 | 8 | 0.00 | 0 |
| 1975 | 1382.7 | 103 | 182 | 13 | 1052.1 | 72 | 97.8 | 12 | 50.8 | 6 |
| 1976 | 1045.7 | 95 | 184.4 | 15 | 807.8 | 72 | 31.3 | 6 | 24.2 | 2 |
| 1977 | 1601.3 | 125 | 206.5 | 25 | 1220.1 | 83 | 124.3 | 10 | 50.4 | 7 |
| 1978 | 2146.3 | 125 | 300.5 | 27 | 1608.9 | 82 | 199.5 | 8 | 35.4 | 8 |
| 1979 | 1068.3 | 80 | 104.1 | 13 | 911.1 | 60 | 11.7 | 5 | 41.4 | 2 |
| 1980 | 1422 | 106 | 283.5 | 22 | 1070.1 | 72 | 34 | 9 | 34.2 | 3 |
| 1981 | 1842.1 | 126 | 547.6 | 35 | 1151.1 | 77 | 5.2 | 1 | 143 | 13 |
| 1982 | 1454.8 | 93 | 258.1 | 22 | 1013.9 | 60 | 19.7 | 2 | 160.1 | 9 |
| 1983 | 1146 | 110 | 257.5 | 21 | 640.5 | 69 | 164.4 | 11 | 83.6 | 9 |
| 1984 | 1989.4 | 108 | 179.1 | 18 | 1726.6 | 80 | 67.9 | 5 | 15.8 | 5 |
| 1985 | 1575.5 | 107 | 163.5 | 15 | 1168 | 76 | 212.6 | 9 | 31.4 | 7 |
| 1986 | 1752.6 | 107 | 291.4 | 22 | 1209 | 65 | 219.6 | 11 | 32.6 | 9 |
| 1987 | 1626.6 | 104 | 196 | 24 | 1321.8 | 65 | 128 | 11 | 20.8 | 4 |
| 1988 | 1596 | 98 | 292 | 16 | 119.4 | 71 | 110.6 | 7 | 6.7 | 4 |
| 1989 | 1805.5 | 100 | 291.2 | 11 | 1368.4 | 77 | 136 | 7 | 9.9 | 5 |
| 1990 | 2336 | 124 | 478.8 | 23 | 1606.6 | 80 | 202 | 16 | 48.6 | 5 |
| 1991 | 1543 | 107 | 275.6 | 23 | 1120.2 | 66 | 111.6 | 10 | 35.6 | 8 |
| 1992 | 1352.6 | 103 | 207 | 20 | 1094.4 | 70 | 21.8 | 7 | 28.8 | 6 |
| 1993 | 2262.8 | 113 | 312.8 | 24 | 1887.6 | 80 | 61.4 | 8 | 1 | 1 |
| 1994 | 1807.4 | 115 | 299.3 | 21 | 1381.4 | 80 | 50.3 | 9 | 76.4 | 5 |
| 1995 | 1715.6 | 104 | 202.8 | 13 | 1202 | 72 | 268 | 14 | 43 | 5 |
| 1996 | 1520.4 | 88 | 163.4 | 9 | 1275.2 | 70 | 51.6 | 4 | 30.2 | 5 |
| 1997 | 1709.3 | 130 | 191.7 | 25 | 1385.2 | 85 | 52.7 | 8 | 79.7 | 12 |

| Year | Annual | | Pre Monsoon (March to May) | | Monsoon (June to September) | | Post Monsoon (October to November) | | Winter (December to February) | |
| --- | --- | --- | --- | --- | --- | --- | --- | --- | --- | --- |
| | Rainfall in mm | Rainy Days (Days/Year) | Rainfall in mm | Rainy Days (Days/Year) | Rainfall in mm | Rainy Days (Days/Year) | Rainfall in mm | Rainy Days (Days/Year) | Rainfall in mm | Rainy Days (Days/Year) |
| 1998 | 1301.5 | 122 | 285.6 | 24 | 748.1 | 65 | 171.6 | 20 | 96.2 | 13 |
| 1999 | 1956.9 | 117 | 323.9 | 17 | 1455 | 83 | 178 | 17 | 0.00 | 0 |
| 2000 | 1293.9 | 110 | 212.9 | 19 | 1017.9 | 79 | 24.7 | 6 | 38.9 | 6 |
| 2001 | 1615.3 | 130 | 354.9 | 32 | 1054.1 | 84 | 206.3 | 14 | 0.00 | 0 |
| 2002 | 1758.9 | 114 | 280.5 | 25 | 1352.5 | 77 | 79.7 | 6 | 44.2 | 6 |
| 2003 | 1542.9 | 132 | 207.9 | 21 | 869.3 | 82 | 450.5 | 22 | 15.2 | 7 |
| 2004 | 1366.1 | 110 | 152.4 | 23 | 1108.4 | 80 | 102.9 | 6 | 2.4 | 1 |
| 2005 | 1696.3 | 112 | 272.6 | 23 | 1985.1 | 68 | 322.9 | 15 | 14.9 | 6 |
| 2006 | 1530.9 | 112 | 192.1 | 19 | 1301.7 | 85 | 37.1 | 8 | 0.00 | 0 |
| 2007 | 2227.7 | 111 | 233.1 | 19 | 1902.4 | 79 | 24.3 | 4 | 67.9 | 9 |
| 2008 | 2160.2 | 121 | 223.4 | 21 | 1814.3 | 91 | 47 | 3 | 75.5 | 6 |
| 2009 | 1283.3 | 92 | 378.6 | 18 | 835.6 | 62 | 66.1 | 11 | 3 | 1 |
| 2010 | 1075.2 | 110 | 210.6 | 19 | 729.5 | 72 | 116.8 | 13 | 18.3 | 6 |
| 2011 | 1645 | 106 | 290.5 | 23 | 1341.3 | 78 | 2.2 | 1 | 11 | 4 |
| 2012 | 1330 | 103 | 175.6 | 14 | 932 | 70 | 96.2 | 7 | 126.2 | 12 |
| 2013 | 1890 | 112 | 198.4 | 13 | 1592 | 83 | 94.5 | 12 | 5.1 | 4 |
| 2014 | 1498 | 98 | 238.1 | 19 | 1113.9 | 67 | 141 | 10 | 5.8 | 2 |
| 2015 | 2066.72 | 123 | 212.4 | 22 | 1783.42 | 80 | 48.6 | 16 | 22.3 | 5 |

*Source: Medinipur Irrigation and Waterways Office (Data processed by the Author).*

■ **Table 4.11:** Daily average rainfall (in mm) in the catchment basins during 5 days preceding the floods and two days succeeding the floods of different magnitude in the Subarnarekha River

| Name of the river | Gauging site | Date of flood | magnitude | Gauge height in m. with date & time | | | Rainfall in mm. for 5 days preceding and 2 days succeeding the flood | |
|---|---|---|---|---|---|---|---|---|
| | | | | Date | Time | Height (m.) | Date | Rainfall (mm.) |
| SUBARNAREKHA | ASUI-DHARAMPUR | 06.07.07 | Medium Flood | 06.07.2007 | 6.00AM | 45.20 | 01.07.2007 | 72.58 |
| | | | | | 9.00AM | 45.42 | 02.07.2007 | 84.30 |
| | | | | | 12.00 PM | 45.62 | 03.07.2007 | 88.40 |
| | | | | | **3.00PM** | **45.82** | 04.07.2007 | 130.50 |
| | | | | | 5.00PM | 45.72 | 05.07.2007 | 260.10 |
| | | | | | 6.00PM | 45.58 | **06.07.2007** | **26.00** |
| | | | | | 10.00PM | 45.50 | 07.07.2007 | 2.00 |
| | | | | | 12.00PM | 45.40 | 08.07.2007 | 0.00 |
| SUBARNAREKHA | ASUI-DHARAMPUR | 19.06.2008 | High Flood | 18.06.2008 | 6.00AM | 45.50 | 13.06.2008 | 42 |
| | | | | | 9.00AM | 46.62 | 14.06.2008 | 46 |
| | | | | | 12.00PM | 46.72 | 15.06.2008 | 78 |
| | | | | | 3.00PM | 46.88 | 16.06.2008 | 164 |
| | | | | | 6.00PM | 46.90 | 17.06.2008 | 97 |
| | | | | | **7.00PM** | **46.92** | **18.06.2008** | **595** |
| | | | | | 10.00AM | 46.35 | 19.06.2008 | 60 |
| | | | | | | | 20.06.2008 | 1 |

**■ Table 4.12:** Daily average rainfalls (in mm) in the catchment basins during 5 days preceding the floods and two days succeeding the floods of different magnitude in the Kangsabati River

| Name of the River | Gauging Site | Date of Flood | Magnitude | Gauge Height in m. | Date | Rainfall in mm. for 5 days preceding and 2 days succeeding the flood |
|---|---|---|---|---|---|---|
| Kangsa-bati | Kalmijole | 03.08.2015 | High Flood | 7.92 | 29.07.2015 | 133.3 |
| | | | | 9.29 | 30.07.2015 | 16.3 |
| | | | | 9.75 | 31.07.2015 | 6.7 |
| | | | | 9.36 | 01.08.2015 | 154.40 |
| | | | | 9.63 | 02.08.2015 | 36.40 |
| | | | | **10.24** | **03.08.2015** | **0.00** |
| | | | | 9.90 | 04.08.2015 | 0.00 |
| | | | | 9.39 | 05.08.2015 | 20.0 |

*Source: Irrigation and Waterways Dept., Govt. Of West Bengal (Data processed by the Author).*

**■ Table 4.13:** Daily average rainfall (in mm) in the catchment basins during 5 days preceding the floods and two days succeeding the floods of different magnitude in the Silabati River

| Name of the River | Gauging Site | Date of Flood | Magnitude | Gauge Height in m. | Date | Rainfall in mm. for 5 days preceding and 2 days succeeding the flood |
|---|---|---|---|---|---|---|
| Silabati | Gadghat | 03.08.2015 | High Flood | 6.95 | 29.07.2015 | 67.80 |
| | | | | 7.52 | 30.07.2015 | 173.20 |
| | | | | 7.76 | 31.07.2015 | 25.20 |
| | | | | 8.04 | 01.08.2015 | 139.00 |
| | | | | 8.81 | 02.08.2015 | 55.00 |
| | | | | **9.84** | **03.08.2015** | **0.00** |
| | | | | 9.79 | 04.08.2015 | 0.00 |
| | | | | 9.29 | 05.08.2015 | 0.00 |

*Source: Irrigation and Waterways Dept., Govt. Of West Bengal (Data processed by the Author).*

■ **Table 4.14:** Daily average rainfall (in mm) in the catchment basins during 5 days preceding the floods and two days succeeding the floods of different magnitude in the Kaliaghai River

| Name of the River | Gaug-ing Site | Date of Flood | Magnitude | Gauge Height in m. | Date | Rainfall in mm. for 5 days preceding and 2 days succeeding the flood |
|---|---|---|---|---|---|---|
| Kali-aghai | Bakhra-bad | 02.08.2015 | High Flood | 8.95 | 28.07.2015 | 19.35 |
| | | | | 9.00 | 29.07.2015 | 7.65 |
| | | | | 9.30 | 30.07.2015 | 6.80 |
| | | | | 9.10 | 31.07.2015 | 19.35 |
| | | | | 9.40 | 01.08.2015 | 35.00 |
| | | | | **9.70** | **02.08.2015** | **51.85** |
| | | | | 9.40 | 03.08.2015 | 9.35 |
| | | | | 8.50 | 04.08.2015 | 5.67 |

*Source: Irrigation and Waterways Dept., Govt. Of West Bengal (Data processed by the Author).*

In study area only one River, Silabati has been affected by the tidal surges at the confluence point of the River Rupnarayan. So, situation like heavy rainfall, tidal surge, low gradient and high underground water table reduces the flood slope and aggravates the flood situation to a great extent.

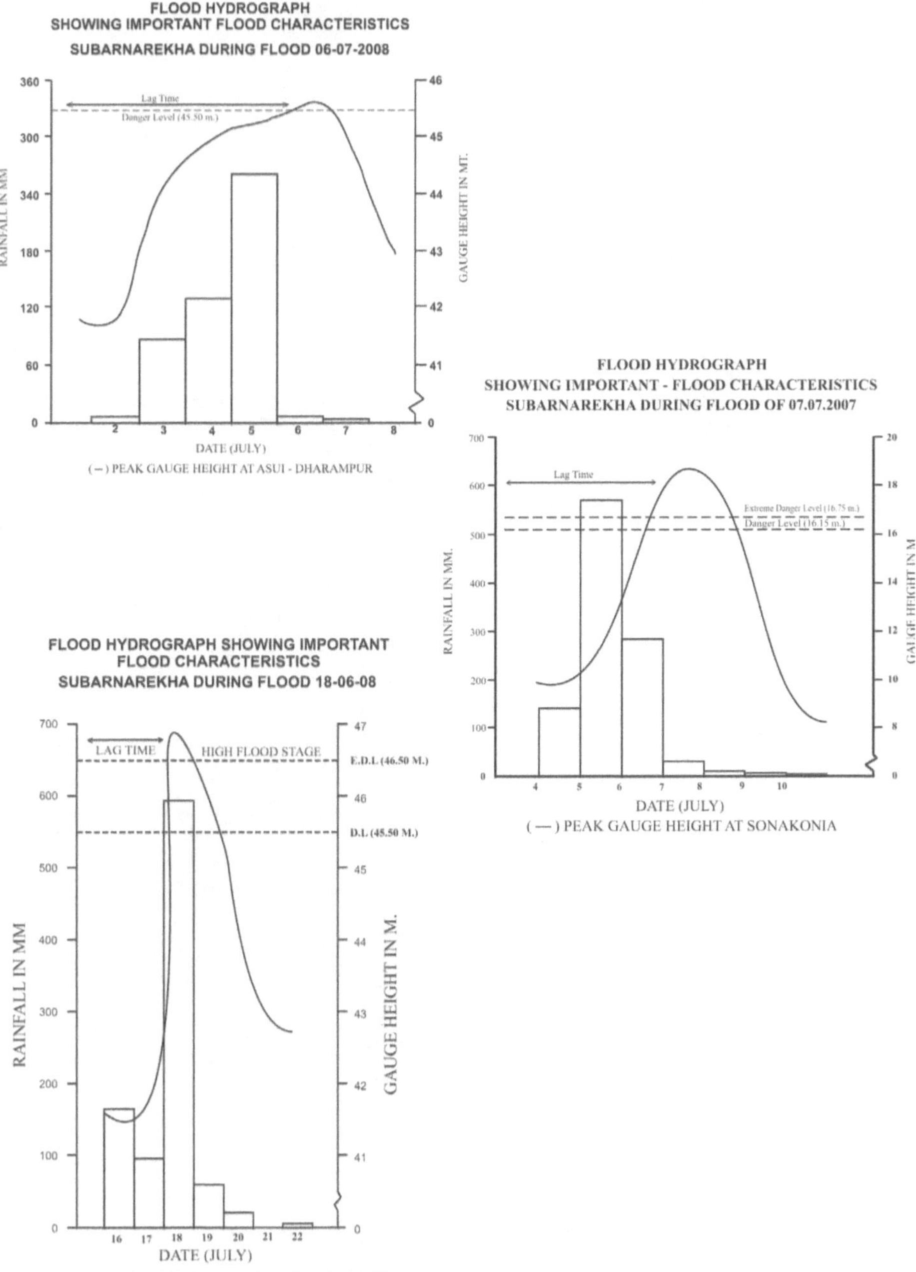



**Fig. 4.11:**  Flood Hydrograph of Subarnarekha River.

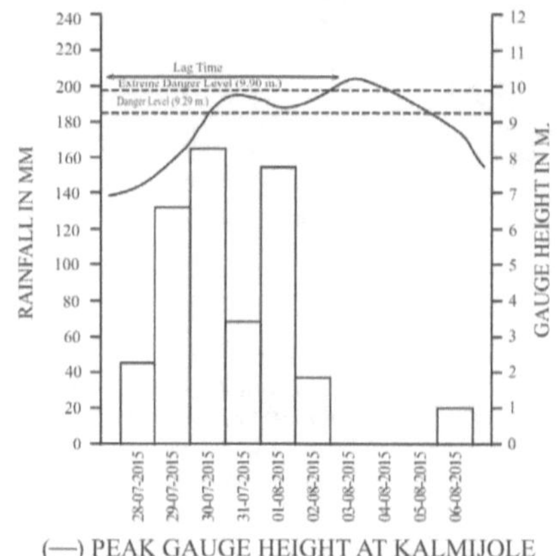


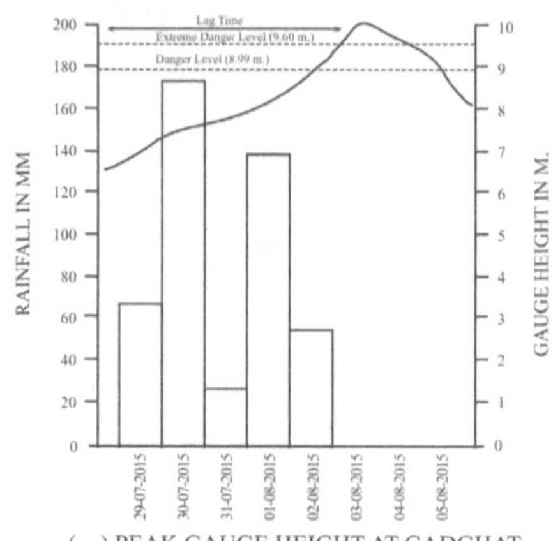


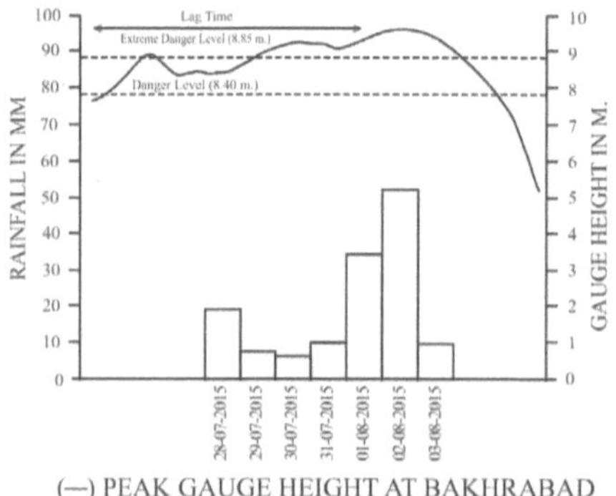


**Fig. 4.12:** Flood Hydrograph of Kangsabati, Kaliaghai and Silabati River.

## 4.5 Hydrological Characteristics

### 4.5.1 Ground Water

In the event of heavy rainfall, underground aquifers are inundated and filled possibly resulting in flooding. Ground water flooding is the emergence of ground water at the ground surface away from perennial river channels and can also include the rising of ground water into man-made ground, including basements and other surface infrastructure (Macdonald et al. 2008). A high ground water level often persists due to extended periods of drainage from the unsaturated zone causing prolonged flooding. Ground water can contribute significantly to river flow during monsoon months. Naturally high ground of river levees can contain river water while low-lying ground beyond can be flooded due to rising ground water. Flooding by the cause of ground water rising due to heavy rainfall or geographical location of the area (concave structure) may last a long time compared to surface water flooding, from weeks to months. Hence, the amount of damage that is caused to property may be substantially higher. Likewise closures of access routes, roads etc. may be prolonged. Ghatal block has been highly affected by this type of condition where level of ground water is very high in monsoon period.

■ **Table 4.15:** Seasonal Ground Water level (m.bgl) at Medinipur Site

| Season Year | Post Monsoon (Rabi) | Pre -Monsoon | Monsoon | Post Monsoon (Kharif) |
|---|---|---|---|---|
| 1996 | 2.98 | 3.04 | 0.91 | 2.94 |
| 1997 | 5.80 | 3.46 | 1.16 | 2.21 |
| 1998 | 3.00 | 2.88 | 1.93 | 2.13 |
| 1999 | 2.77 | 3.33 | 1.03 | 1.50 |
| 2000 | 2.10 | 3.51 | 0.98 | 2.01 |
| 2001 | 2.59 | 3.69 | 1.47 | 2.20 |
| 2002 | 3.24 | 2.89 | 1.18 | 1.54 |
| 2003 | 2.90 | 3.41 | 1.24 | 1.50 |
| 2004 | 3.01 | 3.37 | 1.41 | 1.80 |
| 2005 | 3.30 | 3.80 | 1.37 | 1.48 |
| 2006 | 2.79 | 4.55 | 1.08 | 1.59 |
| 2007 | 3.99 | 5.40 | 1.01 | 2.29 |
| 2008 | 4.89 | 3.34 | 1.42 | 2.14 |

| Season Year | Post Monsoon (Rabi) | Pre -Monsoon | Monsoon | Post Monsoon (Kharif) |
|---|---|---|---|---|
| 2009 | 3.01 | 1.75 | 1.41 | 1.70 |
| 2010 | 2.97 | 2.71 | 1.53 | 2.43 |
| 2011 | 3.42 | 3.88 | 1.06 | 2.30 |
| 2012 | 3.10 | 4.03 | 1.07 | 2.75 |
| 2013 | 3.45 | 4.29 | 4.59 | 1.40 |
| 2014 | 2.89 | 4.16 | 0.83 | 3.11 |
| 2015 | 3.79 | 3.27 | 13.29 | 2.79 |
| 2016 | 3.24 | 3.12 | 0.87 | 2.49 |

*Source: India-WRIS, A Joint Project of ISRO and CWC.*

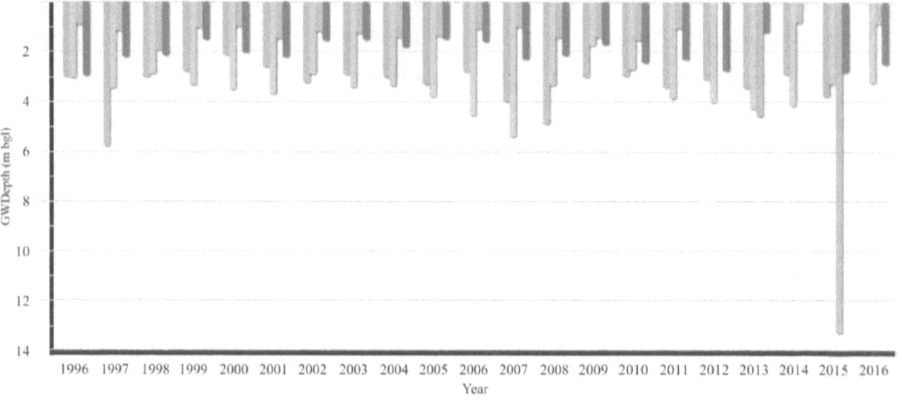

**Fig. 4.13:** Seasonal Ground Water Level in different year.

## 4.6 Other Variable Catchment Basin Characteristics

Apart from the above-mentioned characteristics, there are a number of basin characteristics those effect on flood hydrograph are often complex. These characteristics result from the interaction between climate, soil type, vegetation cover, effect of deforestation and shifting cultivation. These characteristics mostly relate to the catchment basins land use which determines the water retaining capacity of the basins, with low storage potential often resulting in rapid and intensified flooding and reverse is the case with high retentive capacity. But, however, such data are not available at the catchment level to establish the relationship of these variables with that of flood discharge and flood frequency.

## 4.6.1 Soil type and their distribution

In Paschim Medinipur District, most of the laterite soil found in the north western part of the district which is the upper portion of all the river catchment basins. These soils do not have much of water retaining capacity. Some people doing the agricultural practise in the catchment areas with cleaning up of the forest lands has brought about the removal of the top soil increasing thereby surface stoniness and exposure of rock outcrops making the conditions favourable for soil erosion and rapid surface run-off. In the catchment basins the distribution of different types of soil is shown in the Table 4.16.

■ **Table 4.16:** Distribution of the different soil types in the catchment basins

| River Basins / Soil Types | Red Sandy | Red Gravelly | Lateritic | Older Alluvial | Younger Alluvial |
|---|---|---|---|---|---|
| Kangsabati | 244.41 | 7.08 | 611.54 | 1118.96 | 190.47 |
| Kaliaghai | — | — | 469.41 | 1029.09 | 227.044 |
| Silabati | — | — | 835.17 | 883.88 | 312.63 |
| Subarnarekha | 77.27 | 444.39 | 634.25 | 633.51 | - |

## 4.6.2 Land Use Characteristics

The general land use pattern is an outcome of the interactions and interplay of the various physical conditions of the area. The general floodplain land use (one km from active channel) statistics is given in the Table 4.17. The land use pattern is revealed that is nearly around 30.89% bare land in one km land use from active channel. This gives an insight into the nature of land degradation in the catchments whose consequence is the rapid surface run-off favoring the yield of flood water to the plain of Medinipur.

■ **Table 4.17:** Floodplain land use pattern of the catchment basins within the district (one K.M from active channel)

| Catchment Basins | Built-up Area (Sq.Km) | Cultivated Lands (Sq. Km) | Bare Soils (Sq.Km) | Wetlands (Sq. Km) | Rural Settlement (Sq.Km) |
|---|---|---|---|---|---|
| 1 | 2 | 3 | 4 | 5 | 6 |
| Kangsabati | 6.11 (2.54) | 135.17 (56.24) | 13.86 (5.77) | 46.97 (19.54) | 38.25 (15.91) |
| Kaliaghai | 0.78 (0.61) | 86.85 (68.37) | 12.25 (9.64) | 7.37 (5.80) | 19.78 (15.57) |

| Catchment Basins | Built-up Area (Sq.Km) | Cultivated Lands (Sq. Km) | Bare Soils (Sq.Km) | Wetlands (Sq. Km) | Rural Settlement (Sq.Km) |
|---|---|---|---|---|---|
| Silabati | 4.03 (2.07) | 137.49 (70.52) | 7.62 (3.91) | 17.35 (8.90) | 28.48 (14.61) |
| Subarnarekha | 0.56 (0.37) | 38.28 (25.20) | 17.58 (11.57) | 83.27 (54.81) | 12.22 (8.04) |

## Figure within the bracket indicate percentage share of the items.

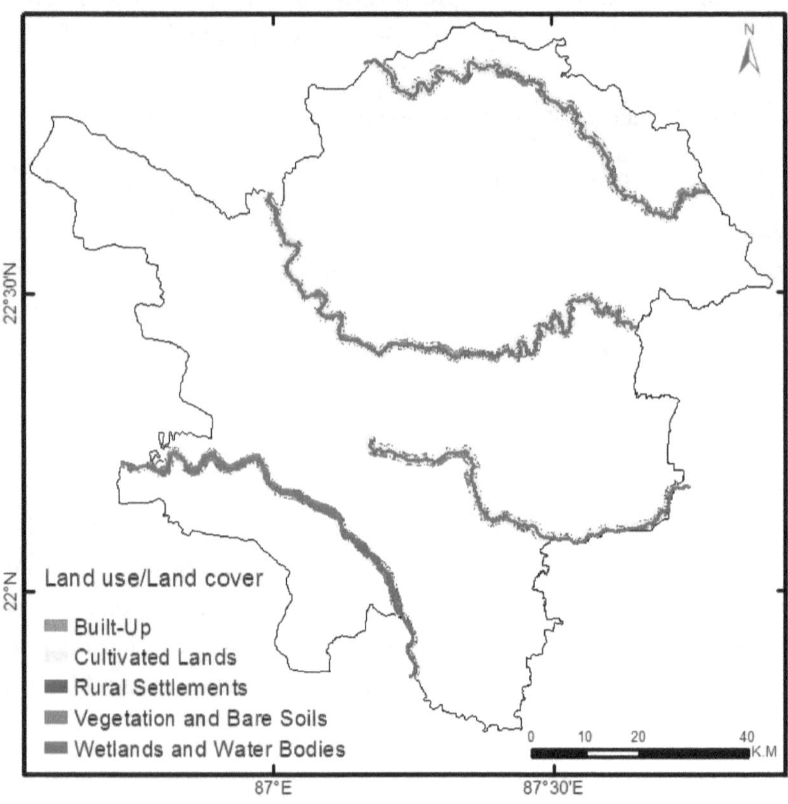


**Fig. 4.14:** Land use and Land cover pattern within one km from active channel.

# VULNERABILITY ANALYSIS AND RISK ASSESSMENT OF FLOOD HAZARDS

CHAPTER

# 05

Physical Vulnerability Analysis: Elevation – Land Use/Land Cover - Distance to active Channels – Geology, Social Vulnerability Analysis: Population Density – Children and Elderly Population/Dependent Population – Gender – Poverty – Type of Housing – Illiteracy – Source of Water – Sanitation – Road Density, Coping Capacity Analysis: Flood Awareness – Literacy Rate – Per Capita Shelter and Hospitals,Composite Vulnerability Index, Result and Discussion: Physical Vulnerability – Social Vulnerability – Coping Capacity – Composite Vulnerability, Flood Risk Mapping.

Flood is one of the most threatens natural hazards for human societies, that can affect people, socio-economic condition, infrastructure and natural environment to a great extent. These events have come to pose greater challenges before humanity with an unprecedented increase in their frequency, intensity and geographical spread over the last few decades. The vulnerability analysis and risk assessment are recognised as an important tool to evolve disaster mitigation and preparedness plans in the hazard prone areas. For disaster prevention, mitigation and preparedness, it is important to identify vulnerable areas and factor configuring disaster risk where the impact could reach to severe magnitude for the affected communities.

Paschim Medinipur is one of the districts of West Bengal in India located in a hot and humid tropical region. The district is endowed with a large network of rivers with four major catchments. The district has been recurrently affected by flood hazards, many of which have turned into disasters with wide spread damage to property and loss of human life. Besides this, the impact on livelihood, damage to housing and crops are also the major concerns of the people of the district.

## 5.1 Concept of Vulnerability and Risk

The vulnerability describes the degree to which an area, people, physical structures or economic assets are exposed to loss, injury or damage caused by the impact of the hazard. According to United Nations Development Programme (UNDP, 1994), vulnerability depends upon the degree of loss to a certain severity level. Risk is viewed as the probability of occurrence or the degree of loss of a specified element expected from a specific hazard. According to Asian Disaster Reduction Centre (ADRC), 2005, describes risk as the overlapping areas of three factors- hazard, exposure and vulnerability- that act simultaneously to generate the risk of natural hazards, which can be expressed as:

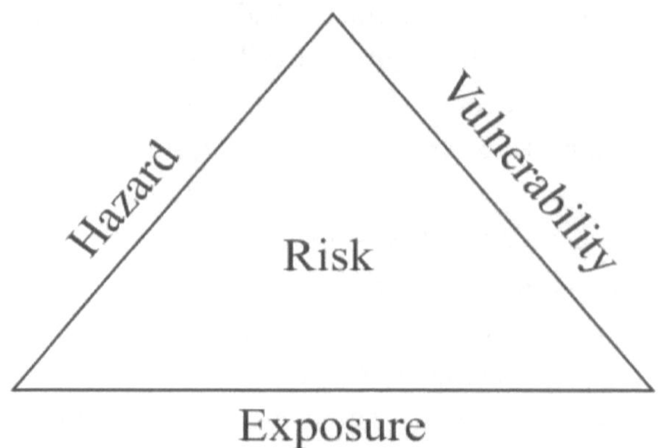


Fig.6.1 Risk Traingle (Adopted from Crichton 2002)

**Fig. 5.1:** Risk Triangle (Adopted from Crichton 2002)

**Risk = hazard * vulnerability** (5.1)
**Risk = hazard * exposure * vulnerability** (5.2)

While hazards are a potential threat to population and the environment, risk is the interplay between hazard and vulnerability. The process of risk assessment involves the quantification of risk by means of hazard assessment and vulnerability analysis. In relation to disaster, risk has been more specifically described as the probability that a disaster will occur, using relative terms as high risk, moderate risk and low risk. For example, the people who live closer to a flood plain are at greater risk than those who live far away. Similarly, people who live in poorly constructed masonry houses near the river bank or flood plain are more at risk than those who live nearby plain in well-built structures. There are three essential components in the determination of risk, each of which should be separately quantified. They are (i) The hazard occurrence i.e. the probability at a location or in a region (ii) The elements at risk i.e. identifying and making an inventory of people, buildings or other elements which would be affected by the hazards if it occurred and where required, estimating their economic value (iii) The vulnerability or other elements would be if they experienced some level of hazard.

## 5.2  Data Base and Function of Analytical Hierarchy Process

A placed-based approach was adopted to evaluate flood vulnerability analysis and risk assessment at the community level. A method comprising the Analytic Hierarchy Process (AHP) and Weighted Linear Combination (WLC) was used to operationalize the conceptual model within a GIS framework. A number of biophysical variables were used to derive the Physical Vulnerability Index (PVI). In addition, nine (9) variables were extracted from diverse sources to derive the Social Vulnerability Index (SVI). To determine the Coping Capacity of a community, four (4) variables were employed and a Coping Capacity Index (CCI) was developed. Using the PVI, SVI and CCI a Composite Vulnerability Index (CVI) was prepared. Four variables were used to assess the physical vulnerability, as the locational factor is an important indicator to depict the susceptibility of humans and properties to floods. A reasonable assumption is that people living in the proximity of active channels or in properties on a floodplain are at a high risk than those living highly elevated areas or away from rivers. Therefore, physical variables have been used to estimate physical vulnerability. Data regarding physical vulnerability assessment were collected from a number of sources. An elevation data collected from SRTM dataset. Land-use and land-cover data obtained from the LISS 3 image and river network vector files/distance to active channel were collected from MBGIS. Geology data were collected from the geology map of Medinipur. To determine the indicators for social vulnerability and coping capacity, a range of variables was constructed from diverse sources. Socio-economic and demographic attributes were collected from the PHED, Govt. Of West Bengal and District Annual Plan, 2015-2016 which represent the population census of 2011.

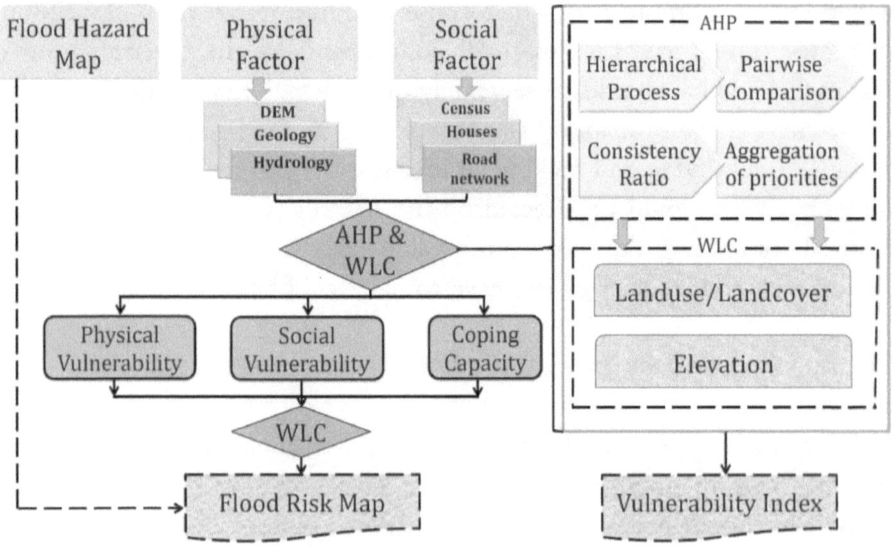


**Fig. 5.2:** Flowchart showing overall methods of the study.

A variety of techniques are available to compute community vulnerability to natural hazards and they can be categorized as inductive or deductive (yoon, 2012). Similarly, variables that are used to derive the vulnerability of an area depend on various factors such as scale of analysis, extent of the study area and the vulnerability of data (Fekete et al. 2010). As mentioned above, this study considers indicators from physical, socio-economic and other sources to examine community vulnerability to floods. Note that the physical and social indicators have been analyzed separately to produce an individual index and the results are then combined to construct a Composite Vulnerability Index (CVI). The basic premise of the work was to create flood vulnerability and risk maps that can easily be interpreted and to allow improved decision making for mitigating flood related damage in Paschim Medinipur District. A placed-based approach is adopted to estimate the vulnerability of communities by integrating spatial and census data. Spatial multi-criteria assessment techniques in the form of Analytic Hierarchy Process (AHP) and Weighted Linear Combination (WLC) were used as a method of analysis. The AHP was first introduced by Thomas L. Satty as a robust and flexible technique for supporting priority setting and improve decision making when the phenomena that is being studied involves both the quantitative and qualitative aspects of a decision (Satty 1977).The AHP is based on multi-criteria that prioritize the criteria identified by different groups of people involved in the decision-making process in order to arrive at the best decision. It also assits in justifying the optimality of the decision (Satty 1980). The AHP allows a problem to be organized as primary and secondary objectives, which is known as the hierarchy and a matrix is subsequently used to weight each factor against every other factor within each level of the hierarchy. Every level in the process is tied with its top and bottom levels, resulting in a clear priority statement for a group or individual (Ramanathan 2001). The following steps are involved in the process:

i.   Structuring a hierarchical decision model
ii.  Development of a pairwise comparison matrix
iii. Obtaining local priorities and checking consistency of comparison and
iv.  Aggregation of local priorities.

The hierarchical decision model is the design phase of AHP in which the top level exhibits the overall goal of the decision. Indicators can be criteria in the upper level of the model and each of them is further broken down into sub-criteria. Each pair of criteria or sub-criteria element is compared in terms of its relative importance using a 9 – points system from 1 (if two indicators equally contribute to the objective) to 9 (when one indicator is strongly favoured over another to meet the objective), (see Table 5.1) and forms a comparison matrix namely, a pairwise comparison (see Table 5.2). A score of 1 denotes equal importance, a score of 3 refers to weak preference, while scores 5 and 7 represent obvious and strong preference. The even numbers (i.e., 2, 4, 6 and 8) are used when a compromise is needed between the odd numbers.

The local priority (weight) for a criterion is computed from a pairwise comparison matrix by normalizing the points in the columns (divide a cell value by the sum of a column) and averaging the normalized points in the row of the criterion. The consistency of the comparisons is evaluated by calculating a Consistency Ratio (CR). If the CR is equal to or less than 0.1, the comparisons are considered consistent, otherwise it would be revised. The CR is defined by the following equation:

**CR = Consistency Index/Random Index**  (5.3)

The Random Index (RI) refers to a randomly generated reciprocal matrix from the 9 – point scale and it can be obtained by referring to the RI table Satty (1980) provides a function of n in relationship (see Table 5.3). The consistency index (CI) is defined as:

$$CI = (\lambda_{max} - n)/(n-1) \tag{5.4}$$

**■ Table 5.1:** Semantic Scale of the AHP method

| Comparative importance | Definition | Description |
|---|---|---|
| 1 | Equal importance | Two indicators equally influence the parent decision |
| 3 | Weak importance | One factor is moderately influential over the other |
| 5 | Essential or strong importance | One factor is strongly favoured over the other |
| 7 | Demonstrated importance | One decision factor has significant influence over another |
| 9 | Absolute importance | Evidence favouring one decision factor over the other is the highest order of affirmation |
| 2,4,6,8 | Intermediate | When compromise is needed, values between two adjacent judgments are used |
| Reciprocals | If $A_i$ is the judgemental value when i is compared with j, then $A_j$ has the reciprocal value when compared to $A_i$ | A reasonable assumption |

*Source: Ramanathan (2001).*

**■ Table 5.2:** Example of a Pairwise Comparison Matrix

| Infrastructure and Lifelines | Sources of Water | Sanitation | Road Density |
|---|---|---|---|
| Sources of Water | 1 | 3 | 4 |
| Sanitation | 1/3 | 1 | 2 |
| Road Density | 1/4 | 1/2 | 1 |

**■ Table 5.3:** Random average consistency indexes for various n

| n | 1 | 2 | 3 | 4 | 5 | 6 | 7 | 8 | 9 |
|---|---|---|---|---|---|---|---|---|---|
| RI | 0.0 | 0.0 | 0.58 | 0.90 | 1.12 | 1.24 | 1.32 | 1.41 | 1.45 |

'n' represent the number of criteria.

Where, $\lambda_{max}$ is the largest eigen value derived from the comparison matrix and n is the number of criteria. Once of the consistency is validated, the final priority of the criteria at the upper level of the hierarchy model is obtained by aggregating the local priorities of the criteria at its lower level. In addition to AHP, WLC is also used in this study. Due to its simplicity, multi-criteria decision analysis in terms of WLC is a frequently used technique within a

GIS (Malczewski 1999, 2004, and 2006). In GIS analysis, each indicator is treated as a data layer. A WLC is conducted by multiplying indicators by the corresponding weights and aggregating all weighted layers. In this study, the following equation was used:

$$VI = \sum_{i=1}^{i} \sum_{i=1}^{i} W_i W_{ij} x \tag{5.5}$$

Where, VI is the Vulnerability Index for physical or social indicator, $w_i$ and $w_{ij}$ are the weights for the $i^{th}$ and $j^{th}$ sub-criterian and x represents the value of an indicator.

## 5.3 Physical Vulnerability Analysis

The study asserts that flood risk in PaschimMedinipur district is not only governed by the socio-economic factors but is also significantly influenced by physical/natural factors. Therefore, four physical variables are considered to derive a PVI (see Fig. 5.3). The distance to active channels was calculated by using river network data, assuming that people who live close to active channels has been an elevated risk compared to those who do not. The Euclidian distance function is used to derive the distance to the active channel. Elevation categories are derived by slicing the DEM data. Geology, land-use, elevation and distance to active channel and elevation category, the intensity of importance was determined based on the relationship between flood hazard categories and elevation and distance to active channel parameters.

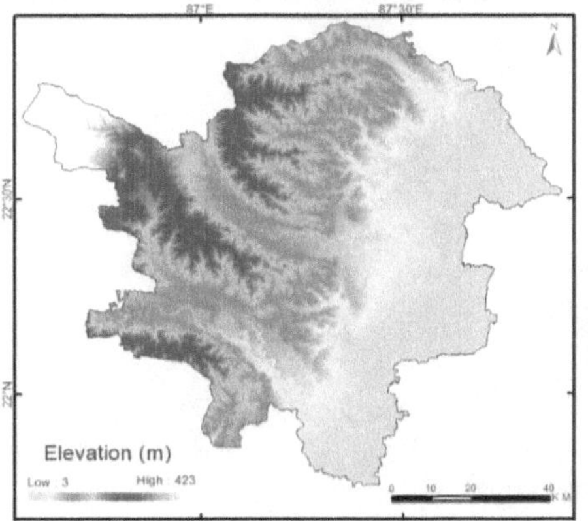


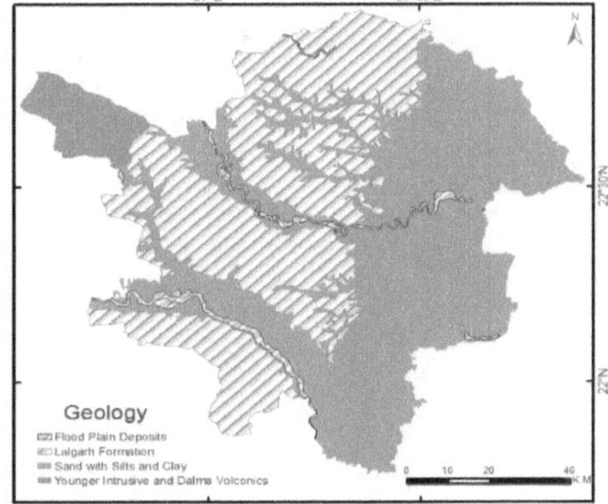

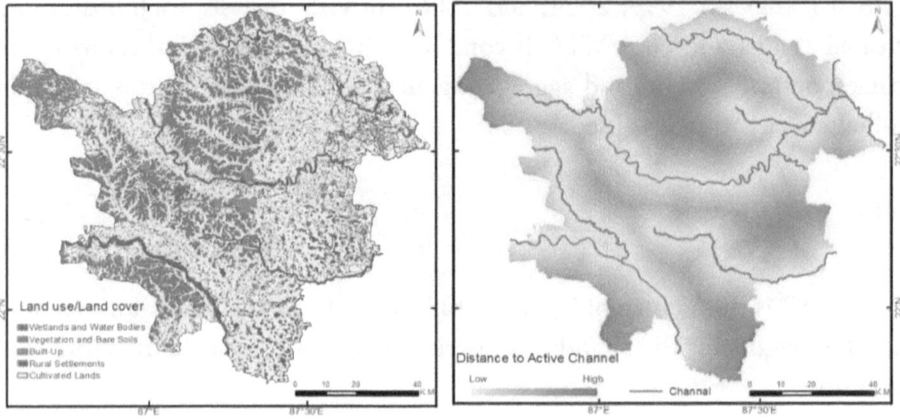


**Fig. 5.3:** Physical Variables.

## 5.3.1 Elevation

Elevation is the most important criteria because it has a tremendous effect on flood hazard in the study area, as most of the areas in southern and south-eastern part of the study area are low lying lands. The elevation category is intersected with the flood hazard map to ensure that the relative weights for each category are justified properly. As expected, the high hazard category is less than 30 m. (see Fig.5.4). Therefore, elevation of less than 30 m. is given the highest weight, while elevation greater than 270 m. is assigned to the lowest weight (see Table 6.4).

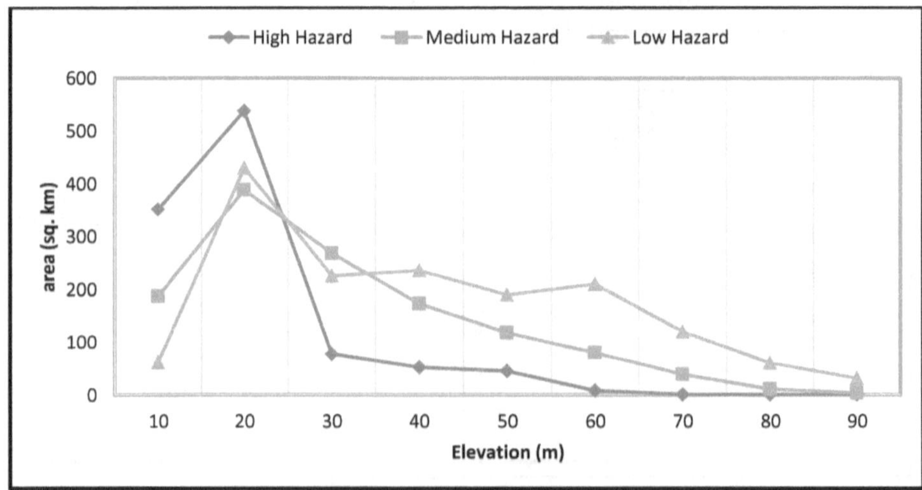


**Fig. 5.4:** Elevation in each hazard zone by area.

### 5.3.2 Land use and Land cover

The land use and land cover data comprise of five categories namely, cultivated rural settlement, wetland and water bodies, vegetation and bare soils and built-up area. Since the potential effects of floods high for the cultivated category in terms of agricultural loss due to floods has a considerable impact on the rural people and also the local economy. That is the causes of cultivated category getting relatively highest weight. Built-up category also potential effects of floods in terms of infrastructural damage and human suffering. Wetlands and water bodies are allocated the lowest weight because they do not pose a threat to people too much; instead they act as a water retention ponds during floods (see Table 5.4).

### 5.3.3 Distance to active channel

People and property are in considerable danger up to 1.5 km away from the existing river networks. However, the maximum weight is allocated to the distance less than.5 km from the rivers and the lowest weight is given to the category with a distance greater than 1.5 km. (see Table 5.4).

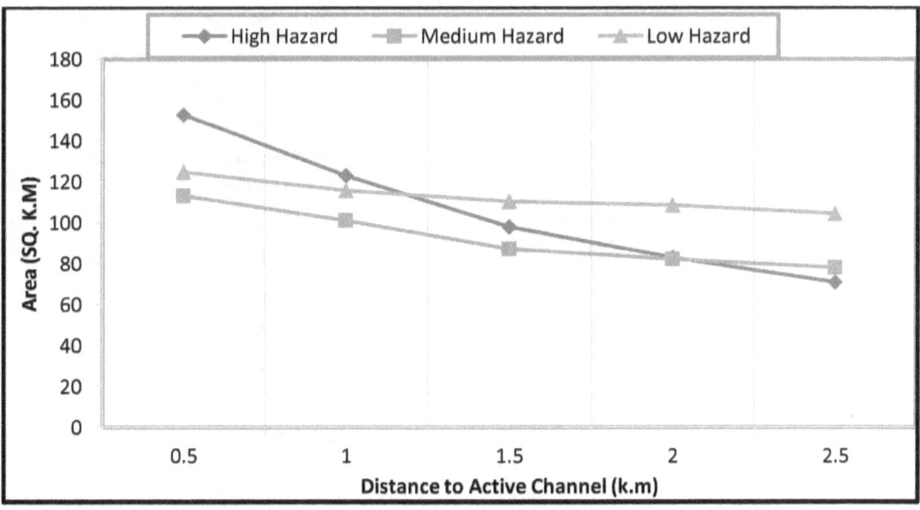


**Fig. 5.5:** Distance categories according to different flood hazard classes by area.

### 5.3.4 Geology

Geologically, the area can be divided into four categories. Younger intrusive and DalmaVolcanics is a highly elevated area and it is not usually inundated during the monsoon season. Therefore, it is assigned to the lowest weight. Flood plain deposit is areas where flood is a normal phenomenon. This is given the highest importance followed by the sand with silts and clays category. Lalgarh formation normally not flooded but during the high flood some parts of the area inundated.

■ **Table 5.4: Physical vulnerability decision hierarchy model**

| 1 | 2 | | 3 | |
| --- | --- | --- | --- | --- |
| | Criteria | Weight | Criteria | Weight |
| Physical Vulnerability Index | Elevation (m.) | 0.483 | <30 | 0.482 |
| | | | 30-60 | 0.299 |
| | | | 60-90 | 0.122 |
| | | | 90-270 | 0.064 |
| | | | >270 | 0.034 |
| | Land-use category | 0.316 | Cultivated | 0.483 |
| | | | Rural Settlement | 0.261 |
| | | | Built up area | 0.141 |
| | | | Vegetation and Bare soil | 0.074 |
| | | | Wetland and water bodies | 0.040 |
| | Distance to active channel (K.M) | 0.145 | <0.5 | 0.470 |
| | | | 0.5-1.0 | 0.300 |
| | | | 1.0-1.5 | 0.160 |
| | | | >1.5 | 0.070 |
| | Geology | 0.056 | Flood plain deposits | 0.560 |
| | | | Sand with silts and clays | 0.230 |
| | | | Lalgarh formation | 0.140 |
| | | | Younger Intrusive and DalmaVolcanics | 0.070 |

Regarding the importance of the criteria at the upper level (level 2), elevation is considered the most important criteria and given the highest weight. The second most important aregiven to land use category because consequent land use change is exacerbating river water flooding in the study area. Flood hazard distribution reveals that the northern and north western portions are not usually inundated, as land elevation is relatively high but the southern and south eastern part of the district normally flooded during monsoon, not only the causes of low land elevation but also protected embankments very week. Therefore, two other parameters, distance from the river and geology are given less importance in the second decision level. The pairwise comparison matrices with CR to evaluate the consistency of the comparison judgements (see Table 5.5). After deriving the weights for each variable using the AHP, WLC was used. So, all variables could be weighted and combined to derive a PVI. Before performing the WLC, the values for elevation and distance to active channels were standardized using the below equation:

$$\rho = \frac{max - x}{max - min} \tag{5.6}$$

Where, 'ρ' is standardized value, min and max represent the minimum and maximum values for each dataset respectively and 'x' is the cell value. Finally, WLC is performed first on the sub-criteria of each indicator and subsequently on the criteria at the upper level of the decision hierarchy model, the resulting index indicated that the higher the value, the greater the susceptibility to flood of a community.

■ **Table 5.5:** Pairwise Comparison Matrix for Physical Indicators (Criteria at level 2 of decision hierarchy model)

| | 1 | 2 | 3 | 4 |
|---|---|---|---|---|
| 1. Elevation | 1 | 2 | 4 | 6 |
| 2. Land-use | ½ | 1 | 3 | 6 |
| 3. Distance to active channel | ¼ | 1/3 | 1 | 4 |
| 4. Geology | 1/6 | 1/6 | 1/4 | 1 |

**CR: 0.05**

■ **Table 5.5:** Pairwise Comparison Matrix for Physical Indicators (Criteria at level 3 of decision hierarchy model)

| Land-use/Land-cover | 1 | 2 | 3 | 4 | 5 |
|---|---|---|---|---|---|
| 1. Cultivated | 1 | 3 | 5 | 6 | 7 |
| 2. Rural Settlement | 1/3 | 1 | 3 | 5 | 6 |
| 3. Built-up Area | 1/5 | 1/3 | 1 | 3 | 5 |
| 4.Vegetation and Bare soil | 1/6 | 1/5 | 1/3 | 1 | 3 |
| 5. Wetland and Water Bodies | 1/7 | 1/6 | 1/5 | 1/3 | 1 |

**CR: 0.07**

| Elevation (m) | 1 | 2 | 3 | 4 | 5 |
|---|---|---|---|---|---|
| 1. <30 | 1 | 3 | 5 | 7 | 9 |
| 2. 30–60 | 1/3 | 1 | 5 | 6 | 8 |
| 3. 60–90 | 1/5 | 1/5 | 1 | 3 | 5 |
| 4.90–270 | 1/7 | 1/6 | 1/3 | 1 | 3 |
| 5.>270 | 1/9 | 1/8 | 1/5 | 1/3 | 1 |

**CR: 0.08**

| Distance to active channel (k.m) | 1 | 2 | 3 | 4 |
|---|---|---|---|---|
| 1. <0.5 | 1 | 2 | 4 | 5 |
| 2. 0.5-1.0 | ½ | 1 | 3 | 4 |
| 3. 1.0-1.5 | ¼ | 1/3 | 1 | 4 |
| 4. >1.5 | 1/5 | 1/4 | 1/4 | 1 |

**CR: 0.07**

| Geology | 1 | 2 | 3 | 4 |
|---|---|---|---|---|
| 1. Flood plain deposits | 1 | 3 | 4 | 6 |
| 2. Sand with silts and clays | 1/3 | 1 | 2 | 3 |
| 3. Lalgarh formation | ¼ | ½ | 1 | 2 |
| 4. Younger Intrusive and DalmaVolcanics | 1/6 | 1/3 | 1/2 | 1 |

**CR: 0.07**

## 5.4  Social Vulnerability Analysis

An efficient social vulnerability assessment for environmental hazards requires good baseline data when the spatial unit includes the local level of analysis (cutter et al. 2003, 2009). This study is based on geographical census data. For social vulnerability analysis nine variables are extracted from the census and relevant spatial databases to determine the human dimensions involved. These variables are divided into three categories: demographic, socio-economic and infrastructures and lifelines (see Fig. 5.6, 5.7, 5.8). It should be noted that BPL households at block level treated as poverty data. The variables are first used to assess their importance in understanding vulnerability using the AHP technique (see Fig. 5.9).

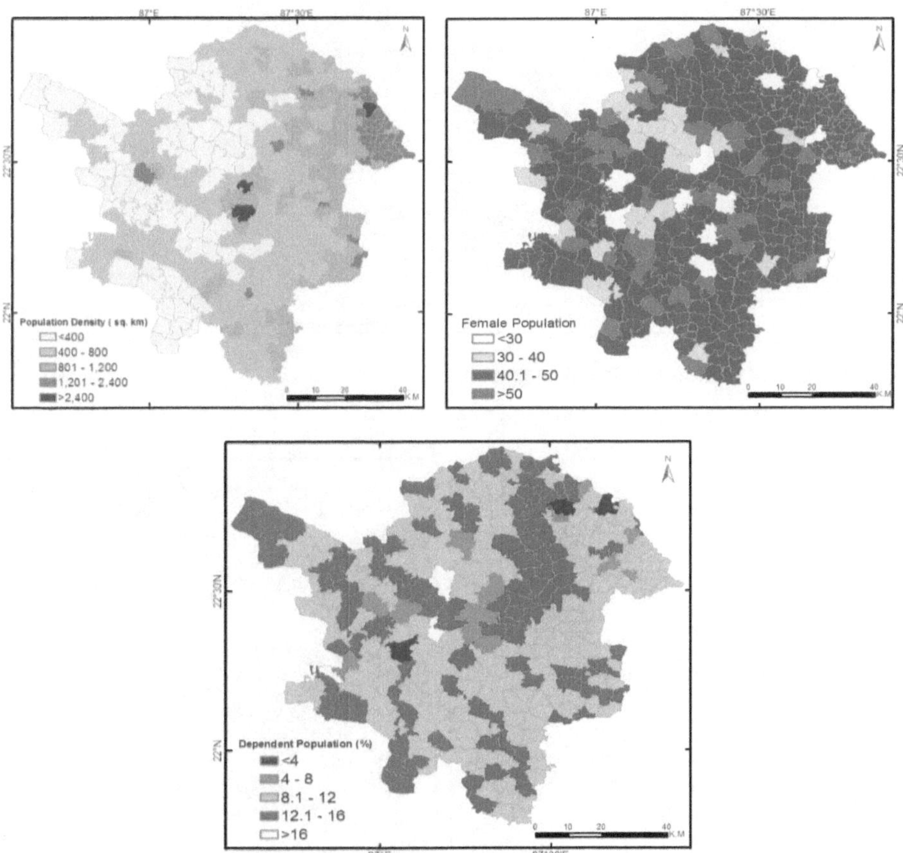


**Fig. 5.6:** Distribution of Demographic Indicators.

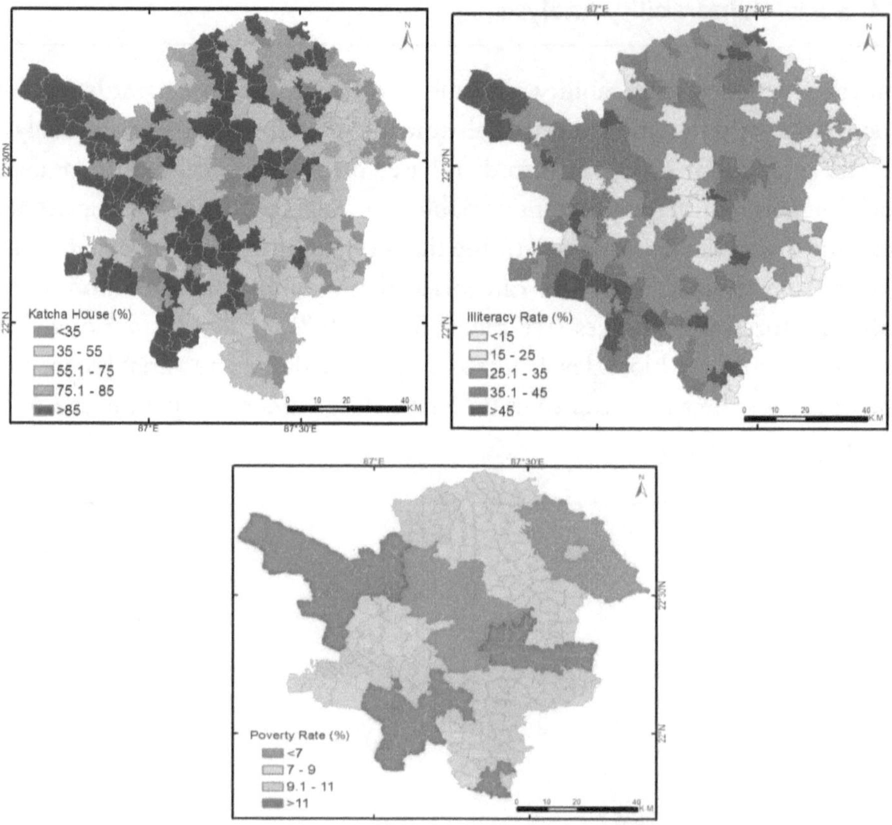

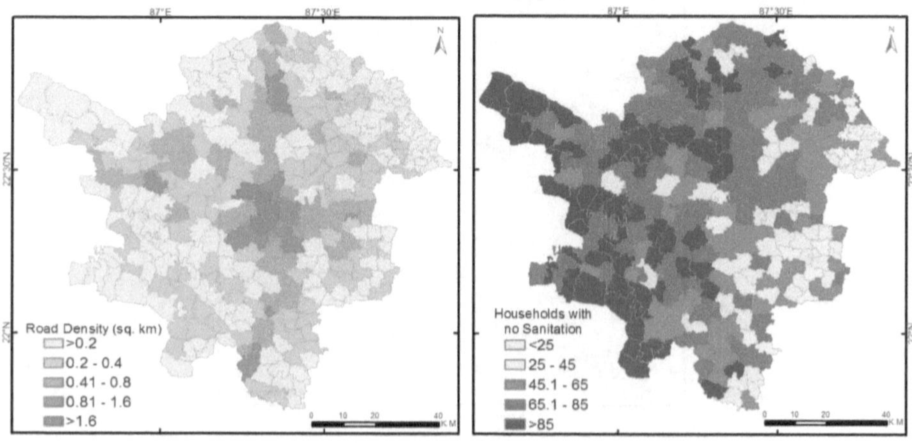



**Fig. 5.7:** Distribution of socioeconomic indicators.



**Fig. 5.8:** Distribution of lifeline and infrastructure indicators.

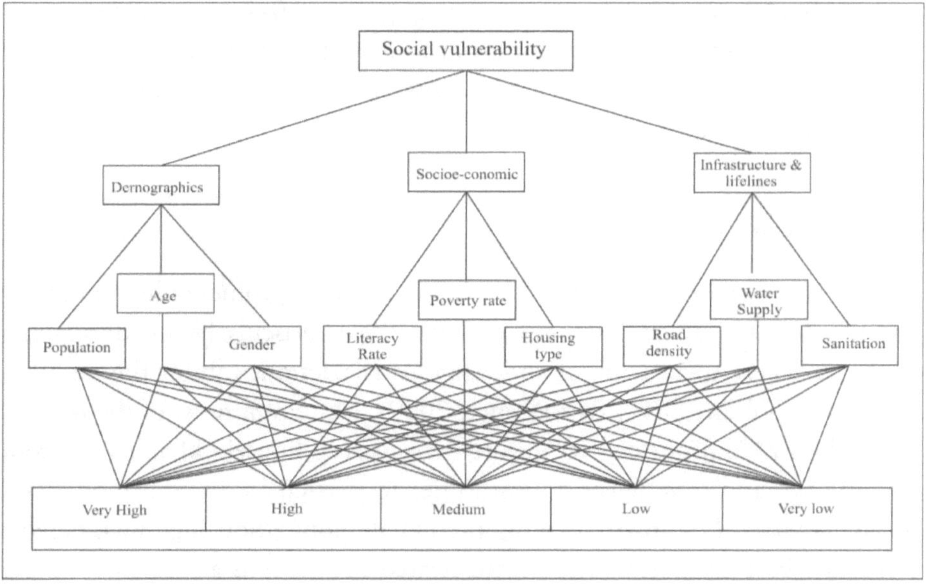


**Fig. 5.9:** Decision hierarchy model for social vulnerability assessment.

## 5.4.1 Population Density

Population density is regarded as one of the most important indicators in determining social vulnerability. Crowdedness caused by high density may introduce many problems during and after a flood event, including evacuation difficulties (Chakrabortyet al.2005) and the increased risk of disease transmission (Anderson 1992). The parameter is also used to assess "elements at risk" while estimating flood risk (Tingsanchali and Karim 2005). Therefore, the indicator of population density was given higher importance at all levels of the decision hierarchy. It was calculated as the total number of people residing in a census tract divided by its total area in sq.km. Higher importance is allocated for higher density, while lower importance is given to lower density (see Table 5.6).

## 5.4.2 Children and Elderly Population/Dependent Population

Age group of 0-14 and above 60 are generally dependent population and they are highly vulnerable to natural hazards because of their restricted mobility and difficulty with evacuation during emergencies. A total number of populations for these groups was extracted and classified into four categories: aged 0-4,

5-9, 10-14 and over 60. Children in the age group of 0-4 in the study area are given maximum weight in the lowest decision hierarchy (See Table 5.6) and the age group of 5-9, 60+ were given subsequent importance in the pairwise comparison (see Table 5.7).

### 5.4.3 Gender

Gender is an important consideration when depicting vulnerability to natural hazards (Cutter et al.2003, Liverman 1990).Particularly in developing countries where socio cultural and religious restrictions inhibit the mobility of women (Sultana 2010, Ray-Bennett 2009). Moreover, most of the females in Paschim Medinipur district devote their lives to household activities from an early age and have fewer opportunities to participate in educational and social activities then males, making the female population highly vulnerable to natural hazards. That's why hazard related mortality is also higher among women than men (Chowdhury et al. 1993). Therefore, higher importance was given to females in the gender variable (see Table 5.6).

### 5.4.4 Poverty

The linkage between hazards, vulnerability and poverty are complex (Few 2003); however, many studies assert that low-income people suffer the most from natural hazards (Dasgupta 2007). For example, an account of UN 2003, the total number of deaths from floods between 1975 to 2000 revealed that the low-income groups had the highest number of deaths while high –income groups accounted for around 1%. The study further ascertained that 50% of the deaths occurred in the low-income category, while 49% occurred in the middle income group. It's clearly shows the association between poverty and flood vulnerability. Higher importance and subsequent weighting are allocated to the greater proportion of poor people in each community and the lowest weight given to the lowest proportion (see Table 5.6).

### 5.4.5 Types of Housing

The quality of housing is an important indicator when assessing vulnerability for a given area (Satterthwaite 2010). Most of the houses in rural area are katcha type and many houses built on floodplains and in close proximity to water bodies tend to exhibit greater vulnerability. Three types of housing information are available in the study area: katcha, semi-pucca and pucca. These housing types were incorporated into the vulnerability evaluation. As katcha houses are poor in quality and subject to severe damage from floods, they were given higher Weight (see Table 5.6) than the other two categories in the pairwise comparison matrix (see Table 5.7).

### 5.4.6 Illiteracy

This variable is certainly important when assessing vulnerability. Educated people are generally more aware of extreme events and they play an important role in the reduction of damage caused by flood (Paul and Routray 2010). The number of illiterate population (males and females) are used with the assumption that illiterate people are dependent on others to prepare and evacuate themselves during a forthcoming disaster. Thus, the highest illiteracy rates of the district are given the highest importance when allocating weight in the decision hierarchy (see Table 5.6)

### 5.4.7 Sources of Water

Access to safe drinking water is an important key indicator for flood risk management. Several studies demonstrated that the outbreak of water-borne disease is widespread during floods due to the increased transmission of pathogens (Tapsell et al. 2002). Mixing of drain water, well water is also polluted in the time of flood. So, drinking water exceeds standard limits and pure drinking water becomes scarce in the time of floods. There are a number of water sources for drinking purposes namely; taps, tube wells, wells, ponds and rivers are available in the study area. Therefore, other water sources received the highest weighting, as people relying on this source like to be at a greater risk of water-borne disease. Well, tube well and tap water's weights are allocated with subsequent importance (see Table 5.6).

### 5.4.8 Sanitation

The sanitation of Paschim Medinipur district is not encouraging, as thousands of people are at risk of communicable diseases after a flood event. Due to the recurring nature of floods, sanitation data per GP is taken into account and classified as access to safe sanitation, no sanitation and other means of sanitation. The no sanitation category was given the most weight, followed by the other mean of sanitation (see Table 5.6).

## 5.4.9  Road Density

Infrastructure facilities such as roads and rail networks are in the category of "lifeline" and play a significant role in evacuation and post event relief and recovery. As these networks are important in determining the lifeline of a community, the density of roads was calculated from the Geo-Eye image with the GP boundary and weighted using the AHP (see Table 5.6).

Table 6.7 represents the pairwise comparison matrices for demographics, socioeconomic and infrastructure and lifeline criteria with their corresponding consistency ratios. The census values for the indicators were first converted into ratios from count and subsequently the weights were assigned to the ratio. The normalization was then performed using the following equation:

$$S = \frac{max - x}{max - min} \tag{5.7}$$

Where, S is the normalized value, min and max represents the minimum and maximum values of the indicator variable respectively and 'x' is the weighted value of the community. The derived social vulnerability index (SVI) indicated that the higher the value, the greater the vulnerability of a particular community.

**■ Table 5.6: Decision Hierarchy Model for Socioeconomic and Infrastructure Vulnerability**

| 1 | 2 | | 3 | | 4 | |
|---|---|---|---|---|---|---|
| | Criteria | Weight | Criteria | Weight | Criteria | Weight |
| Social Vulnerability Index | Demographic | 0.567 | Population Density(km2) | 0.619 | <400 | 0.05 |
| | | | | | 400-800 | 0.06 |
| | | | | | 800-1200 | 0.17 |
| | | | | | 1200-2400 | 0.25 |
| | | | | | >2400 | 0.47 |
| | | | Age in year (Dependent Population) | 0.284 | 0-4 | 0.597 |
| | | | | | 5-9 | 0.231 |
| | | | | | 10-14 | 0.047 |
| | | | | | >60 | 0.125 |
| | | | Gender | 0.097 | Male | 0.250 |
| | | | | | Female | 0.750 |

| 1 | 2 | | 3 | | 4 | |
|---|---|---|---|---|---|---|
| | **Criteria** | **Weight** | **Criteria** | **Weight** | **Criteria** | **Weight** |
| Social Vulnerability Index | Socio-Economic | 0.320 | B.P.L House Hold/Poverty (%) | 0.484 | <7 | 0.053 |
| | | | | | 7-9 | 0.112 |
| | | | | | 9-11 | 0.253 |
| | | | | | >11 | 0.582 |
| | | | Type of Housing (%) | 0.301 | Katcha | 0.690 |
| | | | | | Semi-pucca | 0.244 |
| | | | | | Pucca | 0.066 |
| | | | Illiteracy (%) | 0.143 | <15 | 0.036 |
| | | | | | 15-25 | 0.069 |
| | | | | | 25-35 | 0.136 |
| | | | | | 35-45 | 0.262 |
| | | | | | >45 | 0.497 |
| | Infrastructure and Lifelines | 0.123 | Source of water | 0.620 | Tap Water | 0.063 |
| | | | | | Tube Well | 0.13 |
| | | | | | Well | 0.388 |
| | | | | | Others | 0.428 |
| | | | Sanitation (%) | 0.240 | Sanitized | 0.078 |
| | | | | | No Sanitation | 0.688 |
| | | | | | Others | 0.234 |
| | | | Road Density (%) | 0.140 | <0.2 | 0.042 |
| | | | | | 0.2-0.4 | 0.075 |
| | | | | | 0.4-0.8 | 0.134 |
| | | | | | 0.8-1.6 | 0.264 |
| | | | | | >1.6 | 0.485 |

■ **Table 5.7:  Pairwise Comparison Matrix for Social Vulnerability Indicators(Criteria at level 2 of decision hierarchy model)**

| | 1 | 2 | 3 |
|---|---|---|---|
| 1. Demographic | 1 | 2 | 4 |
| 2. Socio-economic | ½ | 1 | 3 |
| 3. Infrastructure and Lifelines | 1/4 | 1/3 | 1 |

**CR: 0.01**

**■ Table 5.7:** Pairwise Comparison Matrix for Social Vulnerability Indicators (Criteria at level 3 of decision hierarchy model)

| Demographic | 1 | 2 | 3 |
| --- | --- | --- | --- |
| 1. Population Density (km²) | 1 | 3 | 5 |
| 2 Age | 1/3 | 1 | 4 |
| 3. Gender | 1/5 | 1/4 | 1 |

**CR: 0.08**

| Socio-economic | 1 | 2 | 3 |
| --- | --- | --- | --- |
| 1. Illiteracy | 1 | 1/4 | 1/3 |
| 2 B.P.L Households | 4 | 1 | 2 |
| 3. Type of Housing | 3 | 1/2 | 1 |

**CR: 0.02**

| Infrastructure and Lifelines | 1 | 2 | 3 |
| --- | --- | --- | --- |
| 1. Sources of Water | 1 | 3 | 4 |
| 2. Sanitation | 1/3 | 1 | 2 |
| 3. Road Density | 1/4 | 1/2 | 1 |

**CR: 0.02**

**■ Table 5.7:** Pairwise Comparison Matrix for Social Vulnerability Indicators (Criteria at level 4 of decision hierarchy model)

| Population Density (km²) | 1 | 2 | 3 | 4 | 5 |
| --- | --- | --- | --- | --- | --- |
| 1. <400 | 1 | 1/2 | 1/4 | 1/6 | 1/7 |
| 2. 400–800 | 2 | 1 | 1/3 | 1/5 | 1/6 |
| 3. 800–1200 | 4 | 3 | 1 | 1/3 | 1/5 |
| 4. 1200–2400 | 6 | 5 | 3 | 1 | 1/3 |
| 5. >2400 | 7 | 6 | 5 | 3 | 1 |

**CR: 0.063**

| Road Density (km²) | 1 | 2 | 3 | 4 | 5 |
|---|---|---|---|---|---|
| 1. <0.2 | 1 | 1/3 | 1/4 | 1/6 | 1/7 |
| 2. 0.2-0.4 | 3 | 1 | 1/3 | 1/5 | 1/6 |
| 3. 0.4-0.8 | 4 | 3 | 1 | 1/3 | 1/5 |
| 4. 0.8-1.6 | 6 | 5 | 3 | 1 | 1/3 |
| 5. >1.6 | 7 | 6 | 5 | 3 | 1 |
| CR: 0.068 | | | | | |

■ **Table 5.7:** Pairwise Comparison Matrix for Social Vulnerability Indicators (Criteria at level 4 of decision hierarchy model)

| Illiteracy Rate (%) | 1 | 2 | 3 | 4 | 5 |
|---|---|---|---|---|---|
| 1. <15 | 1 | 1/3 | 1/5 | 1/7 | 1/8 |
| 2. 15-25 | 3 | 1 | 1/3 | 1/5 | 1/7 |
| 3. 25-35 | 5 | 3 | 1 | 1/3 | 1/5 |
| 4. 35-45 | 7 | 5 | 3 | 1 | 1/3 |
| 5. >45 | 8 | 7 | 5 | 3 | 1 |
| CR: 0.063 | | | | | |

| Age in year (Dependent Population) | 1 | 2 | 3 | 4 |
|---|---|---|---|---|
| 1. 0-4 | 1 | 4 | 8 | 4 |
| 2. 5-9 | 1/4 | 1 | 5 | 3 |
| 3. 10-14 | 1/8 | 1/5 | 1 | 1/4 |
| 4. >60 | 1/4 | 1/3 | 4 | 1 |
| CR: 0.08 | | | | |

| Poverty (%) | 1 | 2 | 3 | 4 |
|---|---|---|---|---|
| 1. <7 | 1 | 1/3 | 1/5 | 1/8 |
| 2. 7-9 | 3 | 1 | 1/3 | 1/6 |
| 3. 9-11 | 5 | 3 | 1 | 1/3 |
| 4. >11 | 8 | 6 | 3 | 1 |
| CR: 0.04 | | | | |

| Water Sources | 1 | 2 | 3 | 4 |
|---|---|---|---|---|
| 1. Others | 1 | 1 | 5 | 6 |
| 2. Well | 1 | 1 | 4 | 5 |
| 3. Tube Well | 1/5 | 1/4 | 1 | 3 |
| 4. Tap Water | 1/6 | 1/5 | 1/3 | 1 |
| CR: 0.04 | | | | |

| Type of Housing | 1 | 2 | 3 |
|---|---|---|---|
| 1. Pucca | 1 | 1/5 | 1/8 |
| 2. Semi-pucca | 5 | 1 | 1/4 |
| 3. Katcha | 8 | 4 | 1 |
| CR: 0.08 | | | |

■ **Table 5.7:** Pairwise Comparison Matrix for Social Vulnerability Indicators( **Criteria at level 4 of decision hierarchy model)**

| Sanitation | 1 | 2 | 3 |
|---|---|---|---|
| 1. Sanitized | 1 | 3 | 4 |
| 2. Others | 1/3 | 1 | 2 |
| 3. No Sanitation | 1/4 | 1/2 | 1 |
| CR: 0.07 | | | |

## 5.5  Coping Capacity Analysis

To develop the interventions required for effective disaster management, it is important to analyse the status of a community in terms of its capability to endure the effects of environmental hazards (Anderson and Woodrod 1998). This would allow emergency managers to systematically identify the communities with the least capacity to sustain during floods and subsequently prioritize the need to improve their capability to cope with extremes. The selected indicators for coping capacity analysis are the total literacy rate, per capita hospitals, per capita flood shelters and flood awareness (see Fig. 5.10), as shown in the decision hierarchy model (see Table 5.8). For these indicators, higher importance was given to the sub-criteria, with higher values in the pairwise comparison computation (see Table 5.9) so that areas with better coping capacity could be mapped.

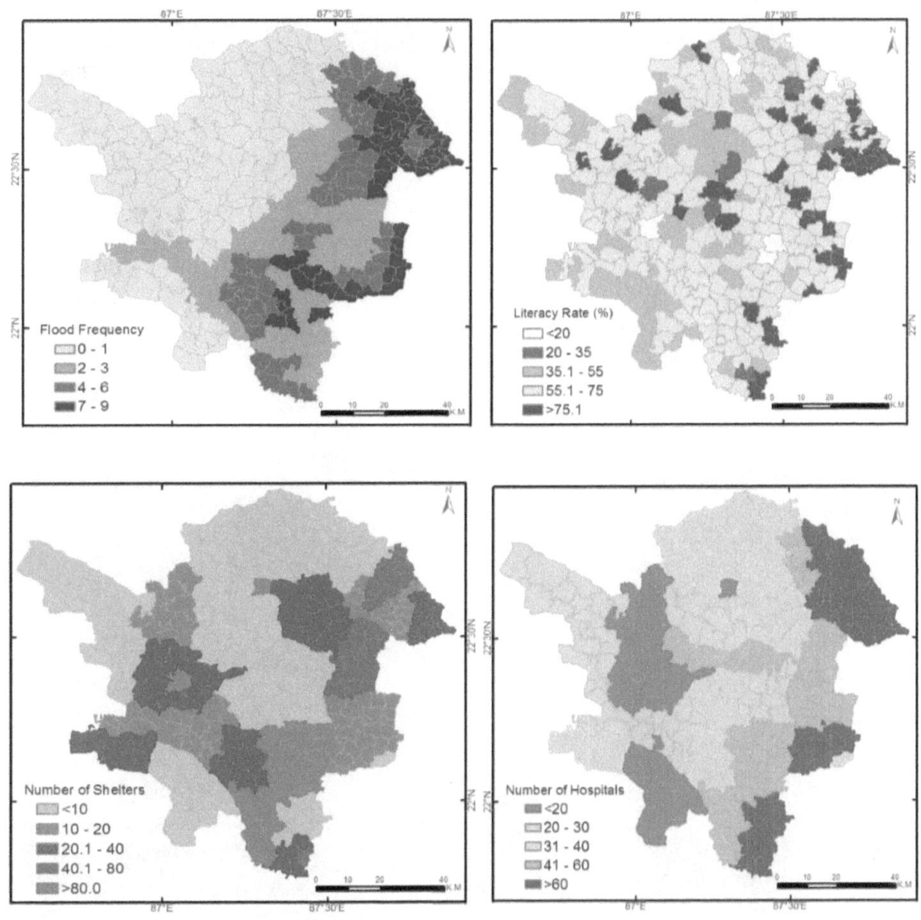



**Fig. 5.10:** Distribution of coping capacity indicators.

**■ Table 5.8:** Decision hierarchy model for Coping Capacity Criteria

| 1 | 2 | | 3 | |
|---|---|---|---|---|
| | Criteria | Weight | Criteria | Weight |
| | Flood Frequency (Awareness) | 0.582 | 0-1 | 0.062 |
| | | | 1-3 | 0.108 |
| | | | 4-6 | 0.267 |
| | | | 7-9 | 0.563 |
| Coping Capacity Index | Literacy Rate (%) | 0.238 | <20 | 0.040 |
| | | | 20-35 | 0.074 |
| | | | 35.1-55 | 0.142 |
| | | | 55.1-75 | 0.248 |
| | | | >75.1 | 0.496 |

| 1 | 2 | | 3 | |
|---|---|---|---|---|
| | Criteria | Weight | Criteria | Weight |
| Coping Capacity Index | No. of Hospitals (%) | 0.070 | <20 | 0.038 |
| | | | 20-30 | 0.054 |
| | | | 31-40 | 0.137 |
| | | | 41-60 | 0.280 |
| | | | >60 | 0.491 |
| | No. of Shelters (%) | 0.110 | <10 | 0.039 |
| | | | 10-20 | 0.056 |
| | | | 20.1-40 | 0.134 |
| | | | 40.1-80 | 0.269 |
| | | | >80 | 0.502 |

■ **Table 5.9:** Pairwise Comparison Matrix for Coping Capacity Indicators **(Criteria at level 2 of decision hierarchy model)**

| | 1 | 2 | 3 | 4 |
|---|---|---|---|---|
| 1. Flood Frequency (Awareness) | 1 | 4 | 5 | 6 |
| 2. Literacy Rate | 1/4 | 1 | 3 | 4 |
| 3. No. of Shelters | 1/5 | 1/3 | 1 | 2 |
| 4. No. of Hospital | 1/6 | 1/4 | 1/2 | 1 |
| **CR: 0.05** | | | | |

■ **Table 5.9:** Pairwise Comparison Matrix for Coping Capacity Indicators **(Criteria at level 3 of decision hierarchy model)**

| Literacy Rate (%) | 1 | 2 | 3 | 4 | 5 |
|---|---|---|---|---|---|
| 1. <20 | 1 | 1/3 | 1/5 | 1/6 | 1/7 |
| 2. 20-35 | 3 | 1 | 1/3 | 1/4 | 1/7 |
| 3. 35.1-55 | 5 | 3 | 1 | 1/3 | 1/5 |
| 4. 55.1-75 | 6 | 4 | 3 | 1 | 1/3 |
| 5. >75.1 | 7 | 7 | 5 | 3 | 1 |
| **CR: 0.07** | | | | | |

| No. of Flood Shelters (%) | 1 | 2 | 3 | 4 | 5 |
|---|---|---|---|---|---|
| 1. <10 | 1 | 1/2 | 1/5 | 1/7 | 1/8 |
| 2. 10-20 | 2 | 1 | 1/3 | 1/6 | 1/8 |
| 3. 20.1-40 | 5 | 3 | 1 | 1/3 | 1/5 |
| 4. 40.1-80 | 7 | 6 | 3 | 1 | 1/3 |
| 5. >80 | 8 | 8 | 5 | 3 | 1 |
| **CR: 0.05** | | | | | |

| No. of Hospitals (%) | 1 | 2 | 3 | 4 | 5 |
|---|---|---|---|---|---|
| 1. <20 | 1 | 1/2 | 1/5 | 1/7 | 1/8 |
| 2. 20-30 | 2 | 1 | 1/4 | 1/6 | 1/8 |
| 3. 31-40 | 5 | 4 | 1 | 1/4 | 1/5 |
| 4. 41-60 | 7 | 6 | 4 | 1 | 1/3 |
| 5. >60 | 8 | 8 | 5 | 3 | 1 |
| CR: 0.07 | | | | | |

| Flood Frequency (Awareness) | 1 | 2 | 3 | 4 |
|---|---|---|---|---|
| 1. 0-1 | 1 | 1/2 | 1/5 | 1/7 |
| 2. 1-3 | 2 | 1 | 1/3 | 1/5 |
| 3. 4-6 | 5 | 3 | 1 | 1/3 |
| 4. 7-9 | 7 | 5 | 3 | 1 |
| CR: 0.03 | | | | |

## 5.5.1 Flood Awareness

The classic natural hazard paradigm shows that prior experience of hazards plays a crucial role in mitigating the negative consequences of floods and preparing against disaster (Paul 1997). Therefore, the flood frequency variable was derived by overlaying multi-temporal flood maps from 2011, 2013, 2015 and 2016 which are collected from BHUVAN disaster series and on the community database. The highest weight was given to this variable among other coping capacity variables in the second level of the decision hierarchy, as disaster preparedness is an important factor for a community to cope with natural disaster. A pairwise comparison matrix prepared for Coping Capacity Index (CCI) by AHP method.

## 5.5.2 Literacy Rate

Education is an important human wealth that allows people to make appropriate decision and takes pertinent mitigation measure to withstand or recover from natural disaster (D'Oyley et al. 1994). It also affects people's lifetime earnings (Cutter et al. 2003). Literature suggests that households with higher levels of education cope better than households with lower level of education (Paul and Routray 2011). To examine this proposition, the total literacy rate was used and weighted for each community to assist in understanding their coping capacity (see Table 5.8). The highest weight was assigned to communities with the highest literacy rate for both males and females, and lowest weight was assigned to those with lower literacy rate.

### 5.5.3 Per Capita Shelters and Hospitals

The availability of shelters and health-care facilities in hazard-prone areas is a vital indicator of coping capacity of a particular community, a factor that gained significant importance for flood management and disaster preparedness planning (Sanyal and Lu 2009; Khan 1991). A database containing the locations of educational institutes, community, religious centres and different medical facilities calculate as the per capita shelters and hospitals in the study area. The higher the numbers of shelters and hospitals in each community, the higher the weight in terms of the third level of the decision hierarchy; however, the highest weight was given to the per capita shelter indicator in the second level of the decision hierarchy (see Table 5.8). The resulting Coping Capacity Index (CCI) indicates that the higher the index, the better the coping capacity of a particular community.

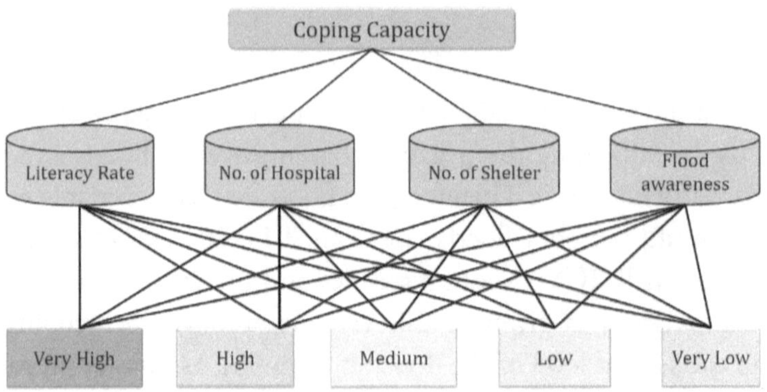


**Fig. 5.11:** Decision hierarchy model for Coping Capacity Analysis.

### 5.6 Derivation of Composite Vulnerability Index (CVI)

A composite vulnerability map was produced by combining vulnerability and coping capacity maps using WLC technique. An equal weighting scheme was adopted for this purpose (Cutter et al. 2003). To combine three maps and estimate CVI, first of all, mean PVI score for each community was derived by intersecting it with the community boundary file. Then, the CCI was linearly inversed so that the lower the CCI value, the higher the contribution of a particular community to flood vulnerability. The following equation was used to derive the overall vulnerability or CVI:

**CVI = 0.33*PVI + 0.33*SVI + 0.33*CCI** (5.8)

It should be noted that the inversed CCI = max − CCI

## 5.7 Flood Risk Assessment

A flood risk map is one of the most important measures for preventing flood loss potential (Yoshino and Yoshikawa 1985). A flood risk map based on fine spatial units (e.g., at the community level) is particularly useful for planners and emergency managers when developing appropriate counter measures. Flood risk is defined in this study as a function of flood hazard and vulnerability (Apel et al. 2009). The following equation is used to derive flood risk map in the study area:

**Flood Risk = hazard x vulnerability** (5.9)

To compute flood risk, the mean hazard value for each community was obtained by overlaying the flood hazard map. Finally, the hazard map was multiplied with the composite vulnerability map to derive the spatial distribution of flood risk in the study area. The resulting flood risk map was reclassified into five classes – no risk, low risk, moderate risk, high and very high risk – according to the intensity of flood risk; thus the map supports visualization of flood risk in the study area.

### 5.7.1 Physical Vulnerability

The PVI map revealed that areas closer to water bodies or near to river with a low elevation (<5 m.) constitute higher vulnerability to flood (see Fig. 5.12). Due to their low elevation and close proximity to river networks communities in these areas are highly susceptible to extreme flood loss also (see Table 6.10). For instance, more than 50% of the population is vulnerable with respect to their locational attribute, as mean distance from active channels. In study area Southern and South-eastern part are in the high to very high vulnerable zones (.82-1.00) in terms of locational and demographic characteristics. In south-eastern direction Ghatal sub-division are highly affected by recurrent flood due to absolute locational factor and also in terms of densely populated and productive nature of the soil. A small percentage of population (2.02%) is in the very low physical vulnerability zone because these zones is highly altitude (>90m). So, those are the locational factor is an important indicator in estimating flood vulnerability in Paschim Medinipur District.

| PV Zone | Value | Population (%) | Mean elevation range (m) | Mean distance to active channel (K.M) |
|---|---|---|---|---|
| Very low | 0-0.26 | 2.02 | >90 | 2 |
| Low | 0.27-0.41 | 37.33 | 60-90 | 1.8 |
| Medium | 0.42-0.57 | 8.33 | 30-60 | 1.5 |
| High | 0.58-0.82 | 32.09 | 5-30 | 0.8 |
| Very high | 0.82-1.00 | 20.57 | <5 | 0.5 |

■ Table 5.10:  Distribution of variables in relation to Physical Vulnerability

## 5.7.2 Social Vulnerability

The SVI map revealed that some of the Eastern, Southern and South-eastern directions of the study area are in the low (0.24-0.36) to very low (0-0.23) social vulnerability in respect of less poverty, high literacy and lower percentage of katcha houses, implying that people in this zone are able to absorb losses relatively quickly. Very high socially vulnerable zone (0.78-1) are distributed along the south and south-eastern margin and also northern and north-western part of the study area. Table 5.11 explains that the social vulnerability of high and very high vulnerable zones is due to high levels of poverty, a large number of katcha houses and high population density. In contrast, access to safe water and sanitation is very low, suggesting a degree of vulnerability to floods. The resulting map also revealed that few communities in western and middle part of the study area very low social vulnerability (0-0.23).

## 5.7.3 Coping Capacity

A coping capacity map showed different results compared to those of vulnerability maps, partly because of the integration of the flood awareness variable into the derivation of the coping capacity of communities. However, a coping capacity indicator can be conceptualized as a form of the adaption capacity of individuals or a community in the study area (Few 2003). Communities that experience floods almost every year exhibit a very high coping capacity (>0.87) and which communities did not experience floods in a regular way, they exhibit a very low coping capacity (<0.31).

**■ Table 5.11:  Distribution of variables regarding the SVI** (*SVI: Social Vulnerability Index*)

| SV zone | Population Density (sq. km) | Poverty (%) | Katcha Houses (%) | Water Sources | | | Sanitation | |
|---|---|---|---|---|---|---|---|---|
| | | | | Tap (%) | Tube Well and Well (%) | Pond and Others (%) | Sanitized (%) | Others and no Sanitation (%) |
| Very low (0-0.23) | 34750.64 | 6.05 | 4.08 | 15.8 | 2.09 | 4.1 | 10.4 | 2.5 |
| Low (0.24-0.36) | 34175.73 | 11.10 | 24.42 | 52.1 | 16.2 | 20.1 | 39.7 | 30.6 |
| Medium (0.37-0.51) | 49960.2 | 18.94 | 30.93 | 25.7 | 38.21 | 35.0 | 33.8 | 30.0 |
| High (0.52-0.77) | 46444.42 | 29.07 | 24.46 | 4.2 | 18.0 | 16.4 | 7.1 | 21.5 |
| Very high (0.78-1.00) | 54297.26 | 34.84 | 16.10 | 2.1 | 25.5 | 24.4 | 9.0 | 15.9 |

## 5.7.4 Composite Vulnerability

This study conceived that the coping capacity is part of vulnerability assessment (UNDP 1992) and should be included in the estimation of the overall vulnerability of a particular area. A CVI was therefore mapped out by combining PVI, SVI and CCI (see Fig. 5.13) and further reclassified according to the severity of vulnerability. The population distribution in each zone indicated that 27 and 15% of people are located in the high and very high zones of vulnerability respectively. The percentage of katcha houses, which are usually home of poor people, is higher in the very high vulnerable zone (39%). In contrast, the number of semi-pucca houses, which are home of middle and lower-middle class households, is highest in the higher vulnerable zone (see Table 5.11). With the forecast increase in Paschim Medinipur's population, the district's flood vulnerability will increase; therefore, it is important to understand the spatial distribution of vulnerable people and property, which could allow an efficient management of future floods.

**■ Table 5.12:  Distribution of variables relating to CVI**

| CVI Zone | Value | Population (%) | Katcha Houses (%) | Semi-Pucca (%) | Pucca (%) | Mean literacy rate |
|---|---|---|---|---|---|---|
| Very high | 0.83-1 | 15.3 | 38.5 | 9.3 | 14.2 | 78.6 |
| High | 0.69-0.83 | 27.2 | 29.3 | 37.4 | 21.1 | 68.5 |
| Medium | 0.45-0.68 | 24.5 | 15.7 | 30.7 | 27.2 | 60.2 |
| Low | 0.20-0.44 | 20.00 | 9.04 | 15.6 | 23.1 | 58.1 |
| Very low | 0-0.19 | 13.00 | 7.1 | 7.0 | 14.4 | 49.6 |

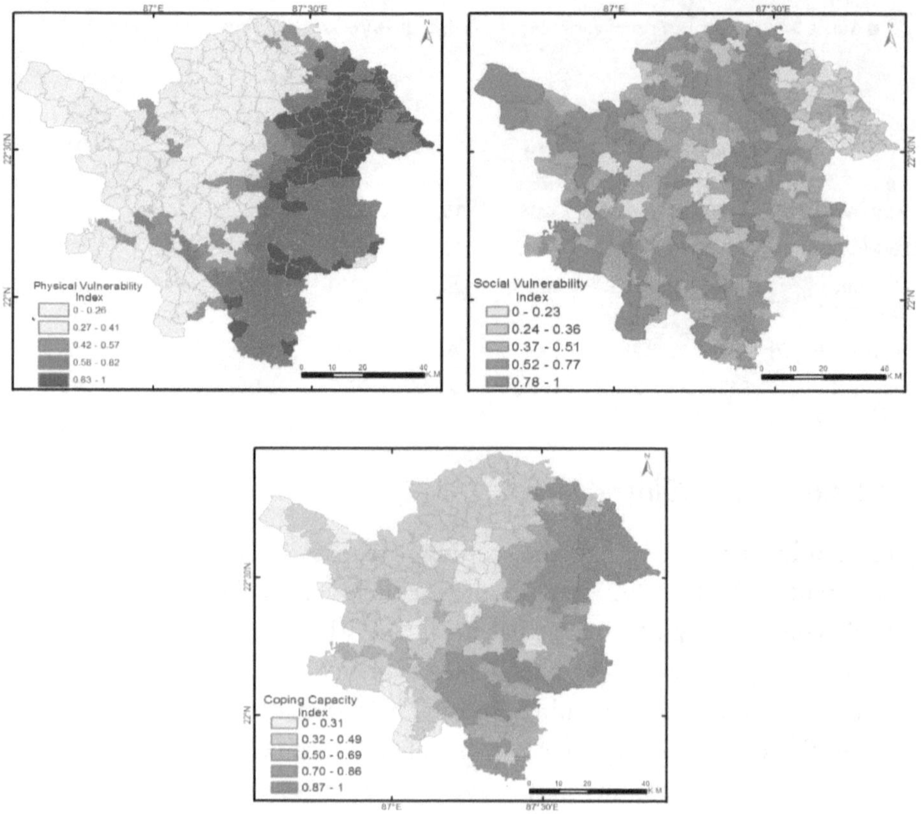

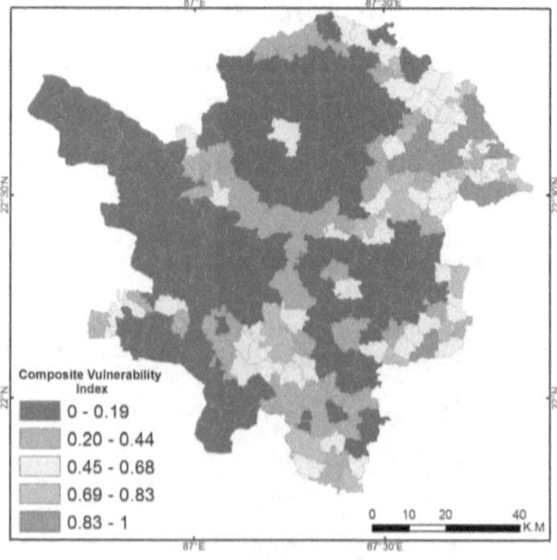

**Fig. 5.12:** Spatial patterns of Physical and Social Vulnerability and Coping Capacity.

**Fig. 5.13:** Spatial pattern of Composite Vulnerability Index at Panchayat level.

## 5.7.5 Flood Risk Mapping

Flood risk map was derived by multiplying the mean hazard score and composite vulnerability map. While hazard represent physical process, flood vulnerability indicates susceptibility to damage and the risk of human lives. To understand the human dimensions of flood risk, population and other parameter were intersected with the derived risk map and statistical analysis was conducted. Most of the elevated places have been no risk and low elevated areas are likely to be higher at the risk spectrum.

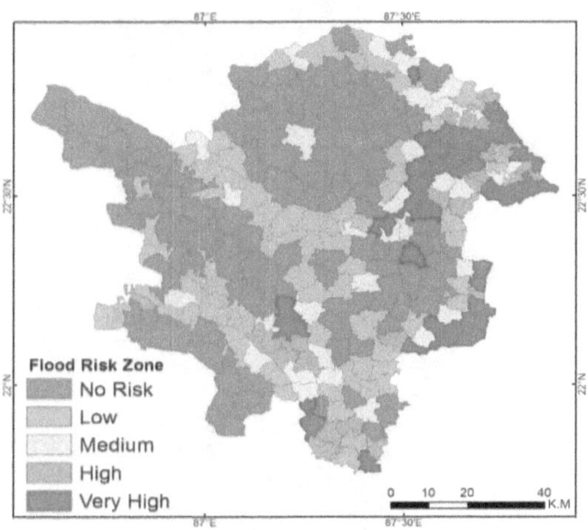


**Fig. 5.14:** Flood risk map of Paschim Medinipur District at Panchayat level.

Using population census data from 2011 and the socio-economic distribution, Table 5.11 summarizes vulnerable subgroups into different flood risk zones. A total of 24.25% of the population lives in high to very high flood risk zones, which is further compounded by the number of females, young (0-14), elderly (>60) and illiterate people. At least 17.76% of housing units (mud house) are located in high to very high-risk zones. As noted earlier, the study is based on 2011 census data and does not take into account potential population growth in the study area, which may underestimate the actual population at risk. However, the flood risk map developed can be used as base line information for the development of adaption measures to mitigate future losses driven by flood hazard.

■ **Table 5.13:** Distribution of variables in different flood risk zones

| Flood Risk Zone | Population | % | Male | % | Female | % | Young (0-14) | % | Illiterate | % | Mud House | % |
|---|---|---|---|---|---|---|---|---|---|---|---|---|
| Very High | 966277 | 17.02 | 519505 | 16.46 | 439511 | 17.42 | 157230 | 16.76 | 245643 | 13.72 | 2332.73 | 11.84 |
| High | 410365 | 7.23 | 213701 | 6.77 | 202664 | 8.04 | 47382 | 7.53 | 114355 | 6.39 | 1166.9 | 5.92 |
| Medium | 433798 | 7.64 | 310635 | 9.84 | 279225 | 11.07 | 74998 | 10.3 | 173684 | 9.7 | 1997.4 | 10.14 |
| Low | 1510312 | 26.6 | 806865 | 25.56 | 516964 | 20.49 | 166582 | 25.46 | 462907 | 25.85 | 5187.44 | 26.33 |
| No Risk | 2358131 | 41.52 | 1305657 | 41.37 | 1084156 | 42.98 | 255095 | 40.12 | 794253 | 44.35 | 9017.95 | 45.77 |

# FLOOD HAZARD MANAGEMENT PRACTICES AND IMPACT OF FLOOD PREVENTION MEASURE ON FLOOD CONTROL

Flood Management in India, District Disaster Management Plans: Changing Context of Disaster Management – General guidelines of DDMP – District Disaster Management Plan: A Model Template, Institutional Mitigation Plan, Existing Flood Management Strategy in Paschim Medinipur District: Construction of Earthen Embankment – Raised Platforms for affected Villages – Bank Erosion and Protecting Works, SWOT Analysis: Pre-disaster Phase – During disaster Phase – Post disaster Phase, Suggested Management Strategies: Watershed Management – Flood Plain Zoning – Flood Forecasting and Warning – Community Participitation – Disaster Prepardness and Response Planning – Flood Fighting – Disaster Relief – Flood Insurance – Crop Management in the Flood Plains. Perspective on community-based management.

Management of flood is a process or strategy that is implemented when any type of flood catastrophic event takes place. The process may be initiated when anything threatens to disrupt normal operations or put the lives of human beings at risk. Flood management of river basins is an ancient and uninterrupted endeavour all over world, works in this line recorded in the histories of most early civilizations. Chinese built the banks of flood 2500 years ago on the Hwang Ho and that the Babylonians diverted the flood waters of the Euphrates into natural dumps to defend the city of Babylon. Nevertheless, it was Egyptian king Amenenhat, who built flood embankments on both sides of the Nile and disarticulate flood waters into lake Moeris (Nixon, 1963). In Britian the Romans pioneered use the flood embankment to reduced flooding from the sea.

Many scientists and agencies like United Nations (1951), Hoyt and Langbien (1955), Lensly and Franzini (1972) have been done immense work for flood hazard mitigation. Pleasant works of Mucklestone (1976),

Thampillai and Mugrave (1985), Ashan (1988) and Roy (1991) on the line of flood hazard management deserve special attention. In Indian context Beraria (1986), Goswami (1982), Misra (1990) and Kar (1997) are also worked of this line. Floods have been frequent phenomena in many segments of Indian rivers which are the result of natural and physical phenomena; causing loss of lives, public property and bringing unuttered misery of the people, especially those in the rural areas. They are too much dependent upon the rainfall characteristics, topographic characteristics and shape and size of river channel. Unsystematic and thoughtless activities of the people aggravate the problems of flood in upper catchment as well as in the flood plains. It should be admitted that there can be no such thing as an "absolute flood control" or "full proof protection" for all magnitudes. So long mankind is not in a position to have some control on modifying the rainfall pattern or its distribution, natural floods bound to occur. It is however well accepted that flood management namely living with flood situation but with maximum mitigation of its adverse effects on mankind, can be achieved (Talukdar, 2005). The concept of flood management aims for such planned measures, which ensure profitable and economic utilization of flood plains and water resource for the benefit of mankind while simultaneously in sorting that during the periods of high floods, there is no severe damage to the extent possible (Chakravarty and Sing, 1998). The disaster due to floods can be mitigated by taking structural and non-structural measure.

## 6.1 Flood Management in India

In India, flood plains are not being developed in a regular way. Therefore, the damage and loss of life, property and cattle due to floods are increasing rapidly. The unprecedented floods of 1954, the Union Minister for Irrigation, Planning and Power, placed before the Parliament on 3rd September 1954, two statements namely "Floods in India – problems and remedies" and "The floods in the country". From that time the National Flood Control Programme was launched in 1954, for the first time in India. Therefore, the Government of India decide to set up the Rashtriya Barh Ayog (National Flood Commission) in 1976 to sprout a coordinate, integrated and specific approach to the flood control problems in the country and to draw out a national plan building for implementation in the future. A large number of flood control works were taken under the direction of Central Flood Control Board and at the state level by the state Flood Control Board. However, this type of provision has not been enough to control the natural hazard like flood. Beside that different five year plans were taken to reducing the floods in view of growing dimension of the problem. In 1987, a National Water Policy was adopted by the National Water Resources Council, Government of India to formulate the plans for flood management. They recommended that "adequate flood cushion should be provided in water storage projects where ever feasible to facilitate better flood management". They also recognised that "physical flood protection works like embankments and dykes will continue to be necessary". Through extensive soil conservation, catchment area treatment, construction of check dams, prevention of deforestation and increase forest area helps the watershed management which could be promoted to reduce the magnitude and intensity of floods. Moreover, for those people who lived in flood plains with built-up settlement and doing economic activity establish a timely warning flood forecasting network which could also be reducing the loss of life and property. Again it was suggested that physical flood protection works like embankments and dykes will continued to be necessary in specific areas, but more emphasis should be given on non-structural measures to minimize the losses and this includes flood plain zoning, land use regulation, flood forecasting, changing crop calendar to suit flood period etc.

## 6.2 District Disaster Management Plans (DDMP)

The district disaster management plan is an operational module for the district disaster management committee to mitigate the intensity of disaster practically with locally available resources. It also assures that immediate response from the existing administrative structure to provide timely relief for disaster-stricken people. For sure it is possible to cut down the impact of disaster by evolving appropriate preparedness, preventive and response plans. Formerly any disaster management known as crisis management function than began with a disaster. Now it is understood that process of mitigation should be performed only after long term preventive and protective measures by adopting appropriate strategies are implemented in the disaster prone areas.

### 6.2.1 Changing Context of Disaster Management

There is a paradigm shift in Disaster Management approach ever since Disaster Management (DM) act 2005 has come into force.

1. From the previous focus primarily on response and relief to prevention and preparedness.
2. Creation of policy, legal and institutional framework, helped by effective statutory and financial support.
3. Building of Disaster Management concerns into the development process and undertaking mitigation measure.
4. Continuous and integrated process of planning, organizing, coordinating and implementing measures in a holistic, participatory, inclusive and eco-friendly manner.

### 6.2.2 General Guidelines of DDMP

1. There shall be a plan of disaster management for the district.
2. It should be prepared by the District Disaster Management Authority (DDMA) consultation with National policy, National Disaster Management Plan and State Disaster Management Plan.
3. It has to be approved by the State Authority.
4. The district plan should include-
   a. Ensure the areas in the district vulnerable to different forms of disasters.
   b. The measure to be taken, for the prevention and mitigation of disaster by the Government Departments at the district level and local authorities in the district.
   c. The capacity building, preparedness and response measures as lay down by the Government Departments at the district level and local authorities in the district to threatening any disaster situation or disaster.
   d. The response plans and procedures in the event of disaster are-
      i. Allocation of responsibilities to departments of the Government at the district level and the local authorities in the district.
      ii. Endeavour response to disaster and relief thereof.
      iii. Procurement of essential resources.
      iv. Establishment of communication links and
      v. The dissemination of information to the people.

    e.   Establish stockpiles of relief and rescue materials or ensure preparedness to make such materials available at a short notice.

    f.   Such other matters as may be required by the state authority.

    g.   The district plan shall be reviewed and updated annually.

## 6.2.3 District Disaster Management Plan: A Model Template

National Institute of Disaster Management (NIDM) under the Ministry of Home Affairs is a pinnacle institute for policy advocacy and capacity building in disaster management of the country. It has been doing pioneering work in areas of disaster management mitigation, preparedness, response, reconstruction and rehabilitation using a multi-disaster risk management framework having the agreement of the Government of India and other stakeholders (Fig.6.1).

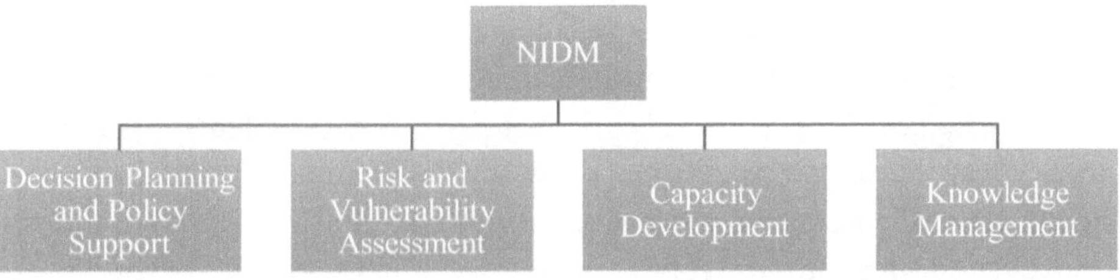


**Fig. 6.1:** A Model Template of DDMP

An assessment of district profile is paramount significance, which provides an overview of the district in terms of physical factors like geographical area, climate, topography, drainage, soils, landholding patterns and socio-economic factors such as economy, literacy, occupational pattern, per capita income, livelihood patterns, and critical establishment etc. for proper assessment of hazard, risk, vulnerability and capacity (HRVC) analysis. Since, HRVC analysis is most important part of the plan as the entire planning process is based on its outcome.

A disaster management plan focusing on hazard, risk, vulnerability and resource assessment which improves the level of response following a calamity on one hand and provides insights to link in with development initiatives on the other hand. The district administration is the nodal point for implementing the all government plans and activities. The district plans developed by district administration are available with NIDM and Ministry of Home Affairs were examined and guidelines for DDMP are evolved (NIDM, 2005).

From HRVC analysis we are knowing that the type of disaster that the district is prone to. We also know that history of hazards, vulnerable areas, impact analysis of the worst cases, the people and infrastructure that is prone to the risk. Whole vulnerability assessment of a hazard prone area deals with the physical, socio-economic, lifeline and infrastructure vulnerability. HRVC analysis should also include resource inventory, capacity analysis, preparedness analysis in terms of network of communication systems, medical facilities, fire stations, flood and cyclone shelters with their capacity, presence of NGO'S and other volunteers etc., so as to enable quick response (NIDM,2005).

### 6.2.4 Institutional Mitigation Plan

The modalities during a disastrous occurrence have immense importance considering the fact. The strategies of each and every government and departments such as army, inter- institutional communication mechanisms and besides them the NGOs and other related social welfare organisations should have to be active and work out side by side in order to get control over the oddities. It will provide certain assistance to the victimised both from psychological and socio-economical perspectives. Hence the mitigation plans and programmes should have to be specific especially sector specific in all concerned as found in the HRVC analysis. It should deal with both structural and non-structural aspects of the situation. For implementing the mitigation modalities, identification of several departments and community mitigation measures should be rational. An organised training strategy has to be formed for every government and non-governmental units in the district. The mitigation plan should follow the followings-

i.    Operational readiness of facilities, equipments and stores.
ii.   Setting up of emergency operating centres, staff, infrastructure, communication etc.
iii.  Updation of resource inventory before flood or cyclone.
iv.   Management/Skills/Simulation training
v.    Community awareness.

### 6.3 Existing Flood Management Strategy in Paschim Medinipur District

The battle against floods is an unceasing struggle since the days immemorial in the part of the teaming millions of West Bengal as well as Paschim Medinipur district to overcome its hazards. And no part of the world has a monopoly of controlling floods to make the people free from the fear to it. Detailed and systematic statistics are not available regarding the incidence to floods, their intensity, duration and subsequent damage to life and property. A large sum of money is being spent to alleviate the sufferings of the people and to compensate the damages and for their controlling measures.

The controlling measures taken by the state Government in the district to provide effective flood protection works have been studied carefully. The prime structural measures undertaken by the government are-

a.  Construction of earthen embankment
b.  Raised platforms for affected villages
c.  Bank erosion and protecting works
d.  Relief Works

## 6.3.1 Construction of Earthen Embankments

Before independence, embankment construction was only available structural measure of flood control. O' Malley in his Gazetteer has recorded that there was 57 km of flood embankment Murshidabad district on the left bank of the Bhagirathi starting from Bhagabangola to Palassey. But during early British Raj days it was not a liability of the state to protect all the flood prone areas. The Zamindars mainly to protect their crops used to construct earthen bundhs based on local knowledge and requirement and many of them very often failed to serve the purpose in long run. This situation most probably was becoming worse with time affecting the revenue earning of the state. So, O' Malley has also recorded that some of the private embankments were not efficient and breached easily and subsequently were taken over by the Government (1910). Till now some of the embankments are Zamindars bundh which are controlled by the local bodies.

Massive programme of structural measures with the construction of embankments, dams and reservoirs were taken up with flood control as one of the major objectives of the district. Construction of embankments to keep the flood water away from the habitation and agricultural fields is the most widely adopted structural measures in the district. The total length of the embankments in the district 257.98 km on the rivers of Kangsabati, Silabati and Subarnarekha which is the under of West Medinipur division. Only the existing embankments were raised and strengthened to combat flood hazard in the district. In spite of such an extensive network, the problems of floods have increased every year, specially because of breaching of embankments.

The embankments under this division have been severely damaged on flood 2013 and 2015 recently. Since couple of years repair to damages of Ex-Zamindars embankments are not undertaken by the concerned panchayet authorities, it is directly controlled by Govt. of Paschim Medinipur district. Cross Bundhs and Fishing Patts on river bed mainly over river Kaliaghai and Kapaleswari at Sabong, Narayangarh, Gobindapur and Gokulpur areas removed regularly before monsoon. To reduce the frequency of repair of wooden bridge, composite bridge technology has been introduced since September 2015.

Some unfavorable effects of embankments also increase with time. The embankments do not allow the sediments come out of the stream and its slow deposition takes place in the river itself. Therefore, river beds have been raised and decrease the carrying capacity of the rivers and enhanced the breaching tendency of embankments. Again, flood affected people occupy embankments with their livestock's. It disrupts the road communication to reach the flood affected people for relief and rehabilitation works as the embankments are used for road communication in the flooded areas. Though breaching in the embankments are the major problems but it's have been adopted as one of the cheap and quick flood management measures. To minimize the flood damages raising the platforms near the flood prone villages are essential.

■ **Table 6.1:** Latest Positions of Embankments in the District

| Irrigation Sub-division | Sl. No | Name of the River/Khal | Name of Embank-ment | Chain age From…To | Length (km) | From….To |
|---|---|---|---|---|---|---|
| Lachmapore | 1 | Cossye (L/B) | Kalichandi flood embankment (Ist phase) | 0.00 to 7.10 km. | 7.10 km. | Srirampur to Amodpural |
| | 2 | Cossye (L/B) | Kalichandi flood embankment (Ist phase) | 0.00 to 17.00 km. | 17.00 km | Patra Bridge to Kalinagar Bridge |
| | 3 | New/Old Cossye (R/B) | TE1H1 | 0.00 to 40.00 km. | 40.00 km. | Okra to Lowada |
| | 4 | Kalaichandi Khal | Kalaichandi flood embankment (L/B, R/B) | 0.00 to 5.64 km. | 11.28 km. | Patra Bridge to Elahigang |
| | 5 | Old Cossye | TE2H2 | 0.00 to 14.00 km. | 14.00 km. | Malihati to Tinua |
| | 6 | New Cossye | TE3H3 | 14 to 26.00 km. | 12 km. | Tinua to Nandabari |

| Irrigation Sub-division | Sl. No | Name of the River/Khal | Name of Embankment | Chain age From…To | Length (km) | From….To |
|---|---|---|---|---|---|---|
| Ghatal | 1 | Old Cossye, Kanki, Silabati, Rupnarayan, Palashpai Khal | Chetua Circuit | 0.00 to 72 km. | 72.00 km. | Katan Bandh – Goura - Kalmijole- Katan |
| | 2 | Durbach-ati(L/S) Rup-narayan(R/S) Palashpai Khal(R/S) | Mohankhali Circuit | 0.00 to 51.00 km. | 51.00 km. | Sibora – via Khukurda – Goura - Sribora |
| | 3 | Old Cossye, Durbachati, Bhasra Khal | Daspur Circuit | 0.00 to 30.00 km. | 30.00 km. | Postanka – Kalmijole – Jotisab - Postanka |

*Source: District Disaster Management Action Plan 2016.*

## 6.3.2  Raised platforms for Affected Villages

During flood episodes the affected people generally takes place on the river embankments along with their livestock. The embankments get damage which creates obstacle to flood fighting and rehabilitation measures. Even after subsidence of flood water people are generally unwilling to go away from the embankments. Insufficiency of the elevated grounds in these areas hampers flood relief and rehabilitation works. To overcome this problem, raised platforms above high flood level to frequent inundation on priority basis.

In view of growing dimension of the flood problems of the district there is the need of construction more earthen embankments so that people can take shelter during flood episodes. Moreover, raised platforms should be handed over the local bodies like Panchayat for subsequent maintenance and kept free from encroachment.

## 6.3.3  Bank erosion and protecting works

Bank side erosion is one of the major problems in the river of the district. It takes away valuable agricultural as well as residential land, houses and towns on its banks and impoverishes the affected people. To prevent bank side erosion of a river is very difficult and costly task. It takes many years before stability can be established and erosion stopped. Likewise, other district of West Bengal, erosion causes of valuable lands and properties in Paschim Medinipur district. The Flood Control Department of the Government is taking different measurement in the district to stop erosion caused by the rivers. These are following-

i.    Revetment
ii.   Timber Spur
iii.  Boulder Bars and Bars with Polythin bags

## 6.3.4  Relief Works

The district level relief committee consisting of official and non-official members including the local legislators and the members of parliament review the relief measures. What kind of things are to be needed during flood season, the committee accounted for that during pre-flood season. Some of the following readiness has to be taken by the Committee during pre – flood season.

■ **Table 6.2:**  Details Bank Protection Work in the bank of River Subarnarekha and Kangsabati under West Medinipur Division

| Sl. No | Vulnerable Area | Length of work | Probable Cost in lakh | Remarks | Nature of Works | Year of Completeness |
|---|---|---|---|---|---|---|
| 1 | River Subarnarekha (R/B), Mouza: Basbetia, Block: Nayagram | 2000 m. | 500 | Bank Erosion | Revetment | On going |
| 2 | River Subarnarekha (R/B), Mouza: Thuria, Block: Nayagram | 3000 m. | 700 | Bank Erosion | Boulder Bars | 2015 |
| 3 | River Subarnarekha (R/B), Mouza: Malam, Block: Nayagram | 700 m. | 175 | Bank Erosion | Boulder Bars | 2015 |
| 4 | River Subarnarekha (R/B), Mouza: Aushapal, Block: Nayagram | 800 m. | 200 | Bank Erosion | Boulder Bars | On going |
| 5 | River Subarnarekha (R/B), Mouza: Kamalpur, Block: Nayagram | 1800 m. | 500 | Bank Erosion | Boulder Bars | On going |
| 6 | River Subarnarekha (R/B), Mouza: Patina, Block: Nayagram | 2000 m. | 500 | Bank Erosion | Revetment | 2015 |

| Sl. No | Vulnerable Area | Length of work | Probable Cost in lakh | Remarks | Nature of Works | Year of Completeness |
|---|---|---|---|---|---|---|
| 7 | River Subarnarekha (L/B), Mouza: Kuthighat, Block: Gopiballavpur II | 750 m. | 100 | Bank Erosion | Boulder Bars | 2014 |
| 8 | River Subarnarekha (L/B), Mouza: Chorchita, Block: Gopiballavpur II | 2100 m. | 600 | Bank Erosion | Revetment | 2014 |
| 9 | River Subarnarekha (L/B), Mouza: Mahapal, Block: Gopiballavpur II | 500 m. | 150 | Bank Erosion | Timber Spur | 2015 |
| 10 | River Kangsabati (R/B), Mouza: Barakuria, Bamuniabandh, Block: Jhargram | 1200 m. | 190 | Bank Erosion | Boulder Bars | 2015 |
| 11 | River Kangsabati (R/B), Mouza: Pairaguri, Satpati, Block: Jhargram | 1500 m. | 300 | Bank Erosion | Timber Spur | 2015 |

*Source: District Disaster Management Action Plan, 2016.*

**Plate: 6.1:** A timber spur to protect the Dherua village on left bank of Kangsabati River.

**Plate: 6.2:** A scene of Boulder Bar to protect the embankment of Subarnarekha River at Gopiballavpur near Subarnarekha bridge.

**■ Table 6.3:** No. of Camping sites for flood affected people, 2016

| Name of Block | No. of camping sites | Suitable places for dropping relief materials during flood |
|---|---|---|
| Ghatal | 45 | 4 |
| Chandrakona – I | 10 | 2 |
| Chandrakona- II | 5 | 2 |
| Daspur – I | 35 | 7 |
| Daspur – II | 39 | 6 |
| Sabong | 32 | 8 |
| Debra | 8 | 9 |
| Kharagpur – I | 9 | - |
| Kharagpur – II | 9 | 3 |
| Pingla | 38 | 11 |
| Datan – I | 63 | - |
| Datan – II | 8 | 2 |
| Narayangarh | 263 | 5 |
| Mohanpur | 28 | 2 |
| Keshiary | 21 | - |

| Name of Block | No. of camping sites | Suitable places for dropping relief materials during flood |
|---|---|---|
| Jhargram | 29 | 4 |
| Binpur – I | 12 | 9 |
| Sankrail | 12 | 8 |
| Nayagram | 10 | 4 |
| Gopiballavpur –I | 30 | 5 |
| Gopiballavpur – II | 19 | 4 |
| Medinipur Sadar | 6 | 10 |
| Garbeta – I | 2 | 11 |
| Garbeta – II | 8 | 2 |
| Garbeta – III | 3 | - |
| Keshpur | 25 | 26 |
| Binpur - II | - | - |

*Source: District Disaster Management Action Plan, 2016.*

■ **Table 6.4:** Stock position of Relief material and food grains for flood, before 2016 flood season

| Items | Available | Further Requirement |
|---|---|---|
| Polysheet | 30137 N.C | 50,000 Pcs. |
| Saree | 3462 Pcs. | 10,000 Pcs. |
| Dhuti | 1155 Pcs. | 10,000 Pcs. |
| Lungi | 2611 Pcs. | 50,000 Pcs. |
| Children Garments | 1300 Pcs. | 20,000 Pcs. |
| Blankets | 555 Pcs. | 10,000 Pcs. |
| Male wrapper | 2660 Pcs. | 10,000 Pcs. |
| Salwar kamij | 1900 Sets | 10,000 Pcs. |
| Punjabi & Paijama | 1800 Pcs. | 10,000 Pcs. |
| Spl. GR (Rice) | 102.1 MT. | 500 MT. |
| Spl. GR (Wheat) | - | 100 MT. |

*Source: District Disaster Management Action Plan 2016.*

## 6.4 SWOT analysis (Strength, Weakness, Opportunities and Threats) of flood hazard management in Paschim Medinipur District

SWOT is an acronym for strength, weakness, opportunities and threats and perhaps the most well known approach for define strategy. The technique is mainly used for analysing the any disaster prone district's internal capabilities (i.e. strength and weakness) in relation to the competitive environment (i.e. opportunities and threats).

■ **Table 6.5:** SWOT Analysis

| Phases of DM | DM activities | | Strength | Weakness | Opportunities | Threats |
|---|---|---|---|---|---|---|
| Pre – disaster phase | 1. Preparedness and planning | A. Flood mitigation meeting | At each level of management committee gather in pre-monsoon period to organise a general meeting with the various task like search and rescue, first aid, early warning system, food management, shelter management, dead body disposal force etc. | There is a dearth of search and rescue, first aid, early warning system, food management, shelter management, dead body disposal which are imperative demand for development of competence and organisation of expertise. | Meeting analysis is the review of best practices approaches, measures and experiences to prevent and fight floods. Efforts should focus on forecasting, protection, prevention as well as mitigation during time of no floods. | Heavy precipitation cannot be managed neither can extreme floods. So, 'we have to learn to live with those events'; otherwise it is very harmful for the community. |
| Pre – disaster phase | 1. Preparedness and planning | B. Vulnerability &Risk assessment | Investigate prominent natural and human caused of flood hazard. Identify the vulnerable zone and groups who need more concern during flood. | When authorities prepared any flood hazard map then they must acknowledge the community statement, otherwise it is not work. | Identifying, categorizing and quantifying elements at risk and their vulnerabilities to floods. | How many people of the community and which groups of the people are most vulnerable during the flood we don't know if we not done vulnerability and risk analysis. So, increased the vulnerability and risk at the community level. |
| | 2. Structural | A. Embankments | To mitigate the flood problems massive structural programme going on construction of embankments and dams. | The embankments do not allow the sediments come out to the streams and their slow deposition takes places in the river itself and river beds have been raised. | It has been adopted as one of the cheap and quick flood management measure to keep the flood water away from the habitation and agricultural fields. | Because of sediment deposition carrying capacity of the river has been decreased and enhanced the breaching tendency of embankments. |

| Phases of DM | DM activities | | Strength | Weakness | Opportunities | Threats |
|---|---|---|---|---|---|---|
| Pre – disaster phase | 2. Structural | B. Prepared river gauge & rain gauge | Every year before the monsoon season the govt. Paints and reconstructions the gauges to know the flood water level. | Sometimes during the flood actual data cannot be collected properly or by the force of water velocity the gauges breaks up. Therefore, it is very essential to build them up in the scientific way. | Accordingly the people will make them safety from the coming flood and also to minimize their damages. | If the common people have no experience about river gauge data then the sudden flood can also increased their damages, even it can take their lives. |
| | | C. Drainage system | Availability of land and large agricultural sector means natural drainage system like swallow are highly feasible. | There are no master plans of drainage system. Disruption of natural drainage systems by unsustainable logging, land – clearing and mining practices. | Incorporate sustainable practices as part of requirements for industrial licenses. Empower local groups that could monitor industrial practices more effectively. | Continual ad-hoc developments that disregard guidelines and master plans. |
| | 3. Non -Structural | A. Cleaning the drainage channel | Cross Bundhs and fishing patts on river bed mainly over river Kaliaghai removed regularly before monsoon. | Increase the deficiency of water for agricultural activities after monsoon. | Increase the channel depth and carrying capacity of the river. | If it is not clear regular basis before monsoon it's prevent the flood water for ease flowing and flood water comes into the habitation and agricultural field. |

Contd…

| Phases of DM | DM activities | | Strength | Weakness | Opportunities | Threats |
|---|---|---|---|---|---|---|
| Pre – disaster phase | 4. Alarming system | A. Early warning mechanism | EWM help the relevant authorities in taking timely preventive measures and thereby reduced the damaged caused by flood. There is already a form of alarm system e.g. to announced by the local authorities and SMS system among different govt. authorities. | Existing warning system is not effective. People vacated their premises late and impulsively ran to any nearest higher ground. Dispersion of people at random places makes them difficult to be reached. | Assessing the current warning system. Developing it further and educating locals on evacuation methods and routes. | Increase the potential damages. |
| | | B. Media and public relation | The dissemination of knowledge during all stages plays a vital role in supporting the management of the calamity, by raising awareness, improving preparedness, especially when conducted through mass media. | People generally look for news that is timely and constantly updated, especially during or immediately after the occurrence of a flood but sometimes it is not happened. | Media can be a decision makers, media should ideally try to build a clear and comparative relationship with the common people who are living with flood. | Under hard conditions like technical problems, bad weather or inaccessibility of some areas media cannot provide correct and reliable information. |

| Phases of DM | DM activities | | Strength | Weakness | Opportunities | Threats |
|---|---|---|---|---|---|---|
| Pre – disaster phase | 5. Infrastructure | A. Transport system | Locals can be highly inventive in improvising local transport systems when there is lack of economic and support from governing bodies. There is a continual tradition of using boats. | Many houses are clustered away from the main road, with only narrow earth tracks as connections. During flood some village are like an island, which can only be reached by boat. | Assessment and monitoring of damages by experts. Educating locals on technical and management skills. | Unseen damages to foundation and grounds. Economic challenges to developing infrastructure. |
| | | B. Sanitation | Some of the houses already have individual septic tanks and residents claim their sanitary system is still usable after floods, only the walls and roof are damaged. | Ad-hoc construction of sanitary system without consideration of possible contamination risks, especially as density increases. | Educating locals on the safe sanitary provisions. | Unseen risk from existing system e.g. contamination of surrounding area and water due to leaching. |
| | | C. Water supply | Villages are used to two sources of water supply: centralised plant and local wells. | Wells are contaminated during flood. Water supply from centralised plant has to be disconnected during disaster. | Harvesting of rainwater which is stored in flood – proof container. | Increase the polluted waters diseases like dermatitis, conjunctivitis, gastrointestinal illnesses etc. |
| Pre – disaster phase | 5. Infrastructure | D. Electricity | Most areas already have electricity connection. | Prolonged loss of electricity. Generators quickly ran out of oil. | Development of independent or decentralised power supply system e.g. low solar panels, waste-to-energy plants | – |
| | 6. Role of NGOs | | In pre – disaster phase different NGO'S generate the awareness, educating and training the local people to fight against flood situation. | Weak coordination among government officials, brief time-spans for relief interventions, neglects the remote and inaccessible disaster-affected areas and neglect of rural urban diversity and primacy of attention to rural areas. | NGOs can play important role in mobilizing communities and introducing innovative approaches based on the good practices followed in other countries. | – |

Contd…

| Phases of DM | DM activities | | Strength | Weakness | Opportunities | Threats |
|---|---|---|---|---|---|---|
| Pre – disaster phase | 7. Capacity Building | A. Training the volunteer for search & rescue B. Training for evacuation C. Training for the structural measure | SIPRD & ILGUS are available for capacity building of govt. officials. Regarding the emergency management most of the training classes and workshop held in state level for the staff. A 'Three Days State Level Training of Trainer on Disaster Risk Reduction Programme in West Bengal at State Institute of Panchayat and Rural Development' with 42 disaster management officers from three DRR district, 2011. | Weak coordination among the different govt. offices. | Increased the capacity to manage the flood situation among the community level. Sustainable disaster risk reduction also increased. | There is a dearth of structured and implemented education, training, increased of communication and equipments, awareness generation and training programme which are urgent need for development of competence. |

| Phases of DM | DM activities | Strength | Weakness | Opportunities | Threats |
| --- | --- | --- | --- | --- | --- |
| **During disaster phase** | 1. Search & Rescue | NDRF team, Army and sometimes Air force have been engaged during emergency of flood for searched and rescued of flood affected people. An air force helicopter rescue 39 people who were trapped inside a two storey house at Pratappur village in the Ghatal sub-division of Paschim Medinipur district in 2017 floods. | Teams which are responsible for search and rescue not properly trained, equipped and developed strategically. Even, lack of coordination among different govt. groups and govt. officials also a drawback of these objectives. | Increased the capacity of speedboats in the district, especially in the vulnerable areas. | People tend to stay at their house during the flood. |
| **During disaster phase** | 2. Relief Distribution<br><br>2. Relief Distribution | I) Govt. distributed the relief material during flood like Water Pouches, Dry Ration, Milk Powder, Chura, Gur, Rice, Dal, Sugar, and Tarpaulin in flood affected areas.<br>II) A lot of NGOs and individuals took their own initiatives.<br>III) Govt. and some agencies offer different forms of shelters –Temporary tents are among the quickest to arrive and erect.<br>a) Temporary plywood houses. | I) Uneven distribution of help due to lack of coordination.<br>II) Wastage and failure to meets needs as help was not given based on a systematic assessment of needs.<br>III) The public are not well – informed of precautionary measures and safe practices.<br>IV) Tent numbers are limited; hence many people still have to live in makeshift shelters.<br>V) Plywood houses take time to construct and require a degree of building skills.<br>VI) Lack of local knowledge and resources for future maintenance. Assumption that all sites and cases are similar. Limit to truck access of mobility.<br>VII) Lack of technical knowledge safe building construction methods and ways to reclaim, handle and rework existing materials. | I)<br>Establishment of a body to assist government in coordination and promote guidelines on precautionary measures and safe practices.<br>II)<br>Improvisation of plywood houses to include salvaged materials to reduce mobilisation time and cost. | I)<br>People tend to use temporary buildings beyond the expected expiry date. |

| Phases of DM | DM activities | Strength | Weakness | Opportunities | Threats |
|---|---|---|---|---|---|
| During disaster phase | 3. Evacuation | Evacuation centres:<br>- Existing relief centers<br>- Schools<br>- Community halls<br>- Mosques<br>- Abandoned buildings<br>- Makeshift shelters on higher grounds<br>There is already a form of alarm system e.g. message system at officials and announcement at GP level. | Difficult for relief teams to access many evacuation centres. Existing alarm system is not effective, people vacated their premises late. | Developing well-equipped existing and new evacuation centres at suitable locations. Assessing the current alarm system. Developing it further and educating locals on evacuation methods and routes. | - |
| | 4. Health &Sanitation | Govt. stock the medicines like antivenin serum, ORS, halogen tablets and certain other life saving medicines for diseases during and post flood and also stock the bleaching powder for proper sanitation. | Lack of public health protection operational plane and reinforcement of hygiene promotion campaign. | To remedies the health vulnerabilities or hazards baseline health data can be used to identify existing health vulnerabilities or hazards. Increased the flood resilience and associated flood resilience. Baseline health assessment. | Increased the water related disease and potential threats to health. |
| During disaster phase | 5. Special care of children, Women and Aged | Govt. priorities the evacuated of children, aged and women person. | No such body of govt. to assist government in coordination and promote guidelines on precautionary measures and safe practices for such type of restricted people during the time of flood. Which happen for them during flood is all about oral. | For restricted people, quick construction of emergency trench latrines or simple pit latrines is encouraged. Establishment of a body to assist government in coordination and promote guidelines on precautionary measures and safe practices for those people. | They are highly vulnerable because of their restricted mobility and difficulty with evacuating during emergencies. |

| Phases of DM | DM activities | Strength | Weakness | Opportunities | Threats |
|---|---|---|---|---|---|
| **Post disaster phases** | 1. Rehabilitation | Site specific and targeted solutions can be more effective and resource – efficient. | a) No proper waste management system.<br>b) Gases from burning plastics are dangerous to health.<br>c) Insertion of new development needs more careful assessment, strategy and execution in order to minimise disruption on existing environment and people. | a) Developing a localised waste management system.<br>b) Large amount of agricultural waste could be utilised for conversion to energy.<br>c) Rethinking land use: how to rehabilitate affected lands. | Possible clash between new planned infrastructure and existing buildings and natural environment. |
| | 2. Relocation | Move settlements to safer areas. Easier application of economics of scale as the same kind of house can be built in bulk. | a) People's psychological and emotional attachment to their land.<br>b) Disrupting source of economy.<br>c) Temporary and permanent relocation is overlooked by most flood victims due to perceived inability to rent new places owing to low incomes, fear of losing income generating ventures that serve as sources of livelihoods.<br>d) From socio cultural view point they also felt uncomfortable with losing ancestral lands and landed properties as well as breaking long-standing ties with their community folks and other networks. | a) Empowering villagers to get involved in the planning, management and execution in the rebuilding works.<br>b) Their contribution can be paid as salary and the skills they acquire can open up future employment opportunities.<br>c) Engagement with local community through regular community discussion and activities. | a) Difficult to maintain due to loss of sense of belonging and ownership among the community.<br>b) Higher grounds face risks of slope failure and landslides during rainy season. |

Contd…

## 6.5 Suggested Management Strategies

The aim of Flood Management is to minimize the existing and future hazards to lives and properties in the most effective ways. Flood management practices adopted in the district as well as in the whole of the West Bengal during last few decades have already been proved improper and inadequate. During the recent years flood damages seem to go on increasing year after year. So, now it is extreme time to change the concept of flood management for the district. Recent thinking of the scientist suggests that instead of keeping flood way keep people away from the flood. Instead of structural measures, attempts are now directed to non-structural measures. Non-structural measures mainly include watershed management, flood plain zoning, improvement of flood forecasting and warning system. In other parts of India also the idea of non-structural management of flood has got much importance in recent times. The strategies for flood management in Paschim Medinipur District have been taken for discussion in the light of recent national thrust on flood management.

### 6.5.1 Watershed Management

What is watershed management? It is nothing but enhanced the land management to stop soil erosion and to lower surface spill off and improve infiltration rate, which help in preserving water and ground water. Soil preservation measures are important for –

a.  Stopping soil erosion
b.  Raising fertility of land
c.  Supplying ground water.

According to Goswami (1992) as a logical step to the flood problem in the North Eastern India created by Brahmaputra River and its tributaries, regional planning on the basis of water management seems to be beneficial for water resources and for alleviation of regional improvement. Some of the important facts in relation to flood management in Paschim Medinipur District are mentioned and proposals are included in the following –

**Afforestation:**
According to the advice of the National Policy, area under forest cover should be nearly equal to area under deforestation i.e. up to the level of 60%. The district has not yet achieved the mark in extending the forest area as per the

suggestion of the National Policy. Another important factor is the health of the forest. Virgin forest cover has prominent positive influence on soil erosion, surface spill off and in preservation of ground water. Illegal entrance to the forest land is one of the burning problems that adversely influence the resources of the forest. The kinds of trees with following qualities are advised for plantation.

i.  Swift growing
ii. Soil forming characterizes
iii. Economic value in the form of fuel, wood and pulp
iv. Delicious food for the domestic animals

To protect the forest areas and to upgrade the health of forest the following criteria may be advised:

i.  To stop destruction of forest in unplanned manner
ii. Plantation should be made in the deteriorated forest areas
iii. To stop illegal entry in the forest areas, Government should take bold steps.
iv. People should come forward to save forest and vegetation efforts should put to make people aware of the need of the tree and save plant to save land as well as other valuable wealth.

## 6.5.2 Flood Plain Zoning

The primary concept of flood plain zoning is to control the land use in the flood plain to lower down the amount of damage. The improvement of flood plain should be in a regulate way to ensure that the present problems and the damages of flood are not risen up and new developmental works do not get seriously affected. The use of land should be controlled by zoning ordinance. But not yet the Central Government as well as the State Government has passed any legislation for flood plain zoning. The Flood Control Department in Paschim Medinipur District is not paying attention towards this concept. For different frequencies, flood prone areas should be identified and demarcated on a large scale map and also on ground. To control the land use in different flood areas, the importance should be given to the following points.

Priority 1: Defense installations, industries, hospitals, electricity installations, supply of water telephone exchanges.

Priority 2: Public institutions, Government offices, Universities, Public libraries and areas of residential.

Priority 3: Parks and Playgrounds, Parking places

According to the field visits, one of the main causes of floods in this district is the obstacle in the drainage system. The areas where building construction and intense urbanisation activities are prohibited should be mentioned as green belts areas. This will not only help to improve drains in future but will also help in reducing the damage due to drainage disturbance. New island in the river (Chars) should be left to nature as far as possible. These areas are very prone to floods every year and no real protection can be given to the people living in these areas.

### 6.5.3  Flood Forecasting and Warning

Flood forecasting and warning has an immense importance in the mitigation plan during flood. During flood, a warning system may save human lives and resources. It may be considered as one of the most effective non-structural measures of flood management. Flood forecasting needs a proper acknowledgement of the hydrologic process of the catchment. Hence, for issuing forecast on the subject appropriate techniques based on in-depth knowledge should have been used. Underrating of flood peak may cause an untold misery whereas overrating results in disassociation of flood decrescent due to the unacknowledgement of forecast. Therefore, forecasting should be sophisticated. At present, there is a flood forecasting centre of CWC at Paschim Medinipur District but needs more sophisticated and modernization.

There is also a need of Co-operation with neighbouring state (For example Jharkhand) to provide better forecasts in the province where the rivers are from those state by origin.

### 6.5.4  Flood Management through Community Participation

Community Participation should be encouraged in order to generate the awareness about flood disaster. At micro level participatory approach through the involvement of local people is truly essential. Active participation in pre and post perilous situations should be applauded. For this, public information system has to be mended so that the people may consider themselves as participants rather than the object of Govt. plan. They should have to be involved in hazard management activities including hazard readiness, combat relief and rehabilitation rather to create only awareness. It would encourage a sense of responsibility that can produce a better community approach and ensure psychological readiness of the local community to cope with hazard occurrence. The following points may summarise the objectives of community participation.

i.   Community participation is an essential component for a successful substitution of relief measures.

ii.  Community participation helps to understand the problems and needs of affected people.

iii. Community participation may minimize the perfunctory charges of relief operations and increased transparency between the provider and the recipient. It may also reduce the chances of corruption on the concerned.

iv.  Community participation provides us with the knowledge of struggle for existence.

According to the researchers flood management through community participation has yet not enticed people living in the flood prone areas. In this connection, Governmental Departments on the concerned matter, as well as the NGO should play an important role in the disaster alarming system and reducing the common mass about the interest of saving human resources.

### 6.5.5 Disaster Preparedness and Response Planning

Disaster Management is a magnificent framework including all aspects of preventive and protective measures, readiness and systematic organisation of relief, rescue and rehabilitation programme to mitigate the hazards of disaster.

In our country disaster management is dependent upon Govt. Departments. It is the responsibility of honourable departments to look after the matter with its true essence. Apart from them voluntary agencies, NGO and co-operative society take the initial parts creating flood awareness among the common mass and leading them towards disaster management. But unfortunately the disaster mitigation system and readiness programme are usually taken place at the time of flood season or hardly just before the season and eventually remain inactive during the year. In a flood prone district like Paschim Medinipur we hardly realise the essence of advance mitigation. Considering the fact, it seems that we need our officers and staff much more concerned with the awareness as well as common mass with the voluntary agencies dealing flood emergencies.

## 6.6 Minimize the flood impact

A strategy to assist the individual and community in the preparatory, survival and recovery after floods, the following measures are usually taken –

### 6.6.1 Flood Fighting

These measures include several activities to minimize the embezzlement during flood. It mainly consists of supervising the flood control systems for any of its weakness during floods such as wash out due to wave action, seepage across the levee, leakage in the dam or over topping the river banks. So, that certain action may be applied immediately to challenge the hazardous occurrence. Apart from that public health measures to prevent health hazards, restoration of water supply and the sewage facilities are important dimensions of flood fighting strategies. These require advanced planning of equipment and readiness to fight against the concerned disaster. In this connection the measures related to the district of Paschim Medinipur should have been followed.

### 6.6.2 Disaster Relief

Considering the matter, basic needs like food, wearing, shelter and medicine are highly essential. We have to reconsolidate the distressed families in order to provide social and welfare services in most effectively. The principle objective is to make the victim enable both individually and socially to become an independent self sustaining as so as possible. The emotional shock disaster death of the victims, separation of family members, ravaged accommodation loss of possessions affect an individual badly and it becomes hard to recover. The agency concerned must be conscious of need to deal with such problem at the level of understanding of the person concerned. In some cases consolation and counselling may affect but in maximum a material help only appears to be effective.

Considering the state in disaster, Government should assume special responsibilities. In emergency cases Government should not hesitate in approaching defence establishment for rendering help during the ravage. The measures adopted to the flood victims of Paschim Medinipur district may be benefited in this concern.

### 6.6.3 Flood Insurance

Flood insurance may be appearing as such a measure that can provide an advantage in modifying the loss. So far it is not adopted in India. Though the Government has applied several strategies to cover the agriculture under this, it is yet to reach the commoners. Researcher found that no such insurances have been issued in much needed condition of the district. So, it may be an urgent to cover agriculture of the district under insurance.

## 6.7 Crop Management in the Flood Plains of Paschim Medinipur District

The economic status of the river basins of Paschim Medinipur District is agrarian in nature. The crops in this area are mainly affected by floodwater and sand casting. Researchers find out some suggestions to cope with floods.

The high flood season coincides with the paddy, the main crop of West Bengal, from June to November. It occupies more than 80% of the entire agricultural area. Rice is the main crop grown in the flood plains of Paschim Medinipur District. Flood occurring in July and late August or early September leave practically no time for replanting of rice seedlings and thereby lead to total crop loss. Therefore, the farmers usually face problems in starting a fresh cultivation after the water being retrained. Wheat, mustard, potato, boro paddy and several vegetables are grown in the cold. The planting of green gram can be adjusted in autumn. The Kharif rice, which possess the major problem, can also be grown in the flood free time zone, provided suitable varieties for pre and post flood seasons and therefore a suitable irrigation, storage and marketing infrastructure can be developed. So, as discussed above change in the existing crop calendar and cropping pattern is highly essential for the district to avoid the impact of flood.

The flood control measures in the form of structural and non-structural measures, considering all impacts on the concerned, can provide reasonable protection during flood occurrence. The district authority not only has to provide relief to the victims but also has to ensure that they do not breach embankments to release accumulated water from their lands. Possible causes of breaches of embankment should be taken into consideration while formulating the flood mitigation projects. The integrated basin management approach based on the principle of soil and water conservation appears to be more appropriate as long-term strategy against recurring flood and sustainable development. Adjusting the cropping time in order to control the impacts of flood and also to ensure better yield is another non-structural measure that would encourage the farmers of the flood prone areas in future. Therefore, in this respect a better co-operation and co-ordination appear to be a long-desired wish to fight against the disaster like flood.

## 6.8 Ghatal Master Plan: A Case Study

Ghatal is situated in Paschim Medinipur district state of West Bengal. If we are going through the river pattern of Ghatal block, the block divided into three parts. Namely, interfluves part of Silabati and Sankari River, interfluves part of Sankari and Darakeswar River and interfluves part of Silabati and Rupnarayan River. Ghatal town situated in the interfluves part of Silabati and Rupnarayan River. If the more rainfall occurs than the normal rainfall by any cause the Block has been flooded. In a year the Block has been flooded 3 to 5 times (Author Field Interview). Mainly excessive monsoonal rainfall from July to September month and additional dam discharge water from Mukutmanipur and

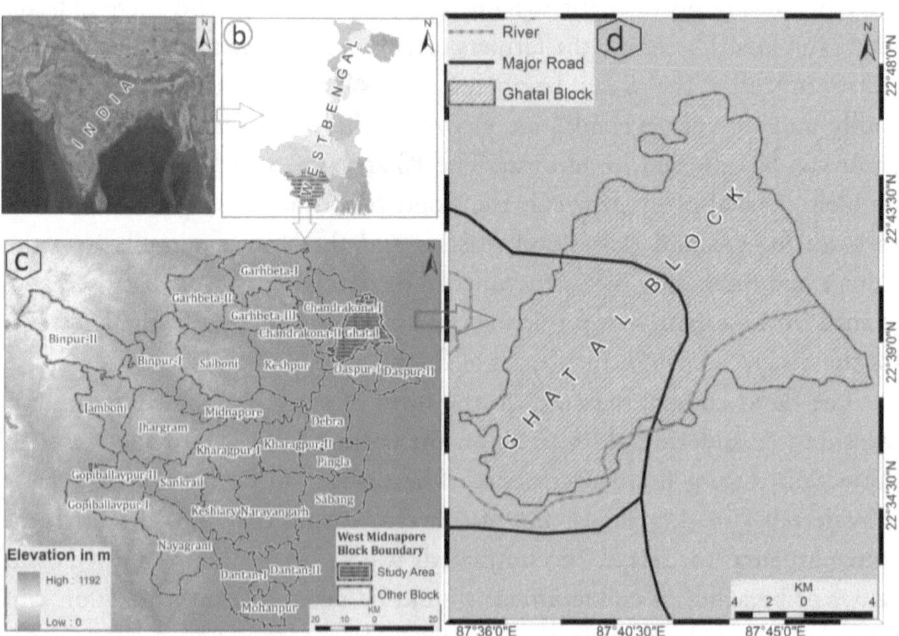

**Fig. 6.2:** Geographical Location of Ghatal Block in Paschim Medinipur District.

D.V.C reservoir are mainly responsible for flooding in this Block and create a great havoc to the people's life. Cyclone formation on the head of Bay of Bengal from the month of October to November is also the cause of flood in this Block.

### 6.8.1 Nature and Causes of Flood in Ghatal Block

If we look the history, we can see that Ghatal and its adjacent area is highly flood prone segment by the River of Silabati and Kangsabati. In British Empire Ghatal Block was divided by many small Jamindars. After starting the permanent settlement the local Jamindars prepared circuit bank in their locality on the rivers in their areas to protect the flood and extend the productive land for which their total income would be increased. As a result when flood water comes from the upstream and high tide water comes from the sea then accumulated water continuously store on the river channel. So, the flood plains area of the river becomes lower in respect to the accumulated water on the river channel. By the gradually assembled of silt in the river bed it becomes a high area than the nearest areas and at the same time the rate of flood increased than the normal situation. As a result in one side these become barrier to discharge excess flood water and in other side as the internal areas of the river bed is lower than the river bank, resulting the critical problem of drainage.

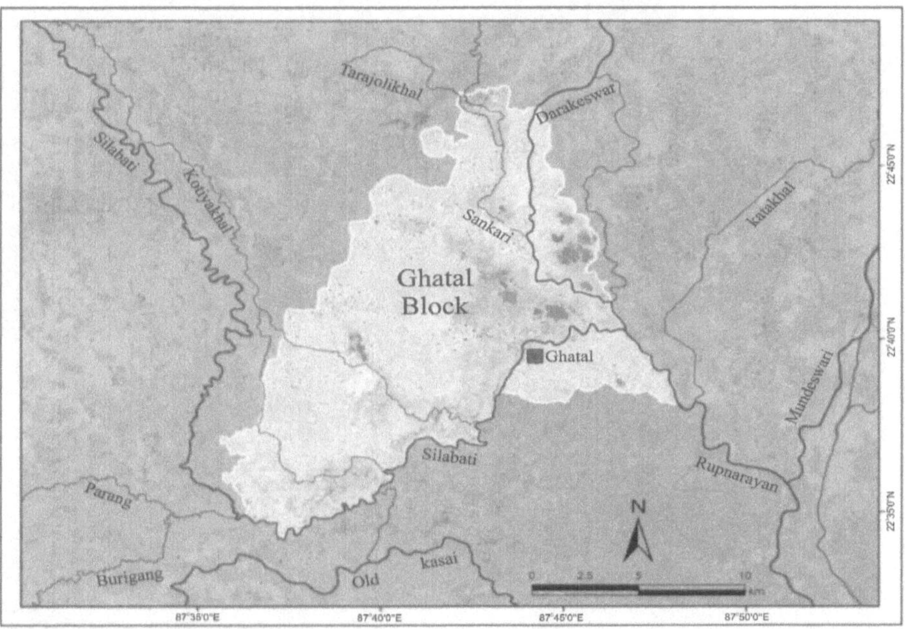


**Fig. 6.3:** Drainage System of Ghatal Block

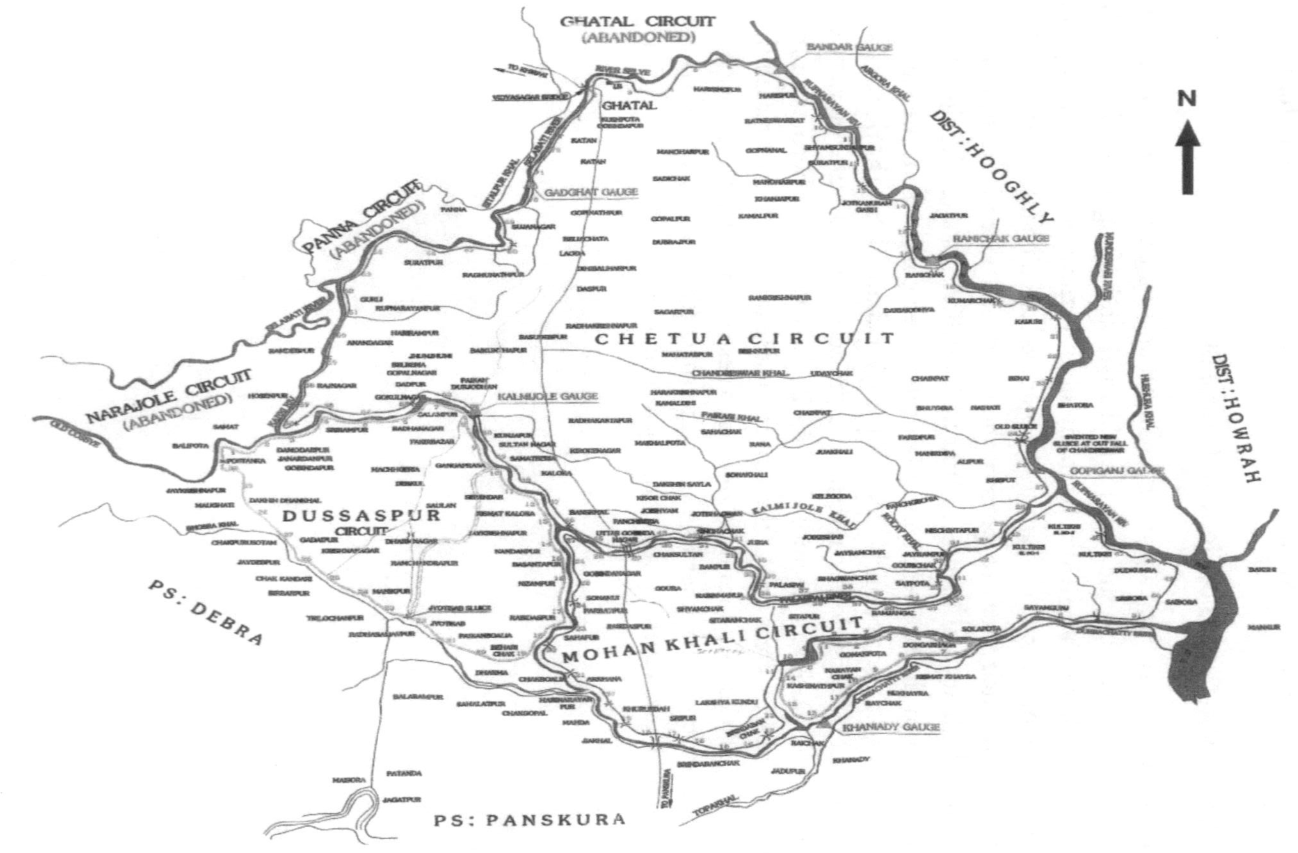


**Fig. 6.4:** Different Circuit around Ghatal Block (Source: Ghatal Irrigation and Waterways Dept.).

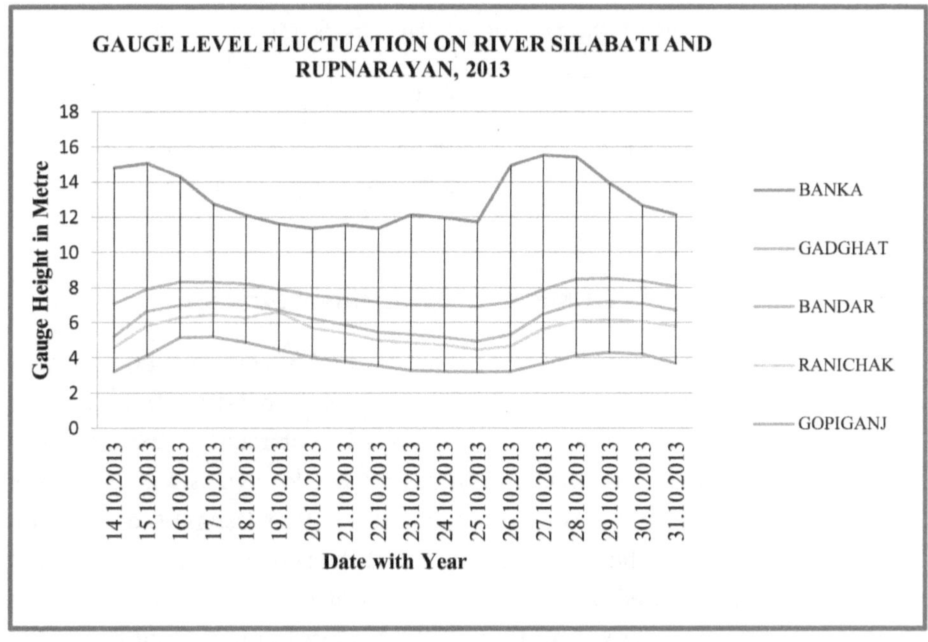



**Fig. 6.5:** Fluctuation of Gauge level during 2013 flood on Silabati and Rupnarayan River.

**▪ Table 6.6:** Depth and Duration of flood water and inundated area in Ghatal Block and adjacent areas.

| Year | More than 30 days | | More than 15 days | |
|---|---|---|---|---|
| | Area (sq.km) | Depth (m) | Area (sq.km) | Depth (m) |
| 1959 | 100 | 2.00 | 184 | 1.50 |
| 1967 | 100 | 2.50 | 69 | 1.50 |
| 1968 | 350 | 2.50 | 308 | 2.00 |
| 1973 | 208 | 3.00 | 150 | 2.00-1.00 |
| 1974 | 61 | 3.00 | 102 | 2.00-1.00 |
| 1975 | 104 | 2.50 | 110 | 2.00-1.00 |
| 1976 | 55 | 2.50 | 104 | 2.00-1.00 |
| 1977 | 100 | 3.50 | 130 | 2.00-1.00 |
| 1978 | 710 | 3.50 | 356 | 2.00-1.00 |
| 1999 | 78 | 3.00 | 100 | 2.00-1.00 |
| 2000 | 80 | 3.00 | 121 | 2.00-1.00 |
| 2007 | 233 | 3.00 | 400 | 2.00-1.00 |
| 2013 | 245 | 3.00 | 275 | 2.00-1.00 |
| 2016 | 368 | 3.85 | 412 | 2.5 – 3.0 |

*Source: WAPCOS and Ghatal Irrigation Office (2011 & 2015, 2016).*

| ■ Table 6.7: Highest flood discharge in different time periods at Silabati Watershed | | | |
| --- | --- | --- | --- |
| | **Time periods** | | |
| Discharge | 25 year | 50 year | 100 year |
| | 2734 cusec | 3428 cusec | 3696 cusec |

*Source: WAPCOS Report, 2009.*

## 6.8.2 Ghatal Master Plan (GMP) as a Management Strategy

Now a day's carrying capacity of Silabati River 650 cms which is totally inadequate to flow the flood water. After a comprehensive study from 1970 to 1976, West Bengal Irrigation and Water Ways Department proposed a plan to mitigate the flood and drainage problem which is known as 'Ghatal Master Plan' (GMP) and in 1976 plan was approved by West Bengal Government. In 1982, 10th February the foundation stone of the project was laid down but that was not implemented. In 1997, again the project was newly prepared and for that estimated cost has was approved 20.82 corers but it was not successful. Considering the physical and socio-economic condition of the region the Central Govt. authorised the responsibilities for preparing a reliable plan to subordinate organisation Water and Power Consultancy Services (WAPCOS). WAPCOS showed the estimated cost for this project in two report Rs. 1460 corers and Rs. 1740 corers in the year of 2009 and 2011 respectively.

Total area of this project is 1659 sq.km and area located in between 22°15′ N to 22°50′ N and 87°15′ E to 87°55′ E. Ten blocks of Paschim Medinipur District and three blocks of Purba Medinipur District are fully or partly included in the project area. In Western, Eastern, Northern and Southern boundary of the project area are Chandrakona-Medinipur road; Rupnarayan River (From Hooghly port to Kolaghat), Panskura-Tamluk road, Denan khal; Part of Ghatal-Chandrakona road, watershed of Silabati and Darakeswar River; Medinipur Khal, Boxi khal and National High Way 6 respectively. Considering the locational importance of Ghatal Sub-division and Ghatal town WAPCOS primarily measured the intensity of the flood which is possible to occur 100 years interval. But geographical structure and location of the region is like that, if embankment is constructed in both the side of the river Silabati than the height of water level in Silabati River is almost 4.5 m. to 5.0 m. from the ground surface. Such a movement is highly dangerous to populous areas like Ghatal. If somehow the embankment breaks any time it may be cause to a major disaster. That's why WAPCOS reformed the plans and they measured the intensity of flood which possible to come 50 years interval instead of 100 years interval. In perspective of this idea WAPCOS formulate a plan to mitigate the flood problem in Kangsabati and Silabati watershed.

■ **Table 6.8:** Included Blocks in Ghatal Master Plan

| District | Name of the Blocks | Included Blocks |
|---|---|---|
| Paschim Medinipur | Daspur -I | Fully |
| | Daspur -II | |
| | Kharagpur –I | Partly |
| | Kharagpur –II | |
| | Debra | |
| | Medinipur | |
| | Chandrakona – I | |
| | Chandrakona – II | |
| | Keshpur | |
| | Ghatal | |
| Purba Medinipur | Mayana | Fully |
| | Panskura | Partly |
| | Kolaghat | |

*Source: WAPCOS Report, 2011.*

According to WAPCOS highest discharge of flood water in Kangsabati and Silabati River 3869 cusec and 3428 cusec in 50 years time. From WAPCOS study it is ensure that to enclosed the flood water in any reservoir and mitigate the flood problem of this region totally impossible. So, they (WAPCOS) are proposed to construct the breakwater, widthing the river channel etc. to minimize the flood problem.

### 6.8.3 Proposal of WAPCOS (2011)

#### 6.8.3.1 Management Proposal of Kangsabati River

i.  To reform the river channels from Medinipur Aniket (Mohanpur) to Kapastikri.

ii. Dam construction on the left bank of River Kangsabati from Kasra to Kapastikri (29.75 km.)

iii.  Renovation of old Kangsabati River from Kapastikri to Gobindanagar where the old Kansabati River is divided into two separate rivers like Palaspai and Durbachoti.

iv.  Construction of a dam with the length of 20 km on the left bank of old Kasai River and reform the right bank of old Kasai River from Kapastikri to confluence point of Kanki River.

v.  To increase the height of dam, strengthening of the river bank and reform the channel of Palaspai River for the length of 19 km.

vi.  To increase the height of dam, strengthening of the river bank and reform the River of new Kasai from Kapastikri to Dhewbhanga for the length of 70 km.

Vii.  To increase the height of dam, strengthening of the river bank and reform the channel of Durbachoti River for the length of 23.9 km.

viii.  To regulate the water flow process in the origins of Palaspai and Durbachoti on old Kasai, place of Gobindapur.

ix.  To construct a water breaker in the place of Kapastikri where old Kasai and New Kasai divided.

x.  To reform the abandoned Narahjole circuit and increased the height from the level of flood water flow.

### 6.8.3.2 Management Proposal of Silabati River

i.  To reform the length of 75 km in the river of Silabati in proposed area.

ii.  To construct a dam from Western part of proposed area to Ghatal – Chandrakona road on the right bank of Silabati River for the length of 70 km.

iii.  To reform the Ketia Khal and construct a dam on the both side of Ketia Khal for the length of almost 36.9 km.

iv.  Formation a sluice gate at the confluence point of Silabati River and Ketia Khal.

v.  To reform the abandoned Ghatal circuit.

vi.  Formation a pump house in the mouth of Narayani Khal for remove the drainage problem of Ghatal Municipality.

vii.  To construct a dam from Ghatal circuit to 13 km length in North-West side which protect the Ghatal and Kharar Municipality to mitigate the flood hazard.

Inspite of the GMP some other necessary action has been taken to save from flood. In previous discussion we say about 'Chatal'. In some places the 'Chatal' has been crossing the road transversely. During flood the 'Chatal' is flooding in every year. So, communications totally depend on boating during flood on this 'Chatal'. Three 'Chatals' are there like this in the left bank of Silabati River. In between two bridges have been completed over two 'Chatals' and another one has been started under the cost of 17 corers (Source: Irrigation and Water Ways, Ghatal.).

### 6.8.3.3 Impact of Ghatal Master Plan (GMP)

To regulate the flood in GMP totally depends on reform the river channel and construction of dam. Although construction of this dam in an unscientific manner is the main causes of flood. So, once again when the dam will be constructed the level of flood water is much higher than the level of ground surface. If somehow earthen dam is broken, it may be the cause of the deadful disaster. If dam is constructed, the suspended sediment of flood water will not get the space to spread over the floodplain. So, it is the cause of increasing the sediment on the river channel and decreasing the depth of channel. So, flood takes a terrible grace in future. Normal slope of ground surface is parallel to the 'Chatal'. That's why it is not ensured that the excessive flood water will not only flow through the river channel. So, GMP is suitable for short term duration to mitigate the flood problem but in long term duration it is very much suspicious that how could GMP mitigate the flood problem. Inspite of that if we want to complete the plan, according to WAPCOS to possess the land permanently 1407 hector and temporarily land 4180 hector which is very difficult in present circumstances of the State Government. So, flood problem of Ghatal Block completely mitigated if GMP executes, this type of publicity is completely wrong. Part of Ghatal Block which is fallen left bank of River Silabati is fully submerged by flood water during flood. If Ghatal Master Plan will be executed the depth and duration of flood water also increased. So, it is doubtful about the positive result if the Ghatal Master Plam (GMP) is executed.

## 6.9 Perspective on community-based management

Over the last three decades, it has become apparent that top-down approaches to disaster risk management that ignore local capacities and resources fail to address the specific needs of vulnerable communities. People-based disaster risk management as an alternative approach emerged in the 1980s and 1990s in response to the limitations of this top-down methodology (ADPC, 2007).

This approach is adopted to foster and institutionalize elements of good governance to empower the community. In this situation, inclusive participation and representation, transparency, accountability and capacity to be resilient to natural disasters are seen not simply as a means to fulfil immediate needs but also to sustain livelihood systems in the face of recurrent floods. The links between community-based interventions and progress in governance are apparent in many successful community-based activities (Haider, 2009). Community-based processes ensure that voices are heard and local communities equipped with the skills and tools to cope with disaster through flood-management initiatives.

Community participation in flood-management activities can be strengthened effectively by adhering to four principles: they are needs-based, effective and efficient, build social capital, and are practical to implement:

➤ Community participation has to match a community's needs in terms of:
  - People/community factors;
  - Vulnerability and risk reduction (and resilience enhancement);
  - Sustainability in activities for infrequent and recurrent events;
  - Establishing public–private partnerships, involving NGOs, private actors and other relevant actors.

➤ Community participation retains its effectiveness and efficiency by:
  - Understanding societal actors and their actions;
  - Synergizing effects of limited financial and human resources;
  - Providing the best mix of community experience and technological knowledge
  - Connecting individual requirements and government preparedness.

➤ Community participation promotes building social capital through:
  - Equitable access – a commitment to ensuring equal opportunity for all community members to participate in decisions;

- Inclusiveness – a commitment to the development of participation strategies for all community members, especially those who, characteristically, do not participate;
- Responsiveness – a commitment to listening and taking action in relation to the views, concerns and experiences of community members;
- Integrity – a commitment to open, transparent and accountable participation practices that enhance trust and confidence in the community.

➢ Community participation ensures practicability for implementation through:
  - Undertaking flood management at each stage (prevention, preparedness, response and recovery);
  - Capacity-building and coordination through dialogue and participation;
  - Creating opportunities for training and drills as realistically as possible.

Community participation has been – at least in principle – for more than 30 years at the core of any development policy and emergency intervention involving people, based on the assumption that a "top-down" approach is not adequate for its implementation. Both development policy and emergency intervention should be coupled by a grassroots or bottom-up approach. This is also true in any policy/intervention in flood management. It is an important step towards enabling communities to be recognized as active actors in this context and to help themselves in this regard and sustain those efforts. It is a process whereby the communities concerned function and contribute to perform a predetermined activity as a cohesive group, while recognizing and enhancing the differences within them.

Each year, there are 50–300 inland floods worldwide, impacting an estimated 520 million people and causing as many as 25 000 deaths (Gore, 2010). The worst natural floods in history, in terms of loss of life, have been those along Chinese rivers: The Yellow River has killed more people than any other natural phenomenon (between 2.5 and 3.7 million in 1931; between 0.9 and 2 million in 1887; and between 0.5 and 0.8 million in 1938). Over the past 4 000 years, it has flooded 1 593 times (Allin et al., 2010).

The worst recent natural floods were the Tamil Nadu floods in India in 2015 (more than 400 deaths); the Kashmir region floods in 2014, meaning

400–500 deaths in India and Pakistan (Burke et al.,2014); the Balkans floods in Serbia, Bosnia and Herzegovina and eastern Croatia in 2014 (almost 100 deaths); and the northern India floods in 2013 (5 700 deaths, while damage to bridges and roads left almost 73 000 people trapped in various places, according to UN-SPIDER (2013); the Greater La Plata floods (Argentina) in 2013 (almost 100 deaths); the Krymsk flood in the Russian Federation in 2012 (almost 200 deaths), the floods in the Democratic Republic of Korea in 2012 (more than 200 deaths), the Nigeria floods in 2012 (almost 100 deaths); the South-East Asian floods in 2011 (1 800 deaths); Tropical Storm Washy floods in the Philippines in 2011 (1 300 deaths); and the Rio de Janeiro floods in Brazil in 2011 (900 deaths).

People can play a key role in the success of many non-structural measures such as awareness generation, popular knowledge valorisation, information dissemination, organizing people, warning and evacuation. These non-structural measures can also contribute to reducing the cost of structural measures (sometimes making them unnecessary or ensuring better monitoring of their impact), such as constructing local flood defences or contributing to design and maintenance of drainage systems.

People/communities are no longer seen as recipients; rather, they have become critical stakeholders who have a major role to play in the management of community floodmanagement programmes. Community involvement is more effective when people are fully conscious, empowered and trained. It is important, therefore, that people be provided with an opportunity to play a more active role and that the government or public officials facilitate and provide catalytic support for community-based flood-management programmes.

The impact of floods on a community is based, among other things, on the historical experience and traditional backgrounds and features of communities. Communities are usually composed of many societal actors more or less firmly bonded to each other and which pursue interests more or less differentiated. We can find cohesive communities, but also cohesive groups inside non-cohesive communities (even with levels of conflict more or less high inside). In the absence of organized community participation (even at the level of specific groups), most of the activities are carried out at individual or household level, driven by individual necessity.

The response to the flood hazards in the Paschim Medinipur district has come up through the action taken in the catchments and along the channels.

The response mostly lies between adjustment and abatement or protection. Since historical times until recently the most frequent choice was that of protection by means of physical controls of the rivers through embankments along the course of the rivers to protect against the destructive inundations. But in the upper part of the all rivers in Paschim Medinipur district are the least protected by the embankments. That is causes of rapid change of river course. The flood detention reservoirs have also been adopted as a means for the moderation of floods. As such the Mukutmanipur dam over Kangsabati River has started functioning in 1956. It has been observed with the Mukutmanipur on the Kangsabati, that the detention reservoirs are capable of moderating the floods in its lower reaches. But, however, the floods of the post-Mukutmanipur period reveal that there is a tendency at the later part of the rainy season to encroach into the space reserved in the flood storage capacity and the floods have a tendency to occur towards the last part of the rainy season.

While concluding on the piece of present work on the floods hazard and their management in the Paschim Medinipur district, it is perceived after a pretty long discussion, that the problem is simple in appearance but very complex in nature. Floods in a certain area can modify developments and aspirations of the human society in the district. The problems of floods are not limited only to physical changes but also to psychology and socio-economy of the floodplain dwellers. The present study tries its best to outline the nature of such a situation with reference to floodplain dwellers of the study area. The facts and phenomena of floods and their impact on human are to be monitored for a very long time and survey works are to be done in details every year after the floods. This type of work may help the planners to work efficiently for flood and floodplain management. Effective functioning of management plans requires participation of the people at large. This in turn requires investigating people's behavior and perception to the floods and their associated problems.

# BIBLIOGRAPHY


**A**

**Agarwal, B.** (1990). Social security and the family: coping with seasonality and calamity in rural India. J Peasant Stud 17(3): 341-412.

**Alam, MJB. Ali, MH.** (2002). Concept of flood shelter to cope with flood. In: Ali MA, Seraj SM, Ahmad, E. (eds). Engineering concerns of flood. Bangladesh University of Engineering and Technology, Dhaka, pp 175-186.

**Anderson, MB.** (1992). Metropolitan areas and disaster vulnerability: a consideration for developing countries, In: Kreimer A, Munasinghe M (eds) Environmental Management urban vulnerability. The World Bank, Washington, DC, pp 77-92.

**Azar, D. Rain, D.** (2007). Indentifying population vulnerable to hydrological hazards in San Juan, Puerto Rico. Geo Journal 69(1-2): 23-43.

**B**

**Barry, R.G.** (1969). Precipitation, Water, Earth and Man – A Synthesis of Hydrology, Geomorphology and Socio – Economic Geography, (ed. R.J. Chorley), Methuen & Co.Ltd., London, 113 – 129.

**Barry, R.G.** (1969). The World Hydrplogical Cycle, Water, Earth and Man – A Synthesis of Hydrology, Geomorphology and Socio- Economic Geography, (ed.R.J.Chorley), Methun & Co.Ltd., London, 11- 30.

**Beckinsale, Robert, P.** (1969). "River Regimes," in Water Earth and Man: A Synthesis of Hydrology, Geomorphology and Socio-Economic Geography edited by R.J. Chorley, Methuen, London, P.455.

**Betal, Himanshu, R.** (2002). Flood problems of Malda – A Geographical analysis, Geographical Review of India, Kolkata, Vol. 64, No – 4, pp. 337-345.

**Beven, K. et al.,** (1989). Floods: Hydrological, Sedimentological and Geomorphological Implications, John Wiley and Sons, New York.

**Beyer, J.L.** (1977). Global Summary of Human Response to Natural Hazards: Floods, Natural Hazards- Local, National Global, (ed.G.F.White), Oxford University Press Inc., New. York.

**Birkmann, J.** (2007). Risk and vulnerability indicators at different scales: applicability, usefulness and policy implications. Environ Hazard 7(1): 20-31.

**Bose, S.C.** (1972). Geography of Himalaya, Thomson Press Limited, New Delhi-21. Brice, J.C., (1974), "Evolution of Meander Loops", Geological Society of America Bull., Vol.85, pp.581-586.

**Boyer, M.C.** (1964). Stream Flow Measurement, Handbook of Applied Hydrology- A Compendium of Water Resources Technology, (ed. Ven Te Chow), McGraw Hill Book Company, New York, Section-XV, 3-41.

**Brice, J.C.** (1981). "Meander Pattern of the White River in Indiana: A Analysis," in Fluvial Geomorphology, edited by Morisawa, M., pp.178-200.

**C**

**Chakraborty J, Tobin GA, Montz BE.** (2005). Population evacuation: assessing spatial variability in geophysical and social vulnerability to natural hazards. Nat Hazard Rev 6(1): 23-33.

**Carson, M.A. and Kirby, M.J.** (1972). "Hillslope Form and Process", Cambridge University Press, Cambridge, UK.

**Chabaux, F. Garnet, M. Pelt, E. France-Lanord, C. and Galy, V.** (2006). MsU-234 U-230 The Disequilibria and Timescale of Sedimentray Transfers in Rivers: Clues from the Gangetic Plian Rivers", Journal of Geochemical Exploration, Vol. 88, Issues 1-3, pp.373-375.

**Chandra, S. Rhodes, E. and Richards, K.** (2007). "Luminescence dating of Late Quaternary Fluvial Sediments in the Rapti Basin, North-Central Gangetic Plains", Quaternary International, Vol.l59, Issue 1, pp.47-56.

**Chandran, R.V.Ramakrishnan, D. Chowdary,V.M. Jeyaram, A. and Jha, A.M.** (2006). "Flood Mapping and Analysis using Airborne Synthetic Aperture Radar: A Case Study of July 2004 Flood in Baghmati River Basin, Bihar", Current Science, Vol.90, No.2, pp.249-256.

**Charlton, R.** (2008)."Fundamentals of Fluvial Geomorphology", Routledge, London, pp.97-148.

**Chen, W. Qinghai, X. Xinging, Z. and Yonghong, M. (1996).** "Palaeochannels on the North China Plain: Types and Distribution", Geomorphology, Vol.18, Issue 1, pp. 207-214.

**Chorley, R.J.** (1968). Models in Geomorphology, Models in Geography, (eds. R.J. Chorley and P. Hagget), Methuen & Co. Ltd., London, 59-96.

**Chorley, R.J.** (1970). The Application of Statistical Methods to Geomorphology, Essays in Geomorphology, (ed. G.H.Dury), Heinemann, London, 275-387.

**Chorley, R.J. et al.** (1969). Water, Earth and Man: A Synthesis of Hydrology, Geomorphology and Socio-economic Geography, Methuen & co. Ltd., London.

**Chow, V.T.** (1956). "Hydrological studies of floods in the United State", International Association of Scientific Hydrology, Vol. 42, No..., pp. 134-170.

**Cox, R.T. Van Arsdale, R.B. and Harris, J.B.** (2001). "Identification of the possible Quaternary deformation in the northwestern Mississippi Embayment is using quantitative geomorphic analysis of drainage basin asymmetry", Bull. Geol. Soc. Am. Vol.113, pp.615-624.

**Cutter, S. Boruff, BJ.Shirley, WL.** (2003). Social vulnerability to environmental hazards. Soc Sci Q 84(2): 242-261.

**D**

**Dalrymple, T.**(1964). Flood Characteristics and Flow Determination, Handbook of Applied Hydrology- A Compendium of Water Resources Technology, (ed. Ven Te Chow), McGraw Hill Book Company, New York, Section-XXV-1, 2-32.

**Das, P.K.** (1968). The Monsoons, National Book Trust of India, New Delhi, pp. 53-55.

**Dawdy, D.R. and Matals, N.C.** (1964). Statistical and Probability Analysis of Hydrologic data –Analysis of variance, Covariances, and Time Series, Handbook of Applied Hydrology – A Compendium of Water Resources Technology, (ed. Ven Te Chow), McGraw Hill Book Company, New York, Section-VIII-3, 69-90.

**De Wiest, R.J.M.** (1965). "Geohydrology", John Wiley & Sons, New York, pp. 99-106.

**Dewan, M. Ashraf.** (2012). Floods in a Megasity: Geospatial Techniques in Assessing Hazards, Risk and vulneeability, Springer Publication, London.

**Dhar, O.N. and Nandargi, S**. (1998). "Floods in Indian rivers and their meteorological aspects", in V. S. Kale (ed.), Flood Studies in India (Memoir No.41), Geological Society of India, Bangalore, p 2.

**Dhar, O.N. and Nandargi, S.** (2003). "Hydro meteorological Aspects of Floods in India", Natural Hazards, Vol. 28, No…, pp. 7-9.

**Dodson, B.** (1996). Vulnerability to flooding in rural Bangladesh: a socioeconomic appraisal. In: Singh RB (ed) Disasters, environment and development (Proceedings of International Geographical Union seminar, New Delhi, 9-12 December 1994). Oxford/IBH Publication, New Delhi/Calcutta, pp 183-195.

**Dogra, B.** (1997) " More floods with Flood Control", Economic and Political Weekly, Vol. 32, No. 18, May 3, pp. 933-934.

**Dury, G.H.** (1969). "Relation of Morphometry to Runoff Frequency", in Water, Earth and Man: A Synthesis of Hydrology, Geomorphology and Socio-Economic Geography, edited by R.J., Chorley, Methuen & Co Ltd., London, p. 425.

E

**Ericksen, N.J.** (1977). Flood Information, Expectation and Protection on the Opotiki Flood Plain, New Zeland, Natural Hazards- Local, National, Global, (ed.J. F. White), Oxford University Press, Inc., New York.

F

**Few, R.** (2003). Flooding, vulnerability and coping strategies: local responses to a global threat. Prog Dev 3 (1): 43-58.

G

**Gardon, N.D. Mcmahon, T.A. and Finlayson, B. L.** (1993). "River Hydrology", John Wiley & Sons Ltd., U.K., pp.316-317.

**Ghosh, A.K.Bose, N. Singh, K.R.P. and Sinha, R.K.** (2004). "Study of SpatioTemporal Changes in the Wetlands of North Bihar through Remote Sensing", paper presented in 131h International Soil Conservation Organisation Conference, Brisbane.

**Goswami, U. Sarma, J.N. and Patgiri, A.D.** (1999). "River Channel Changes of the Subansiri in Assam, India," Geomorphology, Vol.30, Issue 3, pp.227-244.

**Gregory, K.J. and Walling, D.E.** (1973). Drainage Basin Form and Processes: A Geomorphological Approach, Edward Arnold, London.

**Gregory, S.** (1989). "Micro-Regional Definition and Characteristics of Indian Summer Monsoon Rainfall, 1817-1985", International Journal of Climatology, Vol.9, Issue 5, pp.465-483.

**Gupta, A.** (1998). "Geomorphological effects of Floods on Indian Rivers, in Vishwas Kale (ed.), " Flood Studies in India", Memoir 41, Geological Society of India, Banaglore, pp.143-153.

**H**

**Handbook for Predicting Stream Meander**, Migration (2004). National Cooperative Highway Research Program, Transportation Research Board, Washington, D.C., Report no. 533, pp. 1-37.

**Haq, K. Md. F. and Bhuiya, R.H.** (2004). "Delineation and Zonation of Flood Prone Area: A Case Study of Tangail District, Bangladesh, Indian Journal of Regional Science, Vol.36, No.1, pp.20-29. HEC-GeoRAS: An Extension for Support of HEC-RAS using ARCVIEW, User's Manual, Version3.1, October 2002.

**Harding, D.M. and Parker, D.J.** (1977). Flood Hazard at Shrewsbury, United Kingdom, Natural Hazards – Local, National, Global, (ed.G.F.White), Oxford University Press,Inc., New York.

**Higgit, D.L. and Warburton, Jeff.** (1999). "Applications of Differential GPS in Upland Fluvial Geomorphology, Geomorphology, Vol. 29, Issues 1-2, pp.121-134.

**Hooke, J.M.** (2006). "Spatial Variability Mechanism and Propagation of Change in An Active Meandering River", Geomorphology, Volume 84, Issues 3-4, pp.277-296.

**Hosking, J. R.** (1990). L-moment: Analysis and Estimation of Distributions using Linear Combinations of Order Statistics. Journal of the Royal Statistical Society, Series B, 54, 105-124.

**I**

**Islam, MZ.** (1990) Failure of flood embankments: case studies of some selected projects in Bangladesh. Final report, R02/91. Institute flood Control and Drainage Research (IFCDR), BUET, Dhaka

**J**

**Jain, V. and Sinha, R.** (2003). "River System in the Gangetic Plains and their Comparison with the Siwaliks", Current Science, Vol.84, No.825, April, pp. 1025-1033.

**K**

**Kale, V.S.** (1999). "Long Period Fluctuations in Monsoon Floods in the Deccan Peninsula, India, Journal Geological Society of India, Vol. 53, January, pp.S-15.

**Kayastha, S.L.** (1983). "Floods in India: A Study of their Occurrence, Causes, Forecasting and Control," National Geographical Journal of India, Vol. 29, Part 3 and 4, p.l21-141.

**Kayastha, S.L. and Yadav, R.P.** (1980). "Flood Hazard in Lower Ganga-Ghaghara Plain (U.P., India): A Study in Perception and Impact on Socio-economic Development", National Geographical Journal of India, Vol.26, Parts II&I pp.l9-28.

**Kemp, J.** (2004). "Flood Channel Morphology of a Quite River the Lachlan, downstream from Lowra, Southeastern Australia, Geomorphology, Vol. 60, Issues 1-2, pp.

**Kubal, C. Haase, D. Meyer, V. Scheuer, S.** (2009). Integrated urban flood risk assessment- adapting a multi-criteria approach to a city. Nat Hazard Earth Syst Sci 9(6):1881-1895.

**L**

**Law, F.** (1956). The effect of afforestation upon the yield of water catchment areas, Jr. Br. Waterworks Assoc, 38, pp. 489 – 494.

**Leopold, L.B. and Wolman, M.G.** (1957). River Channel Patterns: Braided, Meandering and Straight, U.S. Geol. Survey Prof. Paper 282-B.

**M**

**Mahalonobis, P.C.** (1941). Rainstorms and River Flooda in Orissa, Irrigation and Power Department, Govt. Of Orissa, Bhubaneswar.

**Malczewski, J.** (1999). GIS and multiple-criteria decision analysis. Wiley, New York.

**Malczewski, J.** (2004). GIS based land-use suitability analysis: a critical overview. Prog Plan 62(1): 3-65.

**Malczewski, J.** (2006) GIS based multi-criteria decision analysis: a survey of the literature. Int J Geogr Inf Sci 20(7): 703-726.

**Moline, N.T.** (1977). Perception Research and Local Planning: Floods on the Rock River, Illinois, Natural Hazards- Local National Global, (ed. G.F.White), Oxford University Press, New York.

**Munsi, Sunil Kumar,** (1998). Problems of flood management in India: Policies and Programme, Geographical Review of India, Kolkata, Vol. 60, No. 3, pp. 239-247.

**Murray, J.A. and Sonavane, N.K.** (1969). Statistical Methods Applied to Flood Frequency Analysis, Journal of the Central Board of Irrigation and Power, Vol. XXVI,No. 4, 389-403.

**N**

**Nobel, Charles, C.** (1976). The Mississippi River Flood of 1973 in Geomorphology and Engineering, (ed. Donald R. Coates), Dowden, Hutchinson & Ross, Inc., Pennsylvania, 79-98.

**O**

**Osterkamp, W.R.** (1978). Gradient, discharge and particle size relations of alluvial channels in Kansas, with observation on braiding. American Journal of Science, 278, 1253 – 1268. **Osterkamp, W.R. and Hedman, E.R.** (1997). Variation of width and discharge for Natural high gradient stream channels. Water Resource Research, 13, 256 – 258.

**P**

**Pal, S.K.** (1978). Morphology of the Bramhaputra Flood Plain, (Memiographed), New Delhi. Scope of Intergrating Field Work in Geomorphology, (Memiographed), New Delhi.

**Panda, G. K.** (1994). Community perception and Human adjustment of flood hazards in Orissa coastal plain, Indian Journal of Landscape Systems and Ecological Studies, Kolkata, Vol. 17, No. 2 pp. 62-69.

**Panda, G.K.** (1979). Drainage and Floods in Mahanadi. Delta – A Study in Applied Geomorphology (M.Phil Dissertation), P.G.Department of Geography, Utkal University, Bhubaneswar.

**Panda, G.K.** (1989). The Drainage and Floods in Orissa Coastal Plain – A Study in Applied Geomorphology (Ph.D. Thesis) P.G. Department of Geography, Utkal University, Bhubaneswar.

**Panda, G.K. Satapathy, C.R. and Sinha, B.N.** (1980). Morphometric Analysis of the Drainage Basins and their Geomorphic Significance-A Study on Drainage Basins of Six Major Rivers of Orissa, Eastern Geographical Society, Research Bulletin No. 14, P.G. Dept. Of Geography, Utkal University, Bhubaneswar.

**Paul, SK. Routray, JK.** (2010). Flood proneness and coping strategies: the experiences of two villages in Bangladesh. Disasters 34(2): 489-508.

**Paul, SK. Routray, JK.** (2011). Household response to cyclone and induce surge in coastal Bangladesh: coping strategies and explanatory variables. Nat Hazard 57(2): 477-499.

**Pelling, M.** (1997). What determines vulnerability to floods: a case study in Georgetown, Guyana.Environ Urban 9(1): 203-226.

**Pettitt, A. N.** (1979). An Non-parametric Approach to the Change Point Problem. Applied Statistics, 28 (2), 126-135.

**Q**

**Quirke, T.T.** (1945). Velocity and load of stream. Journal of Geology, 53, 125 – 132.

**R**

**Ramaswamy, C.** (1985). Review of Floods in India during the past 75 Years, Published by the Indian National Science Academy (INSA), New Delhi, pp. 144-151.

**Rasid, H. Haider, W. Hunt, L.** (2000). Post flood assessment of emergency evacuation policies in the Red river delta, Southern Manitoba. Can Geogr 44(4): 369-386.

**Ray- Bennett, NS.** (2009). Coping with multiples disasters and diminishing livelihood resources: Caste, class and gender perspectives: the case from Orissa, India. Reg Dev Dialogue 30(1): 108-120.

**Rayhan, IM.** (2008) Assessing household vulnerability and coping strategies to floods: a comparative study of flooded and non-flooded areas in Bangladesh, 2005. Cuvilier Verlag, Gottingen.

**Remenieras, G.** (1967). Assessment of the Magnitude and Frequency of Flood Flows, United Nations, Water Resource Series No. 3, New York.

**Rodda, John C.** (1969). The Flood Hydrograph, in Water, Earth and Man- A Synthesis in Hydrology, Geomorphology and Socio- Economic Geography, (ed.R.J.Chorley), Methuen & Co. Ltd., London, 405-418.

**S**

**Saaty, TL.** (1980). the analytical hierarchy process. McGraw- Hill, New York.

**Saji, N. H. Goswami, B. N. Vinayachandran, P. N. & Yamagata, T.** (1999). A Dipole Mode in the Tropical Indian Ocean. Nature, 401, 360-363.

**Sales, J. D.** (1993). Analysis and Modeling of Hydrologic Time Series. In D. R. Maidment (Ed.), Handbook of Hydrology (1$^{st}$ ed., pp. 19.1-19.72). McGraw-Hill Inc.

**Santra, S.** (1989). Floods in Howra District, West Bengal: a Geographical Analysis, Indian Journal of Landscape Systems and Ecological Studies, Kolkata, Vol. 12, No. 2, pp. 21-25 Volume I Number I June 2016 Page 57.

**Sanyal J, Lu, XX.** (2006). GIS based flood hazard mapping in Gangetic West Bengal. Singap J Trop Georgr 27(2): 207-220.

**Sanyal J, Lu, XX.** (2009). Ideal location for flood shelter: a geographic information system approach. J Flood Risk Assess 2(4): 262-271.

**Sarkar, S.** (1997). Some consideration on the fluvial dynamics of the River Mahananda, Siliguri, Geographical Review of India, Kolkata, Vol. 59, No. 1, pp.11-24.

**Satty, TL.** (1977). A scaling method for priorities in hierarchical structures. J Math Psychol 15(3): 234-281.

**Sharma, V.K.** (1976). Some Hydrological Characteristics of the Damodar River, Geographical Review of India, Vol. XXXVIII,No.4, 330-343, Calcutta.

**Sinha, B.N.** (1956). Flood Frequencies in Major Rivers of Orissa, Indian Journal of Power and River Valley Development, Vol. VI, No. 7, 5-10.

**Sinha, B.N.** (1973). Floods in Orissa, Paper Presented at the First Annual Conference of the Eastern Geographical Society, Bhubaneswar.

**Sinha, P.C.** (2003). Encyclopaedia of Disaster Management, Hydrological Disaster, Anmol Publications Pvt. Ltd., New Delhi, pp. 48-57.

**Smith, K. and Tobin, G.A.** (1979). Human Adjustment to the Flood Hazard, Longman, London, pp. 31-46.

**Smith, Keith and Ward, Roy,** (1998). Floods: Physical processes and Human Impacts, John Wiley & Sons, Chichester, England, U.K, First Edition, pp. 9-97.

**Stedinger, J. R. Vogel, R. M. & Georgiou, E. F.** (1993). Frequency Analysis of Extreme events. In D. R. Maidment (Ed.), Handbook of Hydrology (pp. 18.1-18.66). McGraw-Hill Inc.

**Subramanian, N.** (1979). Can We Control Floods, Science Reporter, Council of Scientific and Industrial Research, New Delhi, Vol. XVI, No. 5, P. 344.

**Sultana, F.** (2010). Living in hazardous waterscapes: gendered vulnerabilities and experiences of floods and disasters. Environ Hazard 9 (1): 43- 53.

**T**

**Takeuchi, K.** (2001). Increasing vulnerability to extreme floods and societal needs of hydrological forecasting. Hydrol Sci J 46 (6): 869-881.

**Tapsell, SM. Penning-Rowsell, C. Tunstall, SM. Wilson, TL.** (2002) vulnerability to flooding: health and social dimensions. Philos Trans RSoc Lond A 360(1796): 1511- 1525.

**Thornbury, W.D.** (1969). Principles of Geomorphology, John Wiley and Sons, Inc., New York.

**Tingsanchali, T. Karim, MF.** (2005). Flood hazard and risk analysis in the southwest region of Bangladesh. Hydrol Process 19 (10): 2055-2069.

**Tran, P. Shaw, R.Chantry, G. Norton, J.** (2009). GIS and local knowledge in disaster management: A case study of flood risk mapping in Vietnam. Disasters 33(1): 152-169.

U

**United Nations,** (1962). Proceedings of the Fourth Regional Technical Conference on Water Resources Development in Asia and the far East, Flood Control Series, No.19, Bangkok, 105-136.

**UN/ISDR (International Strategy for Disaster Reduction),** (2004). Living with risk: a global review of disaster reduction initiatives. United Nations Publication, Geneva.

V

**Vagas, I.** (1982). Floods of River Tista (in Hungarian). VIZDOC, Budapest.

**Venkata, Bapalu, G. Rajiv S.** (2005). GIS in Flood Hazard Mapping: a case study of Kosi River Basin, India, Conference Proceedings of Map Middle East, UAE, 2005.

W

**Wadia, D.N.** (1976). Geology of India, Tata McGraw Hill Publishing Co. New Delhi.

**Ward, R.C.** (1978). Floods- A Geographical Perspective, the Macmillan Press Ltd., London.

**White, G.F.** (ed.1977). Natural Hazards Research Concepts, Methods and Policy Implications, Natural Hazards- Local, National, Global, Oxford University Press, Inc., New –York.

Y

**Yevdjevich, Vujica, M.** (1964). Statistical and Probability Analysis of Hydrologic Data-Regression and Correlation Analysis, Handbook of Applied Hydrology- ACompendium of Water Resources Technology, (ed. Ven Te Chow), McGraw Hill Book Company, New York, Section – VIII-2, 44-67.

**Yoon, DK.** (2012). Assessment of social vulnerability to natural disasters: a comparative study. Nat Hazard 63(2): 823-843.

**Yoshino, F. Yoshikawa, K.** (1985). Astudy on flood risk mapping. In: Proceedings of the international symposium on erosion, debris flow and disaster prevention, Tsukuba, Japan, pp499-504

Z

**Zenith, E.R.** (1932). Drainage patterns and their significance. Journal of Geology, 40, 498 – 521.

**Reports/Gazetteers**

1. Annual Flood Report - Government of West Bengal.
2. Report of Disaster Management Action Plan – Paschim Medinipur District.
3. Reports of O'Malley – Bengal District Gazetteers.

**Websites**

http://bhuvan-noeda.nrsc.gov.in/disaster/disaster/disaster.php
http://www.bom.gov.au/climate/glossary/soi.shtml
http://www.india-wris.nrsc.gov.in/
http:/www.wbadmip.org/
http:/www.wbphed.gov.in
http:/www.imd.gov.in
**Wikipedia**